Risk Assessment for Domestically Violent Men

The LAW AND PUBLIC POLICY: PSYCHOLOGY AND THE SOCIAL SCIENCES series includes books in three domains:

Legal Studies—writings by legal scholars about issues of relevance to psychology and the other social sciences, or that employ social science information to advance the legal analysis;

Social Science Studies—writings by scientists from psychology and the other social sciences about issues of relevance to law and public policy; and

Forensic Studies—writings by psychologists and other mental health scientists and professionals about issues relevant to forensic mental health science and practice.

The series is guided by its editor, Bruce D. Sales, PhD, JD, University of Arizona; and coeditors, Bruce J. Winick, JD, University of Miami; Norman J. Finkel, PhD, Georgetown University; and Valerie P. Hans, PhD, University of Delaware.

* * *

Risk Assessment for Domestically Violent Men

Tools for Criminal Justice, Offender Intervention, and Victim Services

N. Zoe Hilton, Grant T. Harris,
and Marnie E. Rice

American Psychological Association

Washington, DC

Published by
American Psychological Association
750 First Street, NE
Washington, DC 20002
www.apa.org

To order
APA Order Department
P.O. Box 92984
Washington, DC 20090-2984
Tel: (800) 374-2721; Direct: (202) 336-5510
Fax: (202) 336-5502; TDD/TTY: (202) 336-6123
Online: www.apa.org/books/
E-mail: order@apa.org

In the U.K., Europe, Africa, and the Middle East, copies may be ordered from
American Psychological Association
3 Henrietta Street
Covent Garden, London
WC2E 8LU England

Typeset in Goudy by Circle Graphics, Columbia, MD

Printer: Maple-Vail Book Manufacturing Group, York, PA
Cover Designer: Minker Design, Sarasota, FL
Technical/Production Editor: Harriet Kaplan

The opinions and statements published are the responsibility of the authors, and such opinions and statements do not necessarily represent the policies of the American Psychological Association.

Library of Congress Cataloging-in-Publication Data

Hilton, N. Zoe.
    Risk assessment for domestically violent men : tools for criminal justice, offender intervention, and victim services / N. Zoe Hilton, Grant T. Harris, and Marnie E. Rice. — 1st ed.
        p. cm.
    Includes bibliographical references and index.
    ISBN-13: 978-1-4338-0466-3
    ISBN-10: 1-4338-0466-2
    1. Abusive men. 2. Wife abuse. I. Harris, Grant T. II. Rice, Marnie. III. Title.
    HV6626.H47 2010
    362.82'922—dc22
                                2008055071

British Library Cataloguing-in-Publication Data

A CIP record is available from the British Library.

Printed in the United States of America
First Edition

For our mothers, sisters, and daughters:
Stella, Toni, Petra, Madeleine, and Sophia
—*N. Zoe Hilton*

Margaret and Anne
—*Grant T. Harris*

Marion, Jennifer, Sharyn, and Andrea
—*Marnie E. Rice*

CONTENTS

ACKNOWLEDGMENTS

We are indebted to Detective Chief Superintendent Kathryn J. Lines, bureau commander of the Ontario Provincial Police (OPP) Investigation Support Bureau, for her contribution to the development of the Ontario Domestic Assault Risk Assessment (ODARA) and the collaborative research of the OPP and the Mental Health Centre Penetanguishene (MHCP). We owe a great deal of gratitude and appreciation to our respected friends and colleagues Catherine Cormier, Sonja Dey, Angela Wyatt Eke, and Carol Lang for their contribution to the ideas and work contained in this book.

The Ontario Ministry of Community Safety and Correctional Services (MCSCS), Peel Regional Police, and York Regional Police permitted and facilitated access to offender information. In particular, we thank Kathy Underhill, Tina Gaspardy, Gregory Brown, Ed Gale, Al Cleewer, Karen Noakes, C. Daunt, the staff of the MCSCS archives, and probation and parole offices throughout Ontario, as well as the OPP Behavioural Sciences and Analysis Services data entry, information technology, and Eric Silk Library staff. We also thank Norah Holder and Mary Metcalfe of the Orillia Soldiers Memorial Hospital, Sarah Kaplan and Maureen Hartle of the Cornwall Hospital, Nancy Stirling of Muskoka Interval House, and Natalie Seltzer of Rosewood Shelter and their clients for sharing information pertaining to clinical interviews.

Several of our colleagues reviewed drafts of this book. Michael Seto read large parts of the manuscript and provided insightful suggestions. Carol Lang consulted on the scoring of the practice cases and painstakingly edited the scoring criteria in the appendixes. We also thank Catherine Cormier, Angela Wyatt Eke, Martin Lalumière, Shari McKee, and Vern Quinsey for their comments on draft chapters. Sonja Dey and Amilynn Sharpe carefully examined the entire manuscript for consistency. For the final content of this book, we thank an anonymous reviewer who reviewed the book for the American Psychological Association and Emily Leonard, our cheerful and encouraging development editor.

Many people have been directly involved in our research into domestic violence, and we thank Craig Beach, Stacey Beckles, Leslie Belchamber, Skye Berry, Andrea Boyd, Tamara Burke, Joseph Camilleri, Ashley Caputo, Amanda Cocclioni, Jennifer Ellis, Marnie Foster, Michelle Green, Kelly Grubb, Ruth Houghton, Angela Knowlton, Tracy Lowe-Wetmore, Carolyn Lucarillo, Sarah McGuire, Julie McKay, Andrew Parker, Rob Rawn, Kelly Rawson, and Amilynn Sharpe. We have also enjoyed a productive collaboration with Suzanne Popham, chief psychologist of the Algoma Treatment and Remand Centre, Sault Sainte Marie, Ontario, Canada.

Throughout our research careers, we have benefited from the support of senior administrators at the MHCP. We would also like to thank the staff of MHCP's Learning Resource Group and Clinical Information Services, particularly Pat Reid, upon whose excellent librarian services we have depended; Trent Maracle, who has given tireless support to the ODARA training program; and Barb Desroches, who provided pleasant and efficient access to clinical files over many years.

The research reported in this book was supported by operating funds of MHCP and OPP and by the Social Sciences and Humanities Research Council of Canada.

Finally, we express our gratitude to our spouses, Brad Fisher, Emily Harris, and Greg Rice, for their support, and to Janice Leadbetter for providing loving and reliable child care during the years of research described in this book.

Risk Assessment for Domestically Violent Men

INTRODUCTION

Randy Iles was in his third marriage when he began an intimate relationship with Arlene May. His previous marriages had ended with episodes of child abduction, stalking, and threats with a weapon. He had amassed criminal convictions for harassment, possession of stolen property, breach of probation, and a weapons offense. Witnesses later recalled that Iles's violence toward Arlene began when she became pregnant. Soon after, Arlene went to a shelter for abused women and contacted the police to report an assault. Iles was arrested and attended a bail hearing, but the court was unaware of an outstanding arrest warrant in the neighboring jurisdiction. He was granted bail, ordered to leave the jurisdiction and not to have contact with Arlene, and forbidden to acquire firearms. But he continued to contact Arlene with death threats, and the license enabling him to purchase firearms was never confiscated.

There was a warrant for his arrest for breaching bail conditions when he purchased a gun and ammunition and waited at Arlene's home. When she and her children arrived, he took them hostage. He later released the children, but he shot and killed Arlene and himself. There is enough publicly available information (e.g., Ontario Office of the Chief Coroner, 1998) to score the Ontario Domestic Assault Risk Assessment (ODARA; Hilton et al.,

2004), one of the risk assessments discussed in this book. Had the ODARA then existed, it would have been possible in about 10 minutes to ascertain that Iles was, at the time of his court appearances, in the highest category of risk for repeated assault. Our research also suggests that had this score been presented, the court would have denied bail and held him in custody.

NEED FOR RISK ASSESSMENT

Violence in intimate relationships is noted in the earliest historical accounts (e.g., Hilton, 1991), but views and understandings of such behavior have changed dramatically over our lifetimes. Indeed, in the decade since the May–Iles tragedy, which spurred the Ontario government to action, there has been progress in identifying those men at greatest risk of committing severe violence in intimate relationships and in building more effective responses to this problem.

A pivotal influence on our decision to study men who assault their female partners was a call by the Ontario provincial government for such research in response to the May–Iles tragedy. A high-profile inquiry identified poor communication across jurisdictions and failure to share records as causes of the criminal justice system's failure in this case. It recommended that the Ontario Provincial Police, "in consultation with representatives from shelters, victim services and other authorities in the field of domestic violence, develop a risk assessment instrument" (Ontario Office of the Chief Coroner, 1998, Recommendation H6). The inquiry also recommended that "all police officers should be directed by written policy to conduct a risk assessment in consultation with the victim and Victims Services during routine domestic violence case investigations" (Ontario Office of the Chief Coroner, 1998, Recommendation C4). A government committee subsequently made 11 recommendations for the development and implementation of risk assessments by police, community service providers, and probation, parole, and correctional officers (Baldwin, 1999).

This work led directly to collaboration between the authors of this volume and Kate Lines, then a detective inspector managing what is now the Behavioural Sciences and Analysis Services (BSAS) of the Ontario Provincial Police, as well as a member of that government committee. With expertise in investigation and records management from the BSAS and research and statistical expertise from the Mental Health Centre Penetanguishene (MHCP) Research Department (plus several months developing proposals, submitting grant applications, and ensuring confidential and secure handling of information), a productive and enduring research partnership began. The ODARA (Hilton et al., 2004) was admitted as evidence in court soon after its publication.

The ODARA proved useful in the case of James Hill.[1] On an unusually warm November morning, Hill crouched between the garbage cans outside the shelter where he stayed after a breakup with his girlfriend Angie Tremblay. She was coming to bring him some belongings, and as he waited, she approached on the back of a motorbike driven by a mutual friend, Kyle Morris. Kyle waited while Angie went to the shelter's front door. James sprang out and ran toward Kyle, an iron bar in one hand and a paper bag with eye holes over his head. He clubbed Kyle on the neck and back with the bar. Angie ran to stop James, but he pushed her to the ground. Kyle tore the bag off James and called out his name. James ran off but was soon arrested and charged with assault, mischief, and using a disguise while committing an indictable offense. At a bail hearing 2 days later, the prosecutor submitted James's score on the new ODARA risk assessment tool. The arresting police officer testified that James's score of 8 placed him in the highest category: Only 7% of men with a police report of violence against a domestic partner scored so high. The prosecutor was prepared to call an expert witness, but the defense counsel made no objection, and the court admitted the ODARA score into evidence and detained James in custody to await trial.

SCOPE OF THIS BOOK

This book is about measuring and communicating the risk of wife assault recidivism. We describe the work that we, and our research collaborators and partners, did to develop and test a risk assessment system. We present this system, comprising the ODARA and the Domestic Violence Risk Appraisal Guide (DVRAG; Hilton, Harris, Rice, Houghton, & Eke, 2008), so that others can learn to score, interpret, and communicate the results of these assessments and to incorporate their results into public policy.

Audience

The work we describe in this book has been published in journals addressed to different readerships and presented at training sessions for a variety of audiences: academics, child protection workers, clinicians, lawyers, nurses, physicians, police officers, policymakers, probation and corrections officers, and shelter workers. In this book, we bring our work together in a comprehensive volume and in a format accessible to readers outside our specialized discipline yet suitable for those who want to delve into more detail. We show for the first time how the ODARA and DVRAG are intended to

---

[1]This case description is based on a case for which we prepared expert testimony. All names have been changed.

function as one system of risk assessment across the criminal justice, offender treatment, and victim service sectors and how sharing a common risk assessment method can aid communication and promote an integrated community response to men's violence against their female partners. The full scoring criteria and various interpretation materials (verbal, numeric, and graphic) can be used by all those who need to identify the men most likely to recidivate, whether to make a release decision, determine priority for intervention, or assist a woman with a safety plan.

Terminology

We have found that risk assessment training sessions afford workers from different agencies the opportunity to exchange ideas and opinions about men's violence toward domestic partners. These workers often use different terms for violence, those who perpetrate it, and risk, even though they may share clients and cases. In this book, we use the word *assault* to refer to specific acts of physical violence (listed in Appendix A) involving physical contact with the victim or the use of a weapon to cause or threaten physical harm. We also refer to assaults and other physically violent acts as *violence*. The ODARA/DVRAG system has been created and validated on *samples* (that is, groups of cases used for study) in which the assailant perpetrated assaults against a woman with whom he had lived at any time, as distinct from a stranger, acquaintance, or dating partner; therefore, we refer to such violence as *wife assault* when discussing our research but use the term *domestic violence* when referring to the wider literature or general phenomenon.

Throughout the book, we use the word *risk* to indicate the chance, probability, or likelihood that an event will later occur. Most often, we mean the risk of *recidivism* (the reoccurrence of crime) or of the man being a *recidivist* (a perpetrator who commits another offense) by committing a new act of wife assault. *Risk assessment*, then, is the process or method of evaluating or estimating the likelihood of recidivism. The primary outcome we studied was whether such recidivism occurred, but we also measured the severity and frequency of recidivism and how soon it occurred. The ODARA and DVRAG *rank order* perpetrators, or place them in order from the least to greatest risk.

We acknowledge that many terms are in current use to describe men's violence against female domestic partners and that readers may use different terms from (or even object to) ours. What is most important for effective communication is that the results of risk assessment be reported in terms with a shared understanding. In our actuarial approach, assessment results are reported as numerical scores and percentile ranks with objective interpretations and also are expressed in words or graphs (Appendix F). This communication is possible because actuarial methods entail measuring recidivism in follow-up research using official records or, in some research, victim reports.

Risk Management

Accurate assessment of risk is essential to effective risk management (e.g., Quinsey, Harris, Rice, & Cormier, 2006). This process should begin with the principle that cases at greatest risk of recidivism receive the most comprehensive interventions (e.g., Andrews & Bonta, 2006). As will become evident in this volume, research has not yet established which levels of supervision, which therapies, or which protective actions reduce wife assault. Therefore, saying that risk assessment should consist of specifying conditions under which reoffending will occur or identifying the individual characteristics that require intervention to reduce the likelihood of reoffending, rather than assessing the risk of recidivism, assumes knowledge about conditions or interventions that is not yet in evidence. Such advice contradicts the body of research on the management of violent offenders. Nevertheless, scores on some risk management guides predict recidivism, as we show in chapters 3 and 4.

Applicability

Although our research was conducted in one Canadian province, we took steps to ensure that our findings can be generalized. For example, no perpetrators were excluded on the basis of race, ethnicity, religion, or socio-economic status; the research is based on a diverse population. Furthermore, casting our research nets provincewide meant that both urban and less populated regions, including aboriginal communities, were included. Finally, we validated the ODARA and DVRAG in the Greater Toronto Area, Canada's largest and most ethnically diverse metropolis. Extensive research indicates that the strongest predictors of violent recidivism are the same across cultures. The methods we used to develop the ODARA/DVRAG system were the same as those used to develop actuarial systems that have proved to be valid predictors of recidivism by violent offenders and sex offenders in Canada, the United States, Australia, Asia, and Europe (Quinsey, Harris, et al., 2006; http//mhcp-research.com/ragreps.htm). We hope these tools will help prevent the kinds of serious miscalculation and poor communication that resulted in the May–Iles tragedy. More generally, valid risk assessment is essential to a system that cannot allocate all services equally to all cases but must apportion resources in accordance with risk.

PLAN FOR THIS BOOK

In chapter 1, we describe how and why our efforts focused on the criminal justice system, with men's physical violence against female domestic partners as a priority. We explain our rationale for developing assessments to quantify risk rather than addressing causal explanations and potential interventions. In chapter 2, we give a brief history of violence risk assessment, with an emphasis on empirical methods, follow-up studies, and statistics used to assess accuracy. We show how this research supports empirically derived tools, and actuarial risk assessment in particular, in contrast to professional judgment. Chapter 3 describes the construction and testing of the ODARA. Chapter 4 does the same for the DVRAG and considers an explanation for domestic violence consistent with the large contribution general antisociality makes to its prediction.

Assessing the risk of wife assault recidivism is only the first step in lowering its occurrence; in chapter 5, we turn to communicating risk to practitioners, decision makers, and victims. We also show the pitfalls of avoiding numbers; verbal terms or categories such as "low risk" or "high risk" show poor agreement and can be inappropriately influenced by contextual factors having nothing to do with actual risk. We illustrate the content of a report that uses an actuarial score not altered or adjusted by subsequent professional judgment. Chapter 6 shows how actuarial assessments can be used to develop criminal justice policy intended to reduce wife assault. We describe our experience and offer advice on implementing actuarial risk assessment. Finally, chapter 7 poses and answers some of the most frequently asked questions about using the ODARA/DVRAG system. All scoring criteria, norms, sample reports, and examples of scored cases appear in the appendixes.

1

RISK ASSESSMENT FOR CRIMINAL JUSTICE, OFFENDER INTERVENTION, AND VICTIM SERVICES

When we began the research described in this book, we believed that a specialized risk assessment for domestic violence might be unnecessary and that existing systems for evaluating the risk of violence in general might suffice. We had analyzed the predictive accuracy of the Violence Risk Appraisal Guide (VRAG), an actuarial risk assessment for generally violent recidivism (Harris, Rice, & Quinsey, 1993; Quinsey, Harris, Rice, & Cormier, 2006), among serious wife assaulters drawn from the more than 500 violent offenders on whom the VRAG was first developed and cross-validated. Of the offenders about whom we had information regarding the victims of the offense that precipitated admission to our institution, 88 had assaulted their current or former wife or common-law wife. These men had significantly lower VRAG scores, on average, than the other offenders; indeed, the 80 wife assaulters who had an opportunity to recidivate reoffended with new acts of violence at a rate of only 24%, compared with 44% of the others. The VRAG predicted violent recidivism just as well in the smaller group of wife assaulters as it did in the larger group of other violent offenders (Hilton, Harris, & Rice, 2001).

Grann and Wedin (2002) reported that the VRAG predicted recidivism against spouses (assault and no-contact violations) better than a risk assessment specifically intended to assess the risk of domestic violence, the

Spousal Assault Risk Assessment Guide (SARA; Kropp & Hart, 2000). Most predictors of wife assault recidivism were also known to predict violent recidivism overall (Hilton & Harris, 2005). At the time, though, police services were crafting rudimentary risk assessments for routine use in domestic violence (e.g., Ontario Ministry of the Solicitor General, 2000), and there was widespread use of unvalidated assessments (e.g., Roehl & Guertin, 2000). Although we recognized in 2001 that predicting wife assault recidivism specifically, and distinctly from general violence, was of practical and theoretical interest, we wondered whether it would be necessary or even feasible to have a system to do so.

REASONS FOR DEVELOPING A TWO-PART SYSTEM

We soon learned that many of the best predictors of violence were simply not available to police officers. We saw that some VRAG items (e.g., early childhood problems, psychopathic characteristics, criminal behavior before the age of 16) could not be scored from police records. We discarded our first attempt at a research coding form and went back to the drawing board. As we closely examined the contents of criminal records and narrative police occurrence reports, we saw rich contextual descriptions of perpetrators' conduct, victims' situations, the history of their relationships, and the events that preceded the violence. Much of this content was reminiscent of early work on the context in which wife assault occurs (e.g., Dobash & Dobash, 1979), and it allowed us to explore possible causes of the violence (see chap. 4, this volume). Thus, for both practical and theoretical reasons, we embarked on research using official police records to examine the predictors of repeated wife assault. This work culminated in the Ontario Domestic Assault Risk Assessment (ODARA; Hilton et al., 2004).

After creating the ODARA, we still wondered whether assessors who have the time and ability to gather more information, such as probation or correctional prison officers and forensic clinicians, would be better advised to use existing risk assessments such as the VRAG. During our research with police files, we had gathered corrections records for offenders who had been on probation or in a correctional institution. We scored several other assessments, including the Psychopathy Checklist—Revised (PCL–R; R. D. Hare, 1991, 2003). The PCL–R is the standard tool for measuring the superficial charm, lack of remorse, and versatile criminal behavior that are characteristic of psychopaths, and it is a robust predictor of antisocial outcomes (e.g., Leistico, Salekin, DeCoster, & Rogers, 2007). PCL–R score is also a VRAG item.

Although the VRAG has extensive support from dozens of studies of violent offenders (including wife assaulters), it contains some items that do not help distinguish recidivists from nonrecidivists when it comes to violence against female partners (e.g., having a female victim, ever married). Our research suggested that it is not necessary to score all VRAG items to better predict recidivism if the ODARA score is already available. It was the PCL–R that significantly improved prediction over and above the ODARA and allowed for closer identification of the men most likely to recidivate. The result was the creation of the Domestic Violence Risk Appraisal Guide (DVRAG; Hilton, Harris, Rice, Houghton, & Eke, 2008). The ODARA and DVRAG work as one system for assessing the risk of recidivism among men who assault their female partners.

We developed the ODARA/DVRAG system using the same approach that was used to develop the VRAG and its related instrument for predicting violent recidivism by sex offenders, the Sex Offender Risk Appraisal Guide (Quinsey, Harris, et al., 2006). Our use of actuarial methods reflects our belief that statements of risk should be generated from verifiable facts and should rely as little as possible on opinion or intuition. It is how the items are selected and combined for assessment, rather than which items are used, that definitively distinguishes the actuarial approach. Every item on the ODARA and DVRAG was measured from one point in time and shown to be correlated with subsequent assaults. The particular combination and weighting of items on the DVRAG were determined by the association of each item with recidivism. Using the items merely to guide opinions about risk and altering the actuarial scores on the basis of clinical opinion can both be expected to reduce predictive accuracy. Altered scores essentially constitute a new system that has an unknown relation with the outcome. Correctly used, an actuarial tool permits an interpretation based on comparing the particular case with others in the same class or designated groups. There is no clear interpretation for an altered score, partly because the perpetrator can no longer be directly compared with similar offenders.

In the remainder of this chapter, we tell why we focused our domestic violence research on the criminal justice system, and on risk assessment in particular, with men's physical violence against female domestic partners as a priority. Our previous research on adolescents' self-reported behaviors and attitudes toward partner violence and on the pattern of results typically found in interpersonal violence research serves as an empirical argument for prioritizing research on individual-level factors. In contrast, much previous work on domestic violence has focused on the wider, social level. We also explain our rationale for developing tools to identify individuals in greatest need of intervention rather than first concentrating on causes and potential treatments. Finally, we describe our work with assaulted women and our motivation to make risk assessment accessible to this sometimes overlooked group of decision makers.

Historical reviews of laws limiting violence against women (e.g., Lalumière, Harris, Quinsey, & Rice, 2005) and partner assault specifically (e.g., Buzawa & Buzawa, 2003; Hilton & Harris, 2009a) have indicated clear improvement over time in recognizing women as persons with the right to be free from physical violence. Records of the Massachusetts Bay Colony, for example, indicate that efforts were made not to eliminate domestic violence by men but to limit the physical injury a husband could inflict (e.g., Pleck, 1989). From the 1800s to the mid-1900s, the penalty in Canada for indecent assault on a man was up to 10 years in prison, compared with 2 years for an assault on "his wife or any other female" causing actual bodily harm (Harvey, 1944; J. C. Martin, 1955). Buzawa and Buzawa (2003) reported evidence that deliberate strategies to filter domestic violence cases from police work in the later 20th century effectively discouraged victims from calling police and prevented a timely police response.

Now, in the early years of the 21st century, physical or sexual violence against intimate partners is a crime in all industrialized nations. It is usually defined in the same way as assault against any adult or, in some jurisdictions, as a distinct offense invoking innovative interventions such as court-mandated counseling (Buzawa & Buzawa, 2003). Most police services have at least ostensive presumptive arrest policies for domestic violence. Even so, arrest is not always applied (see chap. 6, this volume). Clearly, frontline police officers make the first of many decisions throughout the criminal justice process as to whether a perpetrator should be arrested and held in custody. A risk assessment instrument would be a valuable tool to aid such decisions.

The contemporary popularity of court-mandated treatment means that most adjudicated cases result in conditional release to the community rather than custodial sentences (Statistics Canada, 2006). Moreover, relatively high risk perpetrators are more likely to receive treatment (Hilton & Harris, 2005). In the Province of Ontario, government-funded Partner Assault Response Services are aligned with the courts so that treatment is a predisposition diversion option and convicted offenders may receive probation rather than a custodial sentence if they agree to attend treatment. Such practice could be improved with formal risk assessments to identify the offenders most likely to recidivate if returned to the community.

Why Focus on Men's Violence Against Women Rather Than Violence by Either Partner?

Our research on risk assessment has focused on partner violence by men and on current or former marital and cohabiting relationships in particular.

From a practical point of view, we, as researchers at a maximum security facility for male offenders, and our collaborators at the Ontario Provincial Police (OPP) Behavioural Sciences and Analysis Services, were familiar with the predominance of men among those suspected or convicted of violent offenses. Official police reports and criminal records indicate that men commit the vast majority of domestic assaults, especially severe violence and homicide (e.g., Li, 2008; Statistics Canada, 2006). Eke, Hilton, Harris, Rice, and Houghton (2008) examined all intimate partner homicides reported in a federal police archive; 85% were committed by men. Although mothers (and disproportionately stepmothers) are responsible for some child homicides, children are still more likely to be killed by men. *Familicide*, in which the partner and children are killed, is almost exclusively committed by men, and in a context of domestic violence (Harris, Hilton, Rice, & Eke, 2007). Male offenders predominate in police records of domestic violence arrests and are more likely to have a criminal history (e.g., Henning & Feder, 2004) and to reoffend (Ménard, Anderson, & Godboldt, 2008) than female offenders. Hospital statistics, too, show the greater cost of violence for women (Stark & Flitcraft, 1996; Zink & Putnam, 2005).

In contrast, studies of self-reported violence give the consistent impression that in the population as a whole, men and women are equally likely to assault their partners (e.g., Archer, 2000; O'Leary, Slep, & O'Leary, 2007). Observational studies of couples in violent marriages or from at-risk cohorts find that women are as likely as men to be verbally hostile and physically aggressive (Capaldi & Crosby, 1997; Jacobson et al., 1994). Some studies report greater injury and fear caused by men's violence (e.g., Cercone, Beach, & Arias, 2005; Hilton, Harris, & Rice, 2000; Jacobson et al., 1994; Melton & Belknap, 2003; Morse, 1995), but many researchers have concluded that domestic violence by women is equally serious (e.g., Langhinrichsen-Rohling, 2005). Shedding some empirical light on this debate, Graham-Kevan and Archer (2003) compared patterns of domestic violence among students, women in shelters, and male prisoners. They found variations in the prevalence of domestic violence reported by men and women as a function of the sample and concluded (as have we; Hilton et al., 2000) that male perpetrators underreport their violence.

In our research with official records of domestic violence, we found that the woman also assaulted the man in about a third of cases. Fewer than 10% of the records indicated that the woman assaulted the man first; in 2%, she was arrested or charged. Our limited information about these women indicates that they were less likely than other victims to have been severely assaulted or to be concerned about future assaults. Houry, Reddy, and Parramore (2006) reported a 9% arrest rate among wife assault victims; women who had a weapon, were using alcohol, were older than average, or were cohabiting with their partner were more likely to be arrested. M. E. Martin

(1997) reported that dual arrests (i.e., arrest of both parties in a domestic dispute) most often resulted in a nolle prosequi (no current prosecution but the potential to reopen the case if the accused commits another offense within a year) at the parties' request.

We attempted to study women perpetrators. First, we tried sampling cases from police records of domestic violence. After identifying 200 reports, however, we found only a handful in which the woman was the primary aggressor. In almost all cases, the police were called because of the man's conduct, and when women did initiate violence, it was usually considered innocuous by both parties. At the other extreme, we and Suzanne Popham, chief psychologist of the Algoma Treatment and Remand Centre (ATRC), a correctional treatment facility, identified the ATRC's entire population of women offenders in a 10-year period. Women's files indicated extensive histories of criminal behavior and substance abuse and childhoods of relentless and sometimes horrific physical, sexual, and psychological abuse (consistent with similar research; e.g., G. L. Stuart, Moore, Gordon, Ramsey, & Kahler, 2006). Among the 180 women, however, only 15% had been charged with offenses related to domestic violence. We do not dispute that women engage in domestic violence and that it can be severe, nor do we condone or minimize it. Our research with female offenders continues, but so does our challenge to find a large enough cohort of female domestic violence perpetrators to investigate their risk of domestic assault recidivism.

Clearly, assessments can have a big impact on police operations, the efficacy of offender interventions, and the safety of potential victims even if they are applied only in cases of violence by men against their female partners. Similarly, research could help alleviate suffering and injury even if it focused, at least at first, on wife assault. Although our decision might be debated, we note that we could locate no empirical data on the predictive accuracy of any form of risk assessment when applied to assaultive women or to violence in same-sex relationships.

Why Use Official Data Rather Than Self-Report Data?

Official criminal records are essential to the accurate prediction of criminal recidivism. Decades of research have shown official criminal history data to be a very strong predictor (e.g., Quinsey, Harris, et al., 2006). Official data, however, are far from being a complete measure of all domestic violence experienced. Estimates of unreported violence far exceed officially reported violence (e.g., the oft-cited average of 35 assaults per police call per woman; Jaffe & Burris, 1984; see also Hirschel & Hutchison, 1996). Official records, though, are likely to be an excellent measure of the violence that comes to the attention of the criminal justice system. Police officers are obliged to submit a report on every incident they respond to, and reports begin with the record of the complainant's call to the dispatch center. They include verbatim statements, so they are not completely influenced by officers' perceptions of severity (contrary to arrests and charges; see chap. 6, this volume) and can be used as a record of whether an act occurred. Police reports are created very close in time to the actual event, so they are unlikely to be subject to memory problems.

Self-Report Data

In contrast, our research with high school students cast doubt on the validity of self-reports as a source of reliable data on the occurrence of violent conduct within a defined period of time. Although self-reports of lifetime prevalence of assault have yielded meaningful results (e.g., Swanson, 1994), they are less suited to risk assessment research that requires a follow-up time frame (i.e., the time elapsed since a particular "index" event, such as the first wife assault). This issue amplifies the normal limitations of human memory. For example, victims sometimes fail to report incidents, sometimes even of serious violence (e.g., Brantingham & Brantingham, 1984; G. S. Goodman et al., 2003; Skogan, 1986). In addition, pressure to remember (e.g., Loftus, 1997) and *telescoping*, or recalling events as occurring at a different time than they actually occurred (e.g., Skogan, 1986, 1990), can inflate the prevalence of self-reports for any time frame.

We observed this problem directly when we varied the time frame we used to solicit adolescents' reports about their experiences of aggression (Hilton, Harris, & Rice, 1998). At first, we used short time frames (1 month or 6 months) on questionnaires, but then we compared these responses with those from longer time frames (up to 12 months) to evaluate whether extrapolation would be valid. In fact, participants generally reported the same amount of violence regardless of the time frame. There was some evidence that the most serious self-reported aggression was sensitive to time frame, but there was no overall effect of time frame. In this study, prorating to 12 months would have produced vastly different estimated annual rates of aggression depending on the time frame in the questionnaire. Short time frame estimates could not be considered more reliable than longer ones. In sum, although self-reports are of theoretical interest—in large part because they are clearly influenced by things other than just whether the behavior occurred—we cannot consider them sufficiently valid for research in which the rate of occurrence of violence in a given follow-up time is an important concern.

Criminal Convictions

We are often asked why we do not use criminal convictions as the measure of recidivism, rather than criminal charges or a police occurrence report alone. A conviction means that the accused person has admitted the behavior or that its occurrence has been proved beyond reasonable doubt. On the other hand, criminal conviction is not a guarantee of guilt—some innocent people are convicted—but most judicial systems are deliberately designed to accept some (and perhaps many; Volokh, 1997) wrongful acquittals to minimize the number of wrongful convictions. Generally law-abiding citizens are sometimes given only a warning for minor offenses even when guilty. Indeed, the concern for victim services is sometimes the opposite: Why have we relied on criminal justice records at all, as only a fraction of domestic assaults come to the attention of police?

Our position is that criminal conviction is neither intended nor believed to be an accurate measure of criminal conduct. In designing a wife assault risk assessment, we strove for a more behavioral criterion: We ensured that all the available information about any incident (either prior or recidivistic) was declared to be an instance of wife assault only if it was clear that behaviors meeting our definition of violence had occurred, whether or not the perpetrator was charged or convicted. This approach was highly reliable; raters independently agreed on this definition. Available research also indicated that it is a valid approach, to the extent that people who commit the most undetected offenses are the same people who commit the most detected offenses (Farrington, 2002). Indeed, the U.S. Sentencing Commission (2004) concluded that convictions underrepresent criminal offending, are correlated with arrest reports, and produce nearly identical findings in recidivism research. Our approach is also conservative because the frequency of reoffending estimated from criminal justice records underestimates actual behavior.

Although our data-gathering approach was the best of the available options, it inevitably entails some measurement error. Error in the measurement of outcome can, of course, plague all research on violent recidivism and, in turn, places an upper limit on the accuracy that one can reasonably expect to observe for any form of risk assessment (Harris & Rice, 2003).

Implications for Risk Assessment

Despite some limitations, official records are a robust measure of criminal behavior. Although they do not capture all violence, they are likely to be especially representative of the most serious. Also, research indicates that perpetrators who self-report the most crime are also the perpetrators with the most extensive criminal history (Farrington, 2002; Huizinga & Elliott, 1986). The pattern of results for predicting official and self-reported violent recidivism has been found to be similar, especially for violence, with a tendency for stronger results for official recidivism data than for interview or self-report (e.g., Bureau of Justice Statistics, 2005; Farrington, 1985; Monahan et al., 2001; C. M. Murphy, Morrel, Elliott, & Neavins, 2003). Thus, a perpetrator's rank order with respect to risk can be expected to be similar whether based on official data or self-report, although estimated likelihoods of recidivism would obviously differ (see chap. 2, this volume). The false negatives that can result from basing prediction only on official data (i.e., failure to identify men who commit new acts of wife assault) are much less likely to affect the rank ordering of offenders with respect to risk. Percentile rank, as we show later, is especially useful for decisions about managing risks.

Official data can also be obtained for a follow-up of many years, in comparison with self-report data, for which attrition rates of up to 50% within a few months are not unusual in domestic violence research (e.g., Bybee & Sullivan, 2005; Gondolf & Deemer, 2004; L. A. Goodman, Dutton, & Bennett, 2000; Weisz, Tolman, & Saunders, 2000). Official data can be gathered with no intrusion and regardless of the perpetrator's current involvement with a domestic partner. Attrition can occur from official follow-up through death or relocation to a different jurisdiction, and we have learned that records in the Canadian national police archive of charges, convictions, and dispositions are not completely comprehensive. This source of data, however, has yielded excellent predictive accuracy in follow-ups of 10 years or more (Quinsey, Harris, et al., 2006; http://www.mhcp-research.com/ragreps.htm). All these considerations weighed heavily in our decision to use official records and frontline police reports in our wife-assault research.

EFFECTIVE CORRECTIONAL PRACTICE: RISK ASSESSMENT FOR OFFENDER INTERVENTION

In Ontario and elsewhere, there is pressure to give therapy to all domestic offenders in the belief that all perpetrators represent a high risk to reoffend. Research on offender treatment, however, has suggested three principles of effective correctional practice: risk, needs, and responsivity (Andrews & Bonta, 2006; Andrews et al., 1990). The first step in planning intervention is to identify the perpetrators at highest risk for whom treatment will be most beneficial. Those who have little likelihood of reoffending at the outset will have little to gain from any intervention. Dollars spent on such men will yield little cost-effectiveness and might increase the likelihood of offending (Bonta & Andrews, 2007). Those who have the greatest likelihood of reoffending will have the most to gain from intervention and should receive the most intensive intervention (including custody, where appropriate) and have the highest priority if there is a waiting list.

The second principle of effective correctional practice is targeting the causes of crime, referred to as *criminogenic needs*. Although the causes of crime generally have yet to be determined, it is certain they are among the correlates of crime. Thus, effective practice requires, at the very least, targeting personal characteristics that are empirically associated with recidivism and usually not intervening with characteristics unrelated to recidivism. For example, having been exposed to violence in one's family of origin is not associated with recidivism (Cattaneo & Goodman, 2005; Hilton & Harris, 2005), and thus treatment targeting the impact of such exposure is unlikely to reduce recidivism. Attitudes and beliefs about abuse, though popular in batterer treatment (Eckhardt, Murphy, Black, & Suhr, 2006), might also be unsuitable targets for intervention (Cattaneo & Goodman, 2005; see Exhibit 1.1). The suggestion that risk assessments should include such attitudes in order to make the assessment more congruent with existing treatment targets (Kropp, 2008b) is antithetical to evidence-based approaches and might lead to wasted resources and avoidable harm. Any intervention should be expected to affect a characteristic that is empirically related to violent behavior (or at least a hypothetical relation not contradicted by empirical evidence). It is important to keep in mind, though, that prediction and causal explanation are separate activities. Not all correlates or predictors of behavior are causes. Valid risk factors offer only a hint about appropriate targets for intervention. Their essential contribution is the crucial task of identifying perpetrators who are the most urgent priority for the most intensive intervention.

The third principle of effective correctional practice is responsivity: Some interventions work better than others, and offenders vary in their response to interventions. Cognitive–behavioral, social learning approaches are generally more effective than insight-oriented counseling or more punitive sanctions (Andrews & Bonta, 2006; Bonta & Andrews, 2007). We discuss evidence regarding the efficacy of domestic violence treatment programs more fully in chapter 6 of this volume. At this point, however, we note that the empirical evidence is equivocal, resting primarily on comparing treatment completers with dropouts (Mears, 2003). Meta-analyses indicate that the few studies attempting random allocation to treatment and control groups yielded zero to small effects, statistically indistinguishable from null effects in most comparisons (Babcock, Green, & Robie, 2004; Feder & Wilson, 2005; see Exhibit 6.2 in chap. 6 of this volume).

It seems to us that one reason treatment might not have been found to be effective is that there are subgroups of perpetrators with differing risk and differing treatment needs. In many studies of partner violence, modest associations are found among numerous variables. As but two examples, Leonard and Senchak (1996) and O'Keefe (1997) both found small ($r = .16$ to $.26$ and $r = .18$ to $.23$, respectively) correlations between relationship violence and past substance abuse. We demonstrated that when a small minority of a sample exhibits extreme and correlated scores on two variables (e.g., substance abuse and violence), modest correlations can be found in the entire large sample even when there is no correlation between the two variables in the great majority (Harris & Hilton, 2001). Such findings suggest that researchers

EXHIBIT 1.1
Attitudes as a Target for Intervention

In our research with high school students, we explored the role of attitudes in the perception of physical, psychological, and sexual aggression by teenagers (Hilton, Harris, & Rice, 2003). Participants (11th-grade students) listened to scenarios portraying intersex conflict between people the same age and then rated their seriousness and whether they themselves had perpetrated the acts portrayed. Boys thought the aggression (especially sexual) was less serious than did girls, and participants considered male-to-female aggression to be the most serious. Boys who reported perpetrating the most aggression rated the aggression in the scenarios least seriously. Do these results, and others showing an association between attitudes and partner violence, point to a viable target for intervention? Could partner violence be reduced by inducing attitude changes in at-risk groups or in the population as a whole? We believe they do not, for a number of reasons.

In our studies, fewer than 10% of boys and 3% of girls endorsed assault (Hilton, 2000), and other studies of adolescents and the community at large failed to show that violence is substantially condoned in Canada and the United States (e.g., Klein, Campbell, Soler, & Ghez, 1997). There is little evidence of a causal relation between supportive attitudes within a group such as high school students and an increased rate of partner violence in that group (and there is some evidence to the contrary; Hilton et al., 2003).

Persuading people to change their attitudes is a complex task (e.g., Schauss, Chase, & Hawkins, 1997). Some educational interventions regarding partner violence have reported effects in the undesirable direction (e.g., Jaffe, Sudermann, Reitzel, & Killip, 1992; Krajewski, Rybarik, Dosch, & Gilmore, 1996; Winkel & deKleuver, 1997; but see Hilton, Harris, Rice, Smith Krans, & Lavigne, 1998; Lavoie, Vézina, Piché, & Boivin, 1995; Macgowan, 1997). Messages intended to increase awareness of partner violence and mobilize sentiment against it, especially addressed to entire student bodies, are, we conclude, unlikely to have any beneficial effect on either attitudes toward or perpetration of partner violence.

We adopt this position despite the encouraging experience we had in the 4 years we spent organizing and providing antiviolence education in Ontario high schools; we were supported by a network of community agencies, everyone felt that we were doing something worthwhile, and we received overwhelmingly positive feedback from the 2,500 students involved. It was definitely a feel-good experience, even though the objective effects were limited to a small increase in adolescents' knowledge of the risks, consequences, and alternatives to violence. Because of these positive findings, we have argued that public education campaigns could benefit victims, especially campaigns that model prosocial behavior (Hilton, 2000), point out the effects on children (Hilton, 1992), or identify risks (Hilton, Harris, & Holder, 2008).

When it comes to modifying perpetrators' behavior, however, the limited association of population attitudes with prevalent behavior, the complexity of attitude change, and the potential for backlash all advise against large-scale campaigns to change attitudes toward and awareness of domestic violence. Instead, we strongly advocate for interventions that adhere to the principles of risk, need, and responsivity, targeting the empirical correlates of violence among the highest risk perpetrators using skills-based, psychosocial, and psychoeducational methods.

should attempt to identify subgroups that might be responsible for a correlation found in a large population.

Attempts to derive typologies classifying all perpetrators into two, three, or four distinct subgroups have met with limited success (e.g., Capaldi & Kim, 2007; Holtzworth-Munroe, Meehan, Stuart, Herron, & Rehman, 2003; Langhinrichsen-Rohling, Huss, & Ramsey, 2000). One consistent subgroup seems to emerge, however, comprising severely antisocial men disproportionately responsible for severe wife assault (Huss & Langhinrichsen-Rohling, 2000, 2006; Swogger, Walsh, & Kosson, 2007). As we discuss in chapter 4 of this volume, such men also seem to represent a qualitatively distinct minority of the offender population (Harris, Rice, & Quinsey, 1994; Skilling, Harris, Rice, & Quinsey, 2002). We propose that greater efforts be made in future studies of wife assaulters to search for subgroups who exhibit different criminogenic needs and responsivity to intervention.

A final lesson from the offender intervention literature in general, where effective interventions have been demonstrated, is that it is difficult to change criminal behavior. Standardized treatment implemented with high integrity by skilled staff is required (Bonta & Andrews, 2007; Quinsey, Harris, et al., 2006). All these requirements mean that a "one size fits all" approach that provides the same intervention to all perpetrators can be justified neither by fiscal responsibility nor by the need to maximize public safety. A valid risk assessment system is essential to the efficacy of domestic violence offender intervention.

EFFECTIVE VICTIM SERVICES: RISK ASSESSMENT FOR SUPPORTING VICTIMS

Several risk assessments have been developed for use in the criminal justice system (reviewed in Hilton & Harris, 2005), but little has been done with victims in mind. J. C. Campbell's (1986, 2004, 2007) Danger Assessment and related victim advocacy is a notable exception. "Home-grown" approaches have been preferred in part because those who work to help victims may feel the outcome of interest is not the same as that predicted by assessments used by criminal justice professionals. Lethal assault, for example, is often a principal concern of victim services and their clients, although it is very difficult to study empirically (see chap. 2, this volume). Other objections are that typical criminal justice tools include items that victim advocates cannot readily assess or exclude factors very common among their clients. Also, some professionals believe clinical experience serves clients better than products created by scientists isolated from the realities of domestic violence. In some cases, assessments and systems used in the criminal justice system are simply not available to those working in the victim service sector.

A common theme in women's experience of the criminal justice system is the feeling of revictimization by the prosecution through lack of information about the court procedure, disempowerment, and even public humiliation (e.g., S. C. Hare, 2006; Hilton & Harris, 2009a; Landau, 2000). Mandatory charging and no-drop prosecution policies, originally intended to increase action against men who assault their partners, also carry bureaucratic and professional implications that sometimes can overshadow the needs of assaulted women (Landau, 2000). Compared with victims of other forms of violence, poor women, ethnic minority women, and women in lesbian relationships are especially ambivalent about the criminal justice system and dissatisfied with every level of its response to partner violence (Hilton & Harris, 2009a).

In our work with victim service providers, we have aimed for a valid and accessible risk assessment that uses the same information the criminal justice system uses but is both practical in a client interview and sensitive to victims' needs for immediate information about the risk of recidivism. The finding that self-reports of violence from perpetrators and victims can be predicted with similar accuracy and by the same variables as criminal record statistics, despite different rates and other characteristics (C. M. Murphy, Morrel, Elliott, & Neavins, 2003), further supports applying a tool constructed using official records to work with victims. Thus, although the normative data provided in this book likely underestimate the occurrence of violence, one can be confident that the highest ranking men are indeed most likely to commit wife assault, whether scored from official data or from a victim interview.

Women who have been assaulted by their partners can predict the repetition of assault reasonably well (as we describe in chap. 2, this volume). Some women, however, deny the seriousness of their situation, are overly optimistic about their ability to end contact with the perpetrator, or—perhaps most important—cannot mobilize the protection and support they require (e.g., J. C. Campbell, 2004; Kim & Gray, 2008; A. J. Martin et al., 2000). Actuarial risk assessment for wife assault is designed to provide an objective, realistic appraisal of the danger a victim faces. It not only helps women make crucial decisions about themselves and their children but also provides evidence to support their need for protection by the criminal justice system, such as increased police patrols and emergency cell phones directly linked to the police.

It is noteworthy that children figure prominently in the appraisal of domestic violence risk; that is, the number of children that the victim or perpetrator have, the victim having a biological child from a previous relationship, and the victim having a child in the home to care for all indicate greater risk that the perpetrator will engage in subsequent wife assault. These items are on the ODARA and DVRAG because they predicted wife assault, but it is important to note that they do not necessarily cause it. We authors differ among ourselves in our hypotheses as to why children play such a prominent role in the prediction of domestic assault. Possible reasons include stress due to parenting, the peak of men's propensity toward violence occurring at an age coinciding with women's childbearing years, or the perpetrator's jealousy aroused by the constant reminder of the victim's sexual relationship with another man. The burden of responsibility for children may make a woman more dependent on financial support and more afraid of a custody dispute and, therefore, less able to leave home than she could if she did not have children. Another possibility is that because wife assault is related to general antisociality, and antisociality is associated with sexual promiscuity from an early age (Harris, Rice, Hilton, Lalumière, & Quinsey, 2007), the highest risk offenders would have had more offspring.

Each of these hypothetical causal pathways could contribute to the violence, or each could be wrong. What matters is that the existence of children is empirically related to wife assault recidivism. Those items' contribution to risk assessment suggests to us that assaulted women, especially those who are mothers, would see face validity in the ODARA.

These child-related ODARA items also attest to the value of domestic violence risk assessment in child protection. One of the first agencies to adopt the ODARA outside the criminal justice system was a child protection service that has integrated this actuarial assessment into their rigorous assessment procedure. In Canada and the United States, exposure to violence between adults in the home is interpreted as child maltreatment or neglect or grounds for increased penalties for domestic violence (e.g., Dunford-Jackson, 2004; Edleson, Gassman-Pines, & Hill, 2006; Rivett & Kelly, 2006). Although this aspect of child protection is controversial, child abuse allegations could be the first opportunity for professional attention and criminal justice help for domestic violence. Indeed, observers have argued that the mother's need for protection, during court proceedings for example, must inform child protection assessments and that the children must also be engaged in safety planning (Hardesty & Campbell, 2004).

In an early study with assaulted women, we were struck by their focus on their children. Most women suffered much physical violence and psychological abuse before eventually leaving the perpetrator for the children's sake. As one woman stated, "I tried and tried before, but when it comes to my kids, no more" (Hilton, 1992, p. 81). Having children to care for meant that women stayed with perpetrators longer than they would have otherwise. One woman said that she could not simply "pick up" and leave because of the disruption for school-age children, another reconciled with her husband because he had temporary custody, and several stayed because the perpetrator threatened to harm the children if the women left. Of those women who indicated a particular decision point for leaving, few left because of a severe assault on themselves, and most left when they realized that their children were also direct or indirect victims of the violence.

Without a shared understanding of the risks of violence in a given case, the criminal justice and victim service sectors—and their clients—can often be at odds as to the need for intervention. The proliferation of idiosyncratic risk assessments, meanwhile, creates a further barrier to effective communication about the risk and the coordination of all responses to the violence. The use of unvalidated tools, moreover, could give victims an inaccurate picture of the risks they face. Invalid assessment entails, by definition, more error than valid assessment, and errors occur in both directions: over- and underestimation of risk. With a common metric such as the ODARA/DVRAG system, both risk assessment and risk communication can be improved.

Because of the need for decision-making aids, empirical bases for effective resource allocation, and accessible information about risk, frontline and in-depth assessments for wife assault recidivism could improve communication and, ultimately, the coordination and effectiveness of responses to domestic violence. With this vision, we began work on the ODARA/DVRAG system.

SUMMARY OF MAIN POINTS

- Our work to develop a risk assessment for predicting domestic assault was influenced by our earlier work with the VRAG, an actuarial tool shown to predict violent recidivism over many follow-up times, using different measures of violent outcome, and in many populations, including wife assaulters.
- Criminal justice responses to domestic violence have increased dramatically over the past generation, and wife assault (men's violence against female domestic partners or former partners) is of particular concern because of its more widespread and serious consequences than women's violence against male partners.
- Official records, although they underestimate the rate of undetected violence, are most appropriate for developing risk assessment tools for the criminal justice system and are not subject to memory problems and other biases associated with self-report.
- Offender intervention should be based on the principles of risk, need, and responsivity; valid risk assessment is the essential starting point.
- A valid risk assessment accessible to those who work with victims and their clients and shared with the criminal justice users can improve risk communication and promote the coordination of all services responding to domestic violence.

2

ASSESSING THE RISK OF FUTURE VIOLENT BEHAVIOR

Early in the 1990s, one of us received an invitation to attend a meeting at which a select group of experts would confer on the identification of risk factors for violent recidivism. Inspired by the possibility of a checklist that could be used to predict violent behavior in forensic populations, we also began a statistical analysis of offender characteristics to examine which ones could adequately distinguish violent recidivists from nonrecidivists. The resulting Violence Risk Appraisal Guide (VRAG; Harris, Rice, & Quinsey, 1993) predicted violent recidivism with a large effect size, a finding that has since been replicated dozens of times, by ourselves and other researchers, in various populations in several different countries, including the United States (Blair, Marcus, & Boccaccini, 2008; M. A. Campbell, French, & Gendreau, 2007; Hanson & Morton-Bourgon, 2007; Quinsey, Harris, Rice, & Cormier, 2006; see current updates at http://www.mhcp-research.com/ragreps.htm). The VRAG's success, we believe, results from reliance on empirical research and an actuarial approach to its creation and interpretation.

We used the same approach for our domestic violence risk assessments, the Ontario Domestic Assault Risk Assessment (ODARA; Hilton et al., 2004) and the Domestic Violence Risk Appraisal Guide (DVRAG; Hilton, Harris, Rice, Houghton, & Eke, 2008). The success of these tools notwithstanding, nonempirical and intuitive approaches to risk assessment remain popular, often because of anxiety about statistics and the scientific method. This chapter provides an overview of the general issues in assessing the risk of violence. We discuss what risk assessment is and show how statements may be made about the risk of violence that individuals pose. We give examples from our own work on the VRAG as well as the empirical literature on domestic violence.

WHAT IS RISK ASSESSMENT?

What a valuable resource is the Internet! As well as offering moment-to-moment updates on the news around the world or the weather outside our windows, it has a great many other uses. With instantaneous search engines, one may automatically peruse the globe for every instance in which the term *risk assessment* is used in the news media. As we write this chapter, there is a story about an air traveler risk assessment to be implemented by the U.S. Department of Homeland Security aiming to evaluate the likelihood that a passenger is a terrorist, partly on the basis of previous meal choices, no-shows, seat selections, traveling companions, and one-way tickets. A small village in northern England must perform a risk assessment for its annual Christmas event; notices must be posted warning that nuts, animal products, and choking hazards may be in the mince pies and that the hot cocoa might be, well, hot. Another story advises those planning for retirement to make financial investments using a risk assessment to balance expected returns against individual tolerance for the possibility of losses. A common theme runs through all these: Risk assessment means making some kind of appraisal now about undesirable events that might happen in the future. What would a risk assessment for future violent behavior accomplish?

The essential purpose of a violence risk assessment is to enable the differential handling of cases. The decision whether to detain accused persons rather than release them with a notice to appear in court, the conditions applied to release on bail, a custodial sentence versus probation, the comprehensiveness of treatment, and the intensity of supervision on parole are all instances in which a distinction is made at least partly on the perceived likelihood of violent recidivism. Considerable research demonstrates that the effects of criminal justice and therapeutic interventions are maximized when the intensity of such interventions is determined by the level of recidivism risk (e.g., Andrews, Bonta, & Wormith, 2006; Andrews & Dowden, 2006).

Thus, the purpose of a risk assessment is to distinguish among cases either with probability statements about future outcomes or with rudimentary labels such as *low risk* or *high risk*. There is also a strong desire to have a risk assessment that provides information about how to lower risk (e.g., Heilbrun, Dvoskin, Hart, & McNiel, 1999). Many risk assessments are conducted with the assumption that if a factor or characteristic is associated with increased risk, then eliminating that factor will directly lower the risk. But many risk factors cannot be changed (as in weather forecasting, genetic factors for illness, or age at first arrest as a risk factor for violent recidivism). Some factors might be changeable in principle but have no known method to bring about that change. For example, there is no evidence yet that therapy aimed at altering the personality traits most associated with violent crime has actually lowered violent recidivism (Harris & Rice, 2006).

Other factors can indicate risk but do not cause it, so altering the risk factor does not affect the risk. A practical example occurred in mid-19th-century London, England, when officials noted that foul odors from poor sewage disposal were associated with the prevalence of cholera and then interpreted the foul odors as causal based on this correlation (Johnson, 2006). They eliminated odors by building sewers to convey sewage into the River Thames, but more people became sick because these sewers contaminated the source of drinking water. Medical science eventually identified drinking water contaminated with the *Vibrio cholerae* bacterium as the cause of cholera, but the human tendency to interpret correlations as causes still confuses the field of risk assessment. Risk assessment's principal function is to quantify future likelihoods regardless of the causal or noncausal nature of the predictors.

A useful risk assessment must rely on accessible information. For the organizers of the English village event, there would be little point to a risk assessment entailing positron emission scanning of the mince pies because the required device is not likely to be available. Similarly, in a risk assessment for use by frontline police officers, a psychiatric diagnosis, no matter what its predictive value, would be of no use because a valid diagnosis requires time and unavailable expertise. The obverse is not true, however; mental health clinicians working in forensic institutions can decide that violence risk assessment should include a measure of criminal history. Even though forensic clinicians might not routinely check their clients' records of criminal activity, they could easily request such information, and in fact, to do so would be very worthwhile. In general, the design of a formal risk assessment system must be sensitive to the information to which users might be expected to have access.

CREATING A RISK ASSESSMENT

One sense of *risk assessment* uncovered by our Internet search is that of an informal, impressionistic evaluation based on personal considerations, experience, knowledge of the field, and ineffable qualities of the situation. This approach is often portrayed in movies by a wise and experienced clinician who says, "Given his history of abuse and rage, I think he's extremely dangerous; you'd better catch him before he kills again." In real life, this case review approach is ubiquitous, and many clinical decisions are based almost entirely on informal appraisals. Many personnel decisions, too, are based on an informal impression gleaned from unstructured interviews. People make similar, intuitive decisions all the time about whom to choose as a domestic partner, what kind of car to buy, which team to bet on, how to vote, and so on.

It probably comes as no surprise to learn that people are usually better off using some kind of formal assessment. For example, decisions about which car to buy could be based on systematically organized data about repair records, fuel mileage, resale value, and insurance rates. Personnel selection should be based on formal measures of aptitude and skills. The advantage of formal or mechanical decision making has been well established (if not well followed) for about 60 years; that is, decisions are better (more reliable, accurate, valid, profitable) when a mechanical, formulaic, or actuarial method is used instead of informal, impressionistic, or intuitive methods (e.g., Ægisdóttir et al., 2006; Dawes, Faust, & Meehl, 1989; Grove, 2005; Grove, Zald, Lebow, Snitz, & Nelson, 2000; Swets, Dawes, & Monahan, 2000).

The Clinical–Actuarial Distinction

Human decision making has been studied for decades and spanned many domains, including selecting people for employment or admission to educational programs, making medical diagnoses and prognoses, forecasting weather, anticipating stock market performance, assessing various risks in the insurance industry, and predicting criminal and violent recidivism (e.g., Swets et al., 2000). Decision making has been classified into two types: *intuitive* and *mechanical*. In the violence risk assessment field, the intuitive type is known as clinical or professional judgment, which includes using informal or intuitive processes to identify relevant information and combine such information to render a decision. One uses professional judgment when one's experience, personal acumen, intuition, clinical observations, theoretical perspective, and memory of research findings and authoritative advice determine which client characteristics and circumstances are synthesized into a decision. When no decision-making method is specified in an assessment, it is usually the case that professional judgment is in operation.

In contrast, the best mechanical decision making minimizes intuitive inferences by basing decisions on empirical relationships between predictor characteristics and outcomes (Dawes et al., 1989). In the actuarial assessment of the risk of violent recidivism, predictor items are based on well-designed follow-up studies that identify which items are actually related to the outcome. This research permits an optimum selection of items based on incremental validity; that is, the most powerful predictors are selected first, and then items are added only when they improve prediction. In the actuarial method, data are entered into formulas, experience tables, or charts that provide information about the prevalence of an outcome (or its base rate) to yield an estimate of the outcome's probability. That is, actuarial assessment yields a numerical value for each case. A professional who measured a standard set of personal characteristics, calculated a total weighted score, and located that total in a table of the measured rates of recidivism in a population of similar offenders would be using the actuarial method (but would, alas, make for dull TV).

Actuarial experience tables indicate the proportion of previously observed cases that met the criteria for subsequent violent conduct within specified periods of opportunity. In addition, the numerical score permits a rank ordering of all cases with respect to their assessed risk. This rank ordering is what permits assignment to offender intervention (custody, community supervision, or treatment) according to risk. Paradigmatic actuarial methods also have accompanying evidence of the potential for reliable scoring and, importantly, predictive validity.

As an actuarial assessment, the VRAG was first published along with details of the follow-up research, including the characteristics of the sample from which the VRAG was developed, the methods used to select its items and measure the outcomes, and the evidence supporting the reliability and validity (see below) of VRAG scores (Harris, Rice, & Quinsey, 1993). Figures that subdivide all possible VRAG scores into categories, give the proportion (with confidence intervals) of offenders in each category that met the research criteria for violent recidivism with various periods of opportunity, and show how VRAG scores are distributed in terms of percentiles were also provided. The dissemination and promotion of a risk assessment system before this sort of supportive evidence is available is antithetical to actuarial methods. Quinsey, Harris, et al. (2006) provided detailed instructions for scoring each VRAG item and computing the total score (including what to do about missing information), recommended formats for reporting and interpreting VRAG scores, and provided answers to technical and interpretation questions. Furthermore, VRAG users can avail themselves of practice materials that allow them to test their own ability to score the VRAG, advice about how VRAG scores should be used in forensic clinical practice, and materials to support a response to challenges to its use on the basis of misinformation or misconceptions (Quinsey, Harris, et al., 2006).

Empirical research has settled the question as to which risk assessment approach is most accurate. The actuarial method is more accurate, particularly regarding the risk of criminal and violent recidivism (Grove et al., 2000; Quinsey, Harris, et al., 2006). Where actuarial systems are available, unstructured clinical judgment is indefensible on both ethical and scientific grounds (Dawes, 2005; Grove & Meehl, 1996). There have been many scientific tests in which "experts" are given information on which to base decisions (e.g., about diagnosis and prognosis, future academic success, vocational performance, the likelihood of suicide or criminal activity) while the same set of facts is subjected to a formula or mechanical process. The researchers then compare the accuracy (usually in terms of the proportion of correct statements) of the predictions. Meta-analyses using common metrics to derive a numerical statement as to whether either has shown an overall advantage have shown that the actuarial approach has a consistent advantage in producing more accurate prediction of outcomes, especially for violent and criminal behavior (Ægisdóttir et al., 2006; M. A. Campbell et al., in press; Grove et al., 2000; Hanson & Morton-Bourgon, 2007). Despite this evidence, some criticisms of actuarial assessment persists (see Exhibit 2.1).

A Word About Unaided Clinical Judgment

We often wonder why clinical judgment is so weak. Surely anticipating violence by others has always had important consequences, so people should have evolved abilities to sense who will be violent. Research has shown that people commonly use simple heuristics or intuitive rules to make even seemingly complex decisions (e.g., Todd & Gigerenzer, 2000, 2007). Such heuristics are often surprisingly effective because the heuristics, having an evolutionary basis, take advantage of actual features of the natural environment. Although these researchers have not studied clinical judgment of violence risk specifically, their research helps explain why it might perform so poorly. For example, clinicians are mistaken about valid risk factors and rarely get feedback about their own predictions (in Gigerenzer's terms, cue validities are erroneous or unknown). In such circumstances, simple heuristics that are helpful in many other real-world contexts (e.g., attend to the single most recognizable factor, imitate other clinicians, imitate high-status clinicians; Gigerenzer, 2008) fail in violence risk assessment. Of note, Todd and Gigerenzer (2000) also discussed actuarial tools as heuristics that outperform apparently more complex cognitive processing.

Contemporary Nonactuarial Approaches

A simple rule for detecting whether a method is actuarial or clinical is that the actuarial method is well specified and, therefore, also amenable to replication, whereas the clinical method is neither clearly articulated nor easily reproduced (Grove & Meehl, 1996). In a system sometimes called a *guided clinical approach* or *structured professional judgment* (e.g., Douglas, Yeomans, & Boer, 2005; Kropp & Hart, 2000), professionals are guided to make decisions without explicit rules but after consideration of a given list of variables. Although total scores on these lists have been shown to predict violent recidivism, including among wife assaulters (e.g., Grann & Wedin, 2002; Hilton et al., 2004), they are not associated with experience tables indicating a rank order or base rates of recidivism and thus cannot be considered actuarial.

EXHIBIT 2.1
Criticisms of Actuarial Risk Assessment

Actuarial approaches are often poorly understood and subject to unfounded criticisms. Below is a sample of criticisms (in italics) that we and others have responded to more fully elsewhere (e.g., Grove & Meehl, 1996; Grove, Zald, Lebow, Snitz, & Nelson, 2000; Harris & Rice, 2007; Hilton, Harris, & Rice, 2006; Meehl, 1973; Quinsey, Harris, Rice, & Cormier, 2006; Rice, Harris, & Hilton, in press; see also chap. 7, this volume).

Actuarial instruments are said to rely on construction research using a single sample that renders them *not generalizable to other populations* (e.g., Douglas & Ogloff, 2003, Douglas, Ogloff, Nicholls, & Grant, 1999). In fact, construction and cross-validation samples were included in the first published accounts of both the ODARA and the DVRAG (Hilton et al., 2004; Hilton, Harris, Rice, Houghton, & Eke, 2008). Whereas the absolute probabilities of recidivism reported for any sample may vary as a function of follow-up time and other variables, the rank order of perpetrators with respect to risk is more stable and generalizable.

Some authors criticize actuarial tools for their focus on the likelihood of recidivism instead of the *nature, severity, frequency, and imminence of violence* (e.g., Dvoskin & Heilbrun, 2001). In fact, ODARA and DVRAG scores are associated with all of these characteristics; indeed, the DVRAG was constructed in part for its association with severity and frequency of wife assault recidivism.

Other authors consider the *rigidity of rules* to be a weakness of actuarial risk assessment, as well as the *exclusion of variables* that might predict recidivism but are not items on the assessment tool (e.g., Douglas & Ogloff, 2003). There is ample evidence, however, that permitting decision makers to deviate from actuarial results or even nonactuarial guidelines produces worse prediction and poorer offender management decisions (Hilton & Simmons, 2001; Krauss, 2004). In contrast, consistent scoring and interpretation and insistence on using only those items shown to have incremental validity make actuarial instruments a strong basis for aiding decision making and developing policy for appropriate and effective allocation of resources.

A related matter is that actuarial tools *focus on the individual.* Two decades ago, we noted the lack of empirical evidence to support policies that promote not only "safety, [but also offender] and staff morale, and treatment effectiveness" (Rice, Harris, Varney, & Quinsey, 1989, p. 24). This sentiment is still in the current literature (e.g., Cooke, Wozniak, & Johnstone, 2008). Unfortunately, this concern has been used to support risk assessments that call for an exploration of intuitive, case-specific "risk factors." Actuarial tools instead measure the individual's risk using characteristics shown to increase predictive power in previously studied groups.

Another misunderstanding stems from the notion that different approaches and variables are needed for *prediction versus management* (e.g., Douglas, Ogloff, & Hart, 2003; Dvoskin & Heilbrun, 2001; Heilbrun, 1997; Kropp, 2008b). Both policy and daily decisions about offender management must be sensitive to the likelihood of violent recidivism. To allocate resources such as custody, treatment, and victim assistance without regard to violence risk would be costly, ineffective, and unfair. Research to find treatable factors that are associated with changes in risk is desirable (e.g., Douglas & Skeem, 2005), but using potentially treatable characteristics to assess risk in the absence of evidence that they improve prediction confuses the two processes. In our considered judgment, most management-oriented risk assessment advice rests entirely on empirically unproved assumptions about whether interventions aimed at specific items actually lower risk. In the meantime, risk assessment tools can be used to evaluate the success of risk reduction policies (as we show in chap. 6 of this volume; see also Kropp, 2008b).

Furthermore, the final professional judgment is based on an unspecified and intuitive weighting of the item list plus an unlimited pool of idiosyncratic case characteristics, rendering it more akin to unstructured clinical judgment than to actuarial approaches (Hilton, Harris, & Rice, 2006).

The Spousal Assault Risk Assessment Guide (SARA; Kropp, Hart, Webster, & Eaves, 1999) was the first scheme that applied a structured clinical approach to domestic violence. The SARA lists 20 items, each scored 0 to 2, that are summed for a total score. Some items are empirically robust predictors of recidivism (e.g., prior assaults, substance abuse, violation of conditional release, personality disorder). Others are not shown to improve the prediction of domestic violence recidivism (e.g., suicidal ideation, child abuse victimization). In its first published study, a judgment of low, moderate, or high risk predicted wife assault recidivism, whereas the total SARA score did not (Kropp & Hart, 2000), but the score has predicted recidivism in six other studies (e.g., Hilton & Harris, 2007; see also Winkel, 2008) with a moderate degree of accuracy (i.e., an average receiver operating characteristic [ROC] area of .62; we explain the ROC later in this chapter).

The authors of the Domestic Violence Screening Instrument—Revised (DVSI–R; K. R. Williams & Grant, 2006) also advised communicating results in these nonnumerical categories because users in field testing said they preferred to do so, even though DVSI–R total scores predicted recidivism better than the nonnumerical categories. Although permitting professional judgment might increase assessors' acceptance of empirically based risk assessment tools, we believe the solution is not to encourage unspecified, idiosyncratic deviations from validated scales; more suitable would be clear and simple actuarial scoring procedures, attention to the effectiveness of risk communication, and appropriate application of actuarial scores (Carter & Hilton, 2008; McKee, Harris, & Rice, 2007; Rice, Harris, & Hilton, in press).

Selecting Potential Predictors

In the absence of data to develop an actuarial tool, the easiest way to compile a risk assessment would be to ask experts in the field—researchers, therapists, victims, advocates, and so on—what they think ought to be included. Items nominated by the most experts would be compiled in a list that constitutes the assessment. As long as all the items were expressed similarly (e.g., "has a history of domestic violence," "has a drinking problem," "victim fears future assaults"), the list could be a checklist. (Note that potential risk factors can be expressed either as strengths or deficits: for example, stable employment, abstinence, conscientiousness, and social support versus frequent unemployment, substance abuse, irresponsibility, and lack of social support.) The more items that were true in a particular case, the greater one could suppose the risk to be. This approach was used to make the first domestic violence risk assessments. For example, the Ontario Provincial Police queried experts to help them compile the Domestic Violence Supplementary Report (DVSR), a checklist that became advised practice for police use at each occurrence of domestic violence by a man or woman (Ontario Ministry of the Solicitor General, 2000). Our research showed that the total number of checked items did a pretty good job of predicting subsequent assaults (Hilton et al., 2004).

The most obvious drawback to this approach is that accuracy (or predictive validity) cannot be assumed and requires a follow-up study. That is, a cohort of perpetrators must be scored on the list and then followed to evaluate the list's level of accuracy in assessing the risk of subsequent recidivism. Because follow-up research is required anyway to validate scores from the list, this approach does not really offer much savings in effort over actuarial methods.

A second drawback is that the experts might miss some important and useful factors that they were unaware of. This approach cannot, by definition, discover new predictors. On the contrary, it can perpetuate "expert" errors. For example, a majority of experts believe that a perpetrator's being suicidal is a risk factor for domestic violence (J. C. Campbell, 2007), perhaps because some high-profile domestic murderers committed suicide. The catch is that behavior observed only after the recidivism occurs is unlikely to predict it; indeed, retrospective collateral reports also indicate that threatened or attempted suicide was not a risk factor in cases of wife murder (J. C. Campbell et al., 2003) and was not statistically associated with murder–suicide after accounting for threats to harm the victim (Koziol-McLain et al., 2007).

Suicidality did not predict recidivism by domestically violent men in our studies or others (e.g., Hilton et al., 2004; Hilton, Harris, & Rice, 2001; Kropp et al., 1999). It is possible that no predictive relationship between suicidality and risk of subsequent domestic violence exists, or perhaps truly suicidal perpetrators are more dangerous but this could not be detected in the research. Some truly suicidal people either do not reveal it or commit suicide and thereby make their risk of recidivism zero. Other perpetrators make insincere threats of suicide to influence the victim's behavior. We hope that future research will investigate this distinction because it is both theoretically intriguing and intensely important to victims faced with a perpetrator's threat of suicide. The same is true of other items included on some rationally developed risk assessments that are not independent predictors of wife assault recidivism (e.g., stress, separation, experience of violence as a child, weapon use; Hilton et al., 2004; Hilton, Harris, et al., 2008; Hilton, Harris, & Rice, 2001).

This limitation illustrates the main problem with generating variables from simple case reviews. Some experts in the field of violence have studied violent offenders intensively, especially those who have committed the worst crimes, such as serial or mass murderers or men who killed their whole families. A real pitfall in this approach is that the meaning of any finding is always unclear. For example, the finding that serial killers report unhappy and disrupted childhoods might seem very significant, but until we know what other criminals report about their childhoods, we cannot say that the finding is even a correlate of serial murder, let alone a predictor. Similarly, the observation that school killers were socially isolated and suspicious beforehand does not help us assess the risk of mass murder until we know about such behavior among students who did not commit mass murder. Unrepresentative but thorough case reviews can identify possible risk factors for further study, but a good prediction study requires a control or comparison group.

We are aware of no study of the ability of shelter workers or other victim counselors to make reliable and accurate predictions of the outcome for their clients; however, there is evidence that victim advocates attend to valid correlates of wife assault recidivism in their predictions, including substance abuse, children in the relationship, and the history of wife assault (Cattaneo, 2007). We think it is likely that these professionals would be well positioned to predict violence because of their exposure to women returning to the shelter after a repeated episode of violence (a form of follow-up) and to clients who can describe detailed histories of their partner's violent behavior.

A few studies indicate that assaulted women themselves can predict reassault, even improving on the predictive accuracy of nonactuarial domestic violence risk assessments (e.g., Cattaneo & Goodman, 2003; Heckert & Gondolf, 2004; Weisz, Tolman, & Saunders, 2000). Women's predictions are associated with their reports of the perpetrator's erratic moods and behavior, substance abuse, employment status, psychological abuse, threats, and violence toward others as well as the severity of domestic assaults (Cattaneo, 2007; Gondolf & Heckert, 2003; E. P. Stuart & Campbell, 1989). Langford (2000) described a constantly changing environment of what we would call "prediction opportunities" and "feedback about outcome" as women appraise the situation and reassess it with each new cue from the perpetrator's mood or behavior. It must be noted, though, that women can underestimate their risk of reassault (Heckert & Gondolf, 2004) and may also be overoptimistic about the likelihood that they will terminate the relationship with their abusive partner (A. J. Martin et al., 2000), so professionals assisting assaulted women should not rely wholly on victims' perceptions of their own safety (Nicolaidis et al., 2003).

In the search for risk factors for recidivism, the best research designs follow a group of violent offenders to determine who later becomes a recidivist or a nonrecidivist. Some research, especially in the early years of attempts to identify correlates of wife assault, compared men with histories of violence with men without such histories (these studies were reviewed in Hilton & Harris, 2005). The main weakness of this approach is that men with histories of violence might or might not be recidivists, so this method tells us only what distinguishes men who do or do not have a violent history, which is quite different from predicting who will be violent again. Other researchers have compared known recidivists with men known to be nonrecidivists (e.g., Kropp & Hart, 2000). This procedure might exclude ambiguous cases or involve some sort of preselection that could restrict the variability of actual recidivism predictors in the sample (for example, does nondomestic violent recidivism exclude a case from study?), with the result that some important risk factors might not be discovered. We have also found that this approach inflates apparent predictive accuracy (Hilton & Harris, 2009b). A follow-up study without prior selection of recidivists is needed to empirically identify valid recidivism risk factors.

Conducting Follow-up Research

A follow-up study begins with a group of individuals all selected to share a common set of relevant characteristics (called a *sample*) and then assessment of one or more outcomes. In our studies of violent recidivism, our samples have included offenders who have all committed an act of violence, and we examine whether they do so again. We measure several (sometimes many) potential risk factors for each offender in the sample and then compare those who recidivated with those who did not on each potential risk factor. Some advantages to this approach to designing a risk assessment should be immediately apparent. Most important, it asks the right question: Which things that could be known at the time of an earlier violent offense are actually informative about the likelihood of recidivism? Because the recidivists and nonrecidivists are not preselected, the effect on recidivism of anything that can be measured at the earlier time can be studied, so there is ample opportunity to discover previously unknown predictors. The size of the effect can be compared for each predictor; some will show a slight difference between recidivists and nonrecidivists, and others might exhibit very large differences. A tool that includes the factors with the largest measurable differences would be the most accurate risk assessment system.

A more subtle advantage of a follow-up study is that it can eliminate redundant risk factors. It is possible for two or more variables to convey the same information. For example, in some of our research, we found that violent recidivists differed from nonrecidivists in their histories of nonviolent crime as well as their histories of violent crime. Thus, knowing an offender's history of violent offending did not help assess the risk of violent recidivism after his nonviolent offending history was already known. Some degree of redundancy among risk factors is a good thing to protect against missing information or measurement error, but when two risk factors convey essentially the same information, assessing them both increases the time and cost of risk assessment (and encourages the faulty perception that there is more information indicating increased risk). A follow-up study allows developers to discover redundancy and to drop one of the fully redundant factors. In this way, developers can select items for a formal risk assessment system on the basis that items must convey at least some nonredundant information before they are permitted. This, in turn, means that a risk assessment need not include every known risk factor; it need include only nonredundant risk factors. An assessment system that used massive amounts of mostly irrelevant information might easily perform more poorly than the intuition of an experienced expert (Gladwell, 2005, provides some unusual examples). In practice, follow-up studies allow risk assessment systems to be much more efficient.

Alternative Approaches to Actuarial Risk Assessment

The well-established advantage of actuarial methods, especially for violence risk assessment, has not led to a wholesale change in practice, in part because of some remaining confusion about what it means to make actuarially informed decisions. For example, one might think that providing forensic decision makers with risk estimates derived from an actuarial system would result in better decision making. In fact, clinical overrides of actuarial scores consistently produce poorer prediction (e.g., Hanson & Morton-Bourgon, 2009). Professionals are sometimes overwhelmed with irrelevant material (or information of unknown relevance) and fail to make any decision or use only the material they have been trained to rely on; even clinicians considered experts do not outperform statistical prediction methods (Ægisdóttir et al., 2006). Clinicians can blend, modify, or discount actuarial assessment so much that their final decisions are no better than professional judgment (e.g., Hilton & Simmons, 2001). Evidently, the effective use of actuarial risk assessment to improve decision making requires some means to prevent the inadvertent or deliberate influence of professional judgment. We note, meanwhile, that some items in an actuarial system, such as diagnostic criteria and the results of psychological tests, could require clinical skills. It is the means whereby such items are selected and then combined that makes the system actuarial.

The statistical method we have described for developing a risk assessment tool identifies only simple additive relationships between the set of risk factors and the outcome variable. Thus, if two factors multiplied together would have made a larger contribution to the prediction of wife assault recidivism, we would not have been able to detect that. Some actuarial risk assessments for general violent recidivism use methods based on a classification tree (e.g., Monahan et al., 2001, 2006). In this approach, risk factors are dealt with in order, and whether any particular risk factor is considered depends on the results for previously considered risk factors. Such an approach can be captured as the multiplication of many risk factors together and has been called *predictive attribute analysis* (e.g., Pritchard, 1977). It contrasts with the linear approach we used in that the linear approach always considers the same factors, and the answers are just added together to get a final score.

Although the classification tree has some appeal (e.g., in being able to incorporate powerful multiplicative predictive relationships), it also has large drawbacks. The interactions create a complicated structure, and a tree assessment often requires computers and special software. For frontline police and criminal justice work, the simple addition of points based on evidence obtained in a routine investigation is much easier to implement. Furthermore, predictive attribute methods tend to produce large predictive accuracy when developed but fail to replicate or predict much less well in subsequent samples (e.g., Monahan et al., 2005; Pritchard, 1977). Thus, the additional accuracy that can be captured by complex higher order relationships comes at a relatively high cost. Although simple linear systems cannot reflect complex relationships (called *higher order interactions* in statistical terminology), it turns out that, for most purposes, they can predict violent recidivism very well.

WHAT SHOULD WE PREDICT?

The decision about what outcome is of interest partly depends on the purpose of the risk assessment. As we describe in chapter 1 of this volume, we made the decision to create a risk assessment to predict wife assault recidivism specifically because existing actuarial assessments for violent recidivism were not always suitable. This decision affected the choice of sample. Other aspects of the decision about what to predict affect the design and how the outcome is measured.

Individual Risk or Group Risk?

There is a sense in which one cannot draw firm conclusions about individuals using group data. For example, data on the level of crime and poverty in various neighborhoods can indicate a relationship between poverty and crime at the neighborhood level but do not allow researchers to conclude that there is necessarily a relationship between poverty and criminality at the individual level. To do so is to commit the *ecological fallacy*: making inferences about individuals on the basis of data collected about groups and not about individuals. As it turns out, research using individual measures of poverty and criminal behavior indicates that poverty is a poor predictor of criminality among individuals, despite being a strong correlate at the group level.

As with the VRAG, scores on the ODARA and DVRAG and data on recidivism were collected on individual perpetrators and were thus not "group" data in the same sense as the neighborhood poverty and crime data in the previous paragraph. It is reasonable to infer the risk represented by one perpetrator from knowledge of how many similar perpetrators (in the group defined by their particular range of scores) were known to have recidivated. Actuarial instruments are designed to make an individual appraisal based on the known outcome of a group of perpetrators obtaining the same actuarial score. Because the follow-up data were also measured at the individual level, they are applied to the prediction of recidivism by a new individual without committing the ecological fallacy.

Any Assault or Assault Severity, Frequency, or Imminence?

In chapter 1, we discussed why we chose to use violent behavior reported in official records rather than either self-report or criminal convictions. A related matter is whether to restrict the definition of violent behavior to only the most serious (i.e., lethal) outcomes. It is, however, unlikely that anyone could develop an actuarial assessment to identify those who will commit a very specific act of violence such as domestic murder, because it is such a rare event in the population. It would be desirable, meanwhile, to identify perpetrators who will cause the most serious personal injury, rather than to target the greater number who will engage in relatively minor aggression, and to identify someone who will act violently soon or frequently, rather than those who will be violent within the coming decade (e.g., Heilbrun et al., 1999). And these considerations might be combined: Is it more important to identify people who will engage in moderately injurious behavior over the next year or to identify the small number who will engage in serious life-threatening violence over the next 5 years? What if some personal attributes predicted frequent and minor violence but were inversely related to the risk of serious, imminent aggression? We hope it is apparent that if these various outcomes were all predicted by different variables, the design of a formal, actuarial risk assessment would have to settle some important, but thorny and value-laden, issues first.

Fortunately, there is good evidence that all these outcomes are related to the same relevant predictor variables. That is, the personal attributes that permit the actuarial identification of at least one assault are the same as those that predict the total number of assaults, their total severity, and how soon they occur (Harris, Rice, & Cormier, 2002; Harris et al., 2003; Hilton, Harris, et al., 2008; Hilton et al., 2004). Fatalities result principally from violence that causes serious injury, which has itself been successfully predicted by actuarial methods (e.g., Harris et al., 2003). Therefore, although these various outcomes seem distinct, they are in fact aspects of the same thing—the risk of violence—and are predicted by the same personal and circumstantial characteristics. In chapters 3 and 4 of this volume, we describe in detail how we measured these outcomes and examined their prediction with respect to wife assault recidivism.

RELIABILITY AND ACCURACY IN RISK ASSESSMENT

Creating a risk assessment is essentially designing a measurement. Most of us assume without much thought that physical things such as distance, temperature, speed, and even time can be measured; everyday life would be impossible without our ability to agree on these measurements. They are, however, relatively modern inventions. The most rudimentary measurements of distance and time are only a few centuries old; more sophisticated measurements of most human traits, characteristics, and predispositions date back only decades. Two essential characteristics of every measurement are its reliability and its accuracy (a central aspect of validity; e.g., Stallings & Gillmore, 1971).

Reliability

Reliability is the consistency with which scores are produced using the measurement. For example, if I climb onto a bathroom scale and it reads 92 kilograms, and I get off and then back on again and it reads 86 kilograms, then 98 kilograms, the scale is not measuring reliably. In violence risk assessment, reliability is usually assessed by comparing the scores that two or more assessors (e.g., clinicians, research assistants) arrive at when evaluating the same individuals independently. This property is known as *interrater reliability* and is usually expressed as a *correlation*, or the extent to which two variables are associated with each other such that as one increases the other one also increases (a positive correlation; e.g., height and weight) or the other one decreases (a negative correlation; e.g., truancy and school grades). The correlation coefficient (represented in this book by the lowercase letter r) is expressed as a number between -1.0 and $+1.0$.

Sometimes reliability is poor because the user is not doing the measurement correctly—for example, leaning against the wall while standing on the bathroom scale. Sometimes poor reliability is an inherent problem with the measurement device itself—a broken spring inside a bathroom scale, for example. In the case of a risk assessment, training users and providing clear scoring instructions can enhance reliability by ensuring the measurement is used correctly, in accordance with its design. Instructions to insert an unspecified amount of personal intuition would be expected to worsen reliability, so on the whole actuarial risk assessments are more reliable than those that encourage the insertion of clinical intuition.

Reliability is a necessary but not sufficient condition for accuracy. Reliability places an upper limit on accuracy. Put another way, a reliable measure can be inaccurate, but an unreliable assessment cannot be accurate. If that bathroom scale gave a different reading every time, it could not be considered an accurate tool, even if one of those readings happened to be correct. Another aspect of reliability is *precision*, or how close, on average, a single obtained score is to the "true" score. If I got on and off my bathroom scale several times and it read 20 kilograms every time, each reading would agree with every other, but it would not be precise. Its readings differ greatly from what would be the true reading, and of course, it also is inaccurate (it does not validly measure my weight). Thus, reliability is essential for accuracy. Establishing accuracy, though, is a separate and more complicated step.

The degree to which an assessment measures what it is supposed to is central to validity. Psychology researchers attend to several measures of validity. The validity that matters most in risk assessment is *predictive validity* (or *criterion-related validity*), the degree to which actual outcomes match predicted outcomes. There are many ways to assess the accuracy of a risk assessment, but the most useful are those that allow comparison from one study or application to another via a kind of common metric. The *relative* (or *receiver*) *operating characteristic* (ROC) curve is the best statistic for this purpose (e.g., Mossman, 1994; Streiner & Cairney, 2007; for a more detailed explanation than provided in this chapter, see Quinsey, Harris, et al., 2006). To explain the information captured by this accuracy statistic, we will use the illustration shown in Figure 2.1.

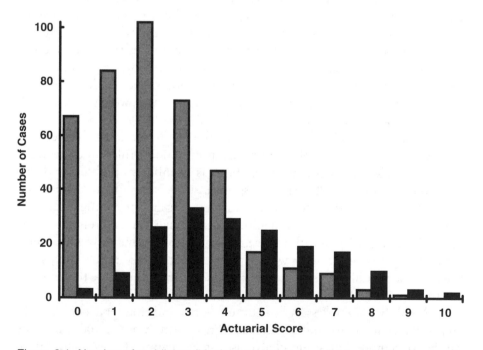

Figure 2.1. Number of recidivists (black bars) and nonrecidivists (gray bars) obtaining each score on an actuarial risk assessment (from a hypothetical sample for illustrative purposes).

Relative Operating Characteristic and Related Accuracy Statistics

Figure 2.1 shows the scores obtained for two groups of (hypothetical) perpetrators: wife assaulters who recidivated during a follow-up period (scores shown in the dark bars) and nonrecidivists (light bars). The two groups overlap, but the mean (i.e., average) score for the recidivists is different from the mean score for the nonrecidivists. A simple t test, described in any undergraduate statistics textbook, can reveal whether this difference is statistically significant according to an arbitrarily selected statistical cutoff point, as can the confidence intervals around each group's average score (see Exhibit 2.2).

Cohen's d (J. Cohen, 1992; Rice & Harris, 2005) is a more useful statistic that tells us how big the difference is. This measure of *effect size* uses standard units that relate to how spread out the group members' scores are proportionate to the number of cases in each group, or the *standard deviations*. In Figure 2.1, for simplicity's sake, each group has the same standard deviation, and the means are one standard deviation apart; thus, $d = 1$.

Base rate is shown in Figure 2.1 by the number of cases in the recidivist group as a percentage of the total number in both groups. In this case, about 30% of the total cases are in the recidivist group, so the base rate is 30%. The simplest measures of accuracy, such as true positives, false positives, and false

---

EXHIBIT 2.2
Confidence Intervals

"Thirty-six percent of 1,000 Canadians randomly polled said they supported the government's current approach to reducing carbon emissions. This proportion is expected to be accurate to plus or minus 3%, 19 times out of 20." Nowadays, we have become accustomed to hearing this sort of research summary, which includes a confidence interval. A *confidence interval* is a point value and an estimate of a range of values capturing the precision of measurement, usually with respect to the "true" value in the population. In general, confidence intervals are smaller (and precision greater) when more measurements are taken (or more people are sampled) and when measurement devices are better (e.g., a stopwatch vs. a grandfather clock).

Confidence intervals also help in drawing conclusions about differences. For example, if the survey were conducted a month later and the result began, "Thirty-eight percent of 1,000 Canadians randomly polled . . . ," the government should not conclude there has been a real increase in the Canadian population's support for its approach to reducing carbon emissions because the new point estimate (38%) falls within the confidence interval of the first estimate (36% ± 3%).

It is common practice in psychological research to accept a 95% confidence interval as the statistical standard; however, it is incorrect to equate this interval with the commonly used 5% alpha level (or *significance* level) used to determine the cut-off point above which an observed result is accepted as chance and below which the result is said to be statistically different from the null hypothesis. In fact, the practice of using *nonoverlapping* 95% confidence intervals as a test of group differences is very conservative. Nonoverlapping 83% or 84% confidence intervals more closely approximate a statistical test with a significance level of .05 (Payton, Greenstone, & Schenker, 2003).

---

negatives, are quite dependent on the base rate, the effect size, or both, so they are not useful for comparing across studies of recidivism. The same is true for correlations, which indicate the degree to which two variables (such as the predictor and the outcome) are positively or negatively related to each other. However, both sensitivity (predicting actual recidivists—i.e., true positives) and specificity (not predicting recidivism in actual nonrecidivists—i.e., 1 − false positive rate) are captured by the ROC statistic.

The ROC expresses the tradeoff between sensitivity and specificity (i.e., giving up sensitivity to avoid false positives versus identifying all recidivists at the expense of false positives). The tradeoff is much less determined by the base rate than are their individual values (Rice & Harris, 1995). The tradeoff can be plotted as in Figure 2.2, which shows the results for the data in Figure 2.1. If there were no overlap between the two groups, the means in Figure 2.1 would be further apart, d would be > 5.0, and every recidivist would have a higher score than every nonrecidivist. Sensitivity would be 1.0, and specificity would also be 1.0. The plot would show an ROC curve traveling up the vertical axis and then extending parallel to the horizontal axis. The

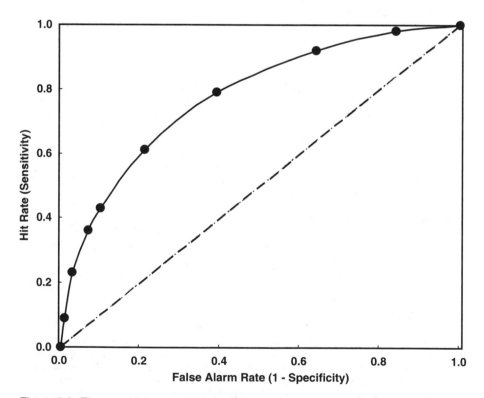

Figure 2.2. The sensitivity–specificity tradeoff illustrated in a relative operating characteristic (ROC) curve (dotted line) for the hypothetical sample in Figure 2.1. Dashed line represents the line of no discrimination equivalent to an ROC curve of .50.

RISK ASSESSMENT FOR DOMESTICALLY VIOLENT MEN

area under the curve would equal 1.0, which is the entire area available and is equal to the probability that a randomly chosen recidivist would have a higher score on the risk assessment than a randomly chosen nonrecidivist.

The accuracy of a risk assessment with an ROC area of 0.5 would be plotted exactly on the diagonal. It would carry a 50% chance of a recidivist having a higher score than a nonrecidivist—no useful prediction at all. The ROC curve plotted in Figure 2.2 indicates an ROC area of .77; that is, there is a 77% probability that the tool used to assess these cases gives a randomly chosen recidivist a higher score than a randomly chosen nonrecidivist. In fact, these data came from the sample of wife assaulters used to construct the ODARA. This accuracy statistic corresponds to a d (effect size) of 1.03; a d of 0.8 is considered "large" (Rice & Harris, 2005). Violence risk assessments consistently yielding effect sizes in this range have great practical value (Harris & Rice, 2007; Quinsey, Harris, et al., 2006).

WHY DESIGN A SPECIALIZED RISK ASSESSMENT?

When we began the research described in this book, no actuarial method existed to assess the risk of domestic violence recidivism. Our review of the literature (Hilton & Harris, 2005) found several follow-up studies identifying some consistent predictors of wife assault recidivism: younger age, lower socioeconomic status, history of marital conflict, verbal aggression or psychological abuse, prior severity of wife assault, and previous arrest for domestic violence. Alcohol abuse, both in the long term and at the time of an incident of assault, was reported to be associated with the occurrence of wife assault (e.g., Fals-Stewart, Leonard, & Birchler, 2005) and had a strong record of predicting violent recidivism in general (Quinsey, Harris, et al., 2006). Both substance abuse and psychopathy (see chap. 4, this volume) were reported to be strongly associated with self-reported violence among men court referred to domestic violence treatment (McBurnett et al., 2001). In fact, an emerging literature was identifying the potential for psychopathy to explain the serious subtype of assaulter identified in batterer typology (e.g., Holtzworth-Munroe, 2000) who exhibit antisocial behavior, severe and general violence, low physiological arousal, substance abuse, and treatment resistance (Huss & Langhinrichsen-Rohling, 2000).

Psychopathy is one of the strongest predictors of violent recidivism (Harris, Skilling, & Rice, 2001). It is characterized by such core features as superficial charm, need for stimulation, callousness, and manipulation and by an antisocial history, including early behavior problems, irresponsibility, impulsivity, and criminal versatility (e.g., R. D. Hare, 1991). Score on the Hare Psychopathy Checklist—Revised (PCL–R; R. D. Hare, 1991, 2003) predicted violent recidivism among wife assaulters, even though they were less likely than other violent offenders to be psychopaths (Hilton et al., 2001; see also Hornsveld, Bezuijen, Leenaars, & Kraaimaat, 2008). Wife assault recidivism itself can be accurately predicted by PCL–R score and the VRAG (Grann & Wedin, 2002) and even by scores on a risk assessment for general criminal recidivism (Hanson & Wallace-Capretta, 2004). The question then arises as to why we would not simply have advised those interested in assessing wife assault risk to use existing actuarial assessments for the risk of violent recidivism or criminal behavior in general.

On the other hand, empirical research supports the notion that abused women know their violent partners best and that this knowledge is useful in assessing risk. Studies have shown that battered women's ratings of likelihood of partner violence were strongly correlated with violence in subsequent months and years (Weisz et al., 2000). General risk assessment tools had no items pertaining to victims' predictions or to the characteristics of perpetrators' relationships or domestic-specific assault history that pervaded the existing literature on attempts to predict wife assault recidivism (reviewed in Hilton & Harris, 2005). As we described in chapter 1, the VRAG predicts recidivism by wife assaulters well, but it could not be used as a frontline police risk assessment because psychopathy and other items (e.g., psychiatric diagnosis, childhood history) require in-depth information not available to these assessors. In the next chapter, we describe our work in developing the ODARA, a frontline tool to assess the likelihood that a man who has been apprehended by the criminal justice authorities for physically assaulting his female intimate partner will do so again.

SUMMARY OF MAIN POINTS

- Risk assessment means making some kind of appraisal now about undesirable events that might happen in the future.
- The main function of violence risk assessment is to enable resources to be apportioned to cases according to their risk.
- Violence risk assessments can be nonactuarial (including clinical or professional judgment and structured professional judgment) or actuarial. Actuarial risk assessment methods have been shown to be more accurate than nonactuarial methods.
- Actuarial risk assessment tools estimate the probability of violence by an individual perpetrator by comparing the individual's score with those of similar perpetrators whose outcomes are known from follow-up research.
- Some items in an actuarial system could be considered clinical, or require clinical assessment, but assessors should not adjust an actuarial risk score based on professional judgment.

- A risk assessment tool built especially to predict wife assault for use by police could include predictors specific to wife assault (e.g., victim predictions) and would be useful only if it included variables police are likely to be able to obtain.
- There is evidence that several outcomes pertaining to violent behavior (e.g., convictions, behavioral evidence of violence, severity of violent behavior, time until violent behavior, lethal violence) are all related to the same predictor variables.
- *Reliability* is the consistency with which scores are produced. It is necessary, but not sufficient, for accuracy.
- *Validity* refers to the degree to which an assessment measures what it is supposed to.
- The area under the ROC curve is a statistic that can be used to compare predictive accuracy across instruments and across studies. It expresses the tradeoff between false positives and false negatives along all possible cutoff scores and indicates the probability that a randomly chosen recidivist scores higher than a randomly chosen nonrecidivist.
- Actuarial experience tables rank order all cases with respect to their assessed risk, permitting assignment to offender intervention (whether custody, community supervision, or treatment) according to risk.

3

CREATING A FRONTLINE
RISK ASSESSMENT

In this chapter, we describe our work developing a frontline actuarial risk assessment for wife assault recidivism. This work necessitated many decisions about what the research procedure would be, which cases would be eligible, how we would measure predictor and outcome variables, what resources could be allocated, and so on. For reasons outlined in chapter 2, we decided at the outset that the risk assessment system would be actuarial, which required us to conduct a follow-up study. We would have to locate a large number of instances of violent behavior meeting a consistent definition of domestic violence and also to find out whether the behavior recurred. In this chapter, we describe how we accomplished these tasks, resulting in the Ontario Domestic Assault Risk Assessment (ODARA; Hilton et al., 2004). We also demonstrate how strongly ODARA scores were associated with subsequent wife assault recidivism (i.e., predictive accuracy), how well users agreed with each other on individual ODARA scores (i.e., interrater reliability), and how the ODARA fared in new tests in similar samples (i.e., cross-validation).

A second fundamental decision we made was that the risk assessment system was to be for use on the front line. That is, although we would use methods of statistical analysis and psychological assessment construction, we did not expect that the principal users of the new system would themselves be psychologists or actuaries. Rather, the idea was that police officers investigating occurrences of domestic violence would use the system to inform decisions about whether to detain men accused of assaulting their partners and whether to offer the victim additional protection. There was some expectation that the system would assist the courts (including prosecutors and the defense) in dealing with the accused, especially for decisions about the applicability of bail, conditions applied to conditional release, and sentencing. We also hoped that victims themselves would benefit from objective information about their partner's likelihood of recidivism when making their own decisions about the relationship or when seeking assistance from the criminal justice system. In later chapters, we discuss the use of risk assessments by mental health professionals and the ways a validated formal risk assessment can be used to evaluate the proficiency of services at the system level.

A FOLLOW-UP STUDY OF WIFE ASSAULT RECIDIVISM

Our primary purpose in developing an actuarial risk assessment, however, was to design a way to help frontline assessors make decisions that are more informed about wife assault risk and to be able to communicate about this risk using a common metric. In this section, we describe the decisions and circumstances that resulted in the method of our follow-up study.

Finding Representative Cases

Deciding to use a follow-up study required us to locate a suitable sample. We were fortunate to form a partnership with the Ontario Provincial Police (OPP). The OPP is the second largest police service in Canada and is the only police service for a large part of the Province of Ontario, Canada's most populous jurisdiction. At the time of our study, the OPP used an electronic archive to record all police contacts; this system housed the verbatim reports of frontline officers, including those of the OPP, First Nations Police Services, and approximately 50 municipal police services. The only police services not subscribing to this archive were those of a few large metropolitan areas, so we supplemented the OPP archive by deliberately sampling from different archives operated by police services in the dense urban area of greater Toronto, Canada's largest and most ethnically diverse city.

Except for this deliberate sampling from urban areas, which was used for cross-validation, we allowed no selection of cases on the basis of region, neighborhood, police detachment, language, or completeness of the report. Ethnicity and racial data were not available to us, so we cannot compare the racial makeup of our research samples with census data. Nevertheless, we were confident that our selection of cases yielded as representative a sample as was feasible with respect to sociodemographic, ethnic, and geographic characteristics of the population of Ontario men with a police record for wife assault during the time of our study. Although such characteristics might affect whether a case of wife assault came to the attention of the police in the first place, the best predictors of violence have demonstrated validity across ethnic and socioeconomic groups (e.g., Bonta, Law, & Hanson, 1998; Walsh & Kosson, 2007).

Using Available Data

The electronic archives contained anecdotal reports of every instance in which police officers had contact with members of the public in the conduct of their duties. The anecdotal accounts identified by full name, date of birth, and address (plus other identifiers) all the people involved (perpetrators, victims, and witnesses), time of day, location, statements by those involved, officers' observations, and the actions they took (e.g., cautioned, arrested, laid criminal charges). Even more valuable was the ability of these electronic archives to link and collate all reports pertaining to any police contact with a single alleged perpetrator, so it was easy to ascertain whether there were prior or subsequent reports of police contact. We were also able to use the national database of criminal charges and convictions maintained by the Royal Canadian Mounted Police, which is readily accessible to frontline and investigating officers across Canada (Canadian Police Information Centre, n.d.) in the same way that regional police records and statewide criminal history databases are in the United States. Professionals working in hospitals, shelters, and even offender treatment programs do not normally have access to these data, but it is possible for them to use the ODARA (we describe an example in chap. 5), and we encourage different sectors to share information in order to implement optimal risk assessment (see chap. 6, this volume).

We also linked police reports to the records of the provincial probation and parole service. Approximately half of the cases identified for the research had some kind of record compiled by these correctional agencies, and the research included information that could be gleaned from these records as long as it would be reasonably available to frontline personnel. An example was whether the perpetrator was unemployed; although not always addressed in the anecdotal police reports, unemployment is something that frontline officers can find out, and therefore we considered it in the research even if the actual data came from correctional files (which themselves are not routinely available to frontline officers). Another example was whether the perpetrator had an alcohol abuse problem. Not all police reports addressed substance use, but this is information that would be reasonably available to investigating officers, and we therefore included it in the research even if it actually came from the correctional files.

The result of these decisions was a research design that considered all information that would be reasonably available to frontline police officers investigating and making decisions about cases of domestic violence. This approach also meant that other frontline personnel such as shelter workers, staff of hospital emergency wards, and other victim support workers could apply the research to their settings because the information could be accessible to them, with the important exception of the perpetrator's criminal record; if a victim were unaware of the perpetrator's criminal history, collaboration with a police service would be necessary.

Case Eligibility

From these vast electronic records, we selected every report classified as a domestic incident. Then we examined each report individually to ensure that the officers' accounts clearly reported that forcible physical contact had occurred in which a man had assaulted his female domestic partner—that is, a woman with whom he lived or had previously lived. In our jurisdiction, a perpetrator may be charged with assault if he threatens to commit a forcible assault, regardless of the effect on the victim; however, we did not use this definition. We included such a case only if a credible threat of death was made with a weapon in hand in the presence of the victim; as it turned out, there were very few of these cases in our sample.

We confined our study to male-to-female violence, by far the most common form in police records. This early decision meant that we could be certain only that our eventual risk assessment system was applicable to the risk of wife assault recidivism. Similarly, we confined our study to couples with a marital or cohabiting history because the nature of the relationship (e.g., just friends, dating, unrequited interest) was difficult to determine otherwise. Not all domestic violence comes to the attention of the police, and thus we could not necessarily be certain that our resulting instrument would apply to the risk of wife assault recidivism among cases without police involvement. Because our primary purpose was a risk assessment for use by the criminal justice system, we decided this definition was acceptable, however, and that we would study the tool's applicability to other cases in later research.

Because of our eligibility criteria and the general approach entailed in the actuarial method (see chap. 2, this volume), we knew from the outset that whatever resulted from this work, we could be certain only that it would apply to the population from which our cases were drawn: men who were or had been living with the victim and who had at least one police report of violence toward the victim. This restriction contrasts with other domestic violence risk assessment tools because of the looser constraints between empirical data and the final assessment in the other tools. Despite the existence of assessment systems intended to be applicable to cases of female perpetrators, dating and/or same-sex couple violence, or nonphysical forms of abusive conduct (e.g., Kropp, Hart, Webster, & Eaves, 1999; Ontario Ministry of the Solicitor General, 2000), no empirical basis for using these systems for such cases yet exists. Unsubstantiated applications are, we would argue, a hallmark of clinical judgment. On the other hand, the Violence Risk Appraisal Guide (VRAG) has been shown to be highly generalizable (see chap. 2, this volume), leading us to be cautiously optimistic regarding the generalizability of actuarial tools.

Although the original intended users of our research were in the criminal justice system, we did not require that the police had laid criminal charges. At first glance this might seem odd; evidence of a charge of assault might increase our confidence that violence had indeed occurred. But consider our purpose in conducting this research: We expected that police officers would use the resulting tool to make decisions during their investigation of domestic violence perpetrators to prioritize cases for interventions such as detaining in a police cell, issuing a warrant for arrest, or transporting a victim to a shelter; such decisions can be made before deciding the final charges. We also expected that bail courts would use the tool to determine whether bail should be granted and other conditions to impose; therefore, we could not require that the index assault resulted in a conviction. This argument is similar to our argument against using criminal convictions for assault as the outcome (see chap. 1, this volume): Had we restricted our initial research to only those men who were criminally charged for or convicted of the index assault, the resulting risk assessment tool would be certain to be applicable only to those persons who would be charged with or convicted of the index assault.

We decided to include all cases in which the police reports clearly and reliably indicated that violence had occurred. Information that gave such indications included formal charges of assault, but also written statements by the investigating officers describing violent behavior, eye witnesses' statements, documentation of injury to alleged victims, and recorded statements by alleged perpetrators admitting to violent behavior. We rejected both cases in which it was unclear whether violence had occurred and the many "domestic disturbances" in which it was clear that it had not. Interrater reliability among our research assistants exceeded .90 (Hilton et al., 2004).

Getting the Work Done

We had a mass of police reports and the ability to link them to case review material in provincial correctional files and to computerized national records of charges and convictions. In fact, that is a long way from a research design. Someone had to read many of these occurrence reports and correctional files and decide exactly, and in precise detail, what pieces of information they were likely to contain. We recall days in a windowless room where we and our research colleagues pored over police documents with the cheerful assistance of an officer on administrative duties. Then a coding manual had to be written exactly specifying how each useable piece of information was to be turned into a number or precise descriptive verbal terms (Exhibit 3.1 shows excerpts from the manual). Practice and testing with drafts of the coding manual had to follow before it was finalized, and formal tests of interrater reliability were conducted. Three students spent a summer coding with our research team, producing data that we used to explore initially promising variables. Because of the months of training required for accurate coding, we replaced summer positions with a full-time research assistant, Ruth Houghton, who became a principal coder along with our colleagues Carol Lang and Catherine Cormier.

Meanwhile, research students read every police occurrence report and screened it for eligibility. Our requests for correctional files were processed by many parole and probation offices as well as staff members at the provincial archives, with the assistance of Ministry of Corrections officials, and we conducted our computer interrogation of each perpetrator's criminal record in the OPP Behavioural Sciences and Analysis Services offices with much assistance from the research manager, Angela Wyatt Eke, and information technology staff. Finally, we and our colleagues had to carefully code more than 1,400 cases and then enter them into a computerized database for analysis; our administrative assistant, Sonja Dey, entered about 3 million data points into dozens of files. This is meticulous work, and we gratefully acknowledge these colleagues.

Identifying Potential Predictors

The next task was to identify and measure the potential risk factors. We cast our nets broadly, including all the recommendations of experts embodied in existing rationally derived systems and previous follow-up studies (Hilton & Harris, 2005), and established risk factors from the research literature on the prediction of violent recidivism in general, including the VRAG. This approach meant coding variables about childhood adjustment, early aggression, and exposure to family violence, as well as symptoms associated with several psychiatric diagnoses. We also included a few variables that reflected our own hypotheses about the causes of domestic violence (e.g., specific aspects of sexual jealousy, including the perpetrator's statement of uncertainty that he is the father of his purported children). However, we confined our analyses for the frontline risk assessment to information that police officers could reasonably be expected to have access to, such as offense details, victim statements, and perpetrator's police record. All the other potential risk factors (e.g., pertaining to psychiatric symptoms and childhood history) were set aside for a study of in-depth predictors (discussed in chap. 4, this volume).

EXHIBIT 3.1
Sample Portions of the Research Coding Manual

Demographic Information for the Index

A "*domestic*" incident is one in which the offender is the perpetrator against his current or previous cohabiting partner and/or her children. The "*index*" incident is the domestic incident which occurred prior to and closest to January 1, 1997 and which involved the use of physical violence by the offender against his current or previous cohabiting partner. "*Physical violence*" includes physical contact with the victim or a credible threat of death with a weapon in hand in the presence of the victim. A "*non-domestic*" incident is one which does not involve the offender's current or previous cohabiting partner and/or her children. Include a non-domestic incident only if the offender physically or sexually assaulted the victim, used weapons during the incident, or was stalking the victim.

OMPPAC (police database) incident report number. Specify the OMPPAC identification number from the OMPPAC incident report (do not include the dash). Code "999" for the first incident report which is not an OMPPAC report, "888" for the second, "777" for the third, etc.

Organization Identification (ORG I.D.). Specify the organization identification (numbers and/or letters) from the OMPPAC report.

Date of index. Code the date the index occurred, not the date that it was reported.

The Victims of the Incident

Relationship of the victims to the offender—Specify the number of victims in each category.

   (1) index partner (victim of the index incident)
   (2) previous partner (previous to the index partner)
   (3) new partner (after the index partner)
   (4) offender's biological child
   (5) child of the index partner (but not offender's child)
   (6) offender's biological family (e.g., mother, father, sister, etc.)
   (7) biological family of the index partner
   (8) offender's friend, acquaintance or neighbour
   (9) stranger
  (10) other (specify)

Physical Injury to the Most Seriously Injured Victim of the Index

VRAG Injury Scale—"Weapon" refers to any object used by the offender to injure the victim, other than his hands or feet.

  1 = no injury
  2 = slight injury, no weapon
  3 = slight injury, weapon
  4 = treated in clinic and released
  5 = victim hospitalized at least one night
  6 = death
  7 = death and postdeath mutilation

DAS Injury Scale

Code "." (NA) if the victim died as a result of her injuries.
  1 = no injuries and/or lasting pain
  2 = bruises, cuts, and/or continuing pain
  3 = severe contusions, burns, broken bones (include cuts requiring stitches)
  4 = head injury, internal injury, permanent injury
  5 = wounds from weapon

(continues)

EXHIBIT 3.1
Sample Portions of the Research Coding Manual   *(Continued)*

The Offender's Use of Physical and Sexual Violence During the Index
Offender used physical and/or or sexual violence against the victims of the index (y/n)—If "yes", code below:

minor violence (y/n)—*"Minor violence"* includes:—held the victim down—threw something at the victim that could hurt—twisted the victim's arm or hair—pushed or shoved the victim—grabbed the victim (include "pulled" and "dragged")—slapped the victim ("slapped" includes any hitting other than punching. include "striking".)—other minor violence (include "shaking".)

severe violence (y/n)—*"Severe violence"* includes:—used a knife or gun on the victim ("used" implies actual or attempted contact with the victim's body. include discharging a gun while pointing it at the victim.)—punched the victim with his fist or hit the victim with something that could hurt—choked the victim (include "grabbed by the neck or throat" or "headlock".)—slammed the victim against a wall—"beat up" the victim—burned or scalded the victim on purpose—kicked the victim—other severe violence (include "picked up and threw"; "head-butting"; "pushed down the stairs"; biting.)

sexual violence (y/n)—*Sexual violence* includes any use of force (by any means) to coerce the victim into having sexual contact when he/she does not want to include any sexual contact with children whether or not force is used.

Measuring Recidivism

The next step was to define the outcome. Our cohort was selected from the register of cases that were in the police record system several years before we began gathering data. For each perpetrator, the incident of wife assault that occasioned a police report closest to but no later than a specified date (the end of 1996) was declared to be his index offense; thus, by definition, every case had at least one instance of wife assault. After we identified men with an eligible index assault, we followed them through subsequent records and found that about one third (30%) of cases reappeared in police records with at least one subsequent instance of wife assault, which we defined as *recidivism*. Thus, we used a follow-up method; we did not select recidivists a priori or attempt a follow-back study.

For the recidivistic offenses, we coded several related outcome measures: a dichotomous variable indicating the occurrence of at least one subsequent instance of wife assault in the record, the total number of such offenses, the total amount of injury caused in such subsequent offenses based on two scales (J. C. Campbell, 2007; Quinsey, Harris, Rice, & Cormier, 2006), and the seriousness of the reoffending based on a standard definition of the severity of violent acts (Straus, 1979; Straus, Hamby, Boney-McCoy, & Sugarman, 1996) and the Cormier–Lang weighted score for each criminal charge (Harris, Rice, & Quinsey, 1993; Quinsey, Harris, et al., 2006). Finally, we derived a measure of the time between the index assault and the resolution of subsequent criminal charges for recidivism. We decided that the primary outcome measure would be dichotomous: An offender either committed subsequent wife assault or he did not. In our prior research with the VRAG, this measure was the simplest to obtain, and it correlated highly with other outcome measures (e.g., number of subsequent offenses, severity of recidivism, time until recidivism; Quinsey, Harris, et al., 2006).

Having all the perpetrator incidents linked to each other in the police records system meant that the people who coded the outcome were not blind to the measurement of the potential risk factors (and vice versa), which is a possible source of methodological bias. We decided against attempting a masked coding procedure for all cases because a fully trained researcher would have had to read through all the material to identify the index and separate information about potential predictors from recidivism, a tricky task because police reports at every incident usually referred to previous incidents. It would have required one of our research coders to be dedicated to this task at the outset, adding months or years to the project. Instead, we conducted a test of interrater reliability on 24 blinded cases (Hilton et al., 2004) to ensure that the accuracy we reported for the resulting risk assessment tool did not benefit from any such threat to internal validity; reliability coefficients were .90 for ODARA score and .91 for recidivism. In fact, the ODARA predicted recidivism with the same accuracy in these blinded cases as it did in the unmasked test (Hilton et al., 2004).

To be counted as a recidivist, a perpetrator had to have clear evidence in the police records of a later assault against a female domestic partner using the same definition as that for case eligibility. We did not contact victims, perpetrators, family members, neighbors, local police, probation officials, or anyone else to find out about any subsequent domestic violence that did not appear in the criminal justice or police records. Thus, our recorded rates of repetition of domestic violence almost certainly underestimate the actual rates (even granting that some men subsequently charged or convicted were innocent of any recidivism). At one level, this limitation is serious and of indeterminate magnitude. The ODARA's norms could not be used to make statements such as "This man is a member of a group of wife assaulters who had a 22% likelihood of subsequent wife assault . . ." without the qualification ". . . that came to the attention of police." At another level, however, the problem of undetected recidivism is much less serious because there is good reason to believe that those persons who commit the most officially detected crimes are the same as those who engage in the most undetected crimes (Farrington, 2002; see chap. 2, this volume). Furthermore, had we included incidents of recidivism that were not reported to police, the resulting tool would have less ready application to the criminal justice system. Our later research has examined the utility of the ODARA to victim services and their clients who do not normally have access to the databases we used to develop the ODARA (discussed in chap. 5, this volume).

Detecting Actual Predictors

The next task was to select the most efficient list of valid predictors of wife assault recidivism using multivariate statistical analyses. All these analyses used dichotomous wife assault recidivism as the dependent variable. The predictors were selected from among the variables that pertained to the time up to and including the index assault, before subsequent recidivism. Thus, we used a prediction method; we did not examine which variables were correlated with prior violence (i.e., "postdiction"). More than 30 independent variables were significantly correlated with the outcome, and we used several steps to identify the best of these predictors.

First, we subdivided them into sets of similar variables: perpetrator's history of previous domestic violence (e.g., number and severity of prior assaults), his other criminal history (e.g., correctional sentences, parole violations), sociodemographic variables (e.g., age, employment status), characteristics of the relationship (e.g., duration, separations), victim's circumstances (e.g., social support, having young children at home), and details of the index assault (e.g., injury, a weapon used). We tested the potential predictors within each set in repeated random samples of two thirds of the 589 cases. From each set, we discarded potential predictors (even those that were significantly related to the outcome) unless they made a statistically significant incremental contribution in most subsample tests. This test of incremental contribution used multivariate logistic regression, a statistical technique that uses many repeated calculations to hold one or more variables constant while examining the additional effect of another in their combined association with the outcome variable. Finally, we tested all the variables that survived this analysis together and retained only those that made a significant independent contribution in the total sample. A list of 13 items resulted (see Appendix A).

In our analyses, some valid risk factors that passed all our tests had stronger relationships with the outcome than others. For example, the perpetrator's substance abuse was twice as strong a predictor as whether he threatened to harm or kill anyone in the index offense. We could have given each item a weighting that reflected the strength of this relationship in construction (as we had done in the construction of the VRAG). However, previous research (Wormith & Goldstone, 1984) has shown that whereas these linear relationships are remarkably robust (i.e., replicate in repeated retesting), weightings are much less robust. The accuracy sacrificed by giving each item the same weight tends to be small, a finding we also found to be true for the ODARA. Similarly, the loss in accuracy sacrificed by making each item binary (dichotomous or yes–no) also tends to be small (Grove & Meehl, 1996). Thus, to make the final risk assessment as easy as possible to implement, we decided to forgo the small increment in

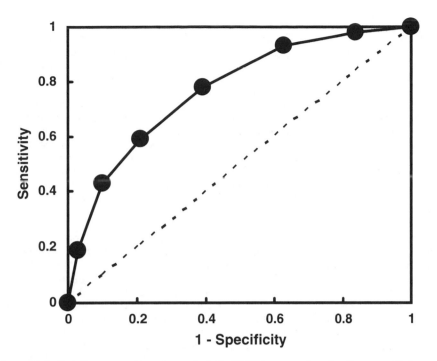

Figure 3.1. Relative operating characteristic (ROC) curve showing the sensitivity and specificity of the Ontario Domestic Assault Risk Assessment (ODARA) at each cutoff score.

predictive accuracy that we could have achieved using more complex scoring procedures, and instead we made each item weight the same and each item have only two possible answers: 0 or 1. The result was the 13-item ODARA, which has a total possible score ranging from 0 to 13. The ODARA score yielded a large effect in discriminating wife assault recidivists from nonrecidivists in the construction sample of 589. Figure 3.1 illustrates the predictive accuracy of the ODARA in the construction sample, and Exhibit 3.2 provides further explanation.

THE ONTARIO DOMESTIC ASSAULT RISK ASSESSMENT

Our actuarial approach to designing a risk assessment and identifying individual items revealed some surprising findings. First, some variables expected to be good predictors were, in fact, not significantly related to recidivism. An example was injury to the victim in the index assault. Another was whether the perpetrator threatened suicide or appeared to be suicidal at the time of the index assault. Other variables were related to recidivism but did

EXHIBIT 3.2
Further Psychometric Properties of the Ontario Domestic Assault Risk
Assessment (ODARA) in the Construction Sample

Figure 3.1 illustrates the linear relationship between ODARA category and the probability of wife assault recidivism. As illustrated in chapter 2 of this volume, adopting different cutoff scores would yield different true positives and false alarm rates. For example, if every case scoring above 3 were predicted to recidivate, whereas all below 4 were predicted not to recidivate, there would be a hit rate (sensitivity) of .63 and a false alarm rate (1 – specificity) of .22. Sensitivity–specificity pairs can be derived for all possible ODARA cutoff scores and then plotted to reveal a symmetrical relative operating characteristic (ROC) curve subtending a proportional area of .77.

By customary standards, this ROC falls in the range of a large effect size (Rice & Harris, 2005). Recall that this ROC area can be interpreted as a probability of .77 that a randomly selected recidivist would have a higher score than a randomly selected nonrecidivist.

There are other ways to capture predictive relationships. For example, we could compute the average difference in ODARA score between those who recidivated and those who did not (Cohen's d, described in chap. 2); in the case of the ODARA construction sample, $d = 1.03$. The Pearson product–moment correlation coefficient for the association between the seven ODARA categories and dichotomous recidivism in the ODARA construction sample was .44, $p < 001$. Or we can adopt a cutoff above which all cases are expected to recidivate and calculate how often that expectation is correct. This statistic is the positive predictive power (PPP). Similarly, negative predictive power (NPP) characterizes the accuracy of the expectation that all those at or below the selected cutoff will not recidivate. Unlike the ROC, PPP and NPP depend on the overall base rate; therefore, they do a generally poorer job of characterizing predictive accuracy.

not improve the risk assessment after the 13 selected items were included. The perpetrator's unemployment and sexual jealousy are examples; both were positively related to recidivism in our study, but neither assisted with the assessment of risk over and above the ODARA items. ODARA users are often troubled by the omission of these two variables, especially experienced practitioners who have been attending to these "risk factors" for years or who are familiar with assessment systems that not only include them but permit users to weight them highly (e.g., Kropp et al., 1999).

Why did we not add a component to the ODARA scoring instructions that gave users permission to consider any non-ODARA items they thought relevant and make an adjustment to the score (e.g., up or down one or two ODARA categories) on that basis? We had, in fact, done that in our early work on using the VRAG (Webster, Harris, Rice, Cormier, & Quinsey, 1994). Such permission might seem at first to have no risks and considerable benefit to the acceptability of the ODARA, as actuarially oriented users could rely on the unadjusted score while intuitively oriented users would have permission to incorporate other material and adjust the total score. However, because we had found no evidence that clinicians could improve on the predictive accuracy of the VRAG by allowing a clinical override (and, in fact, made worse risk management decisions; Hilton & Simmons, 2001), we recommended in subsequent publications about the VRAG that clinicians use only the actuarial score (Quinsey, Harris, et al., 2006). For the same reason, we do not advise any postscoring adjustment to the ODARA score. A meta-analytic study confirmed that unadjusted actuarial scores were the best predictors of domestic violence (see Exhibit 3.3).

Characteristics of the Ontario Domestic Assault Risk Assessment

The final instrument had an average ODARA score of 2.89, with a standard deviation of 2.14, in the construction sample. We tested its interrater reliability (again, by getting two people to code a set of cases and then comparing their answers) among experienced police officers. The interrater reliability coefficient was .95 (Hilton et al., 2004) and far above the minimum level expected for a useful assessment.

The second, and more difficult, aspect of evaluating an assessment's value is accuracy, or the extent to which it measures what it purports to measure. It is common for test designers to establish what is known as *concurrent validity* by showing that the new test is correlated with existing tests designed to assess the same thing. In the case of the ODARA, we showed that it yielded

EXHIBIT 3.3
Collecting and Comparing Research Findings

Throughout this book, we summarize bodies of research results in a narrative way. That is, we report on the overall size and direction of research findings rather informally, apparently based on our overall impressions of the accumulated research. Just as there is a better way to make risk-related decisions (i.e., statistical, actuarial), readers might ask whether there is a more precise way to summarize research findings. And the answer is affirmative: When there are enough well-conducted studies, meta-analysis provides a statistical way to summarize all the findings. Meta-analysis helps compensate for low power due to small samples in individual studies and can even test for possible sources of differences among research results. Sampling characteristics of the original studies can preclude meaningful statistical inference, but the descriptive benefits of meta-analysis remain (e.g., Berk, 2007).

Meta-analyses support conclusions about the general superiority of actuarial methods over informal clinical judgment in general (e.g., Ægisdóttir et al., 2006; Grove, Zald, Lebow, Snitz, & Nelson, 2000), among general and sex offender risk assessments (M. A. Campbell, French, & Gendreau, in press; Hanson & Morton-Bourgon, 2009), and even among the few studies of domestic violence risk assessments (Hanson, Helmus, & Bourgon, 2007). In their analysis of 11 studies, Hanson et al. (2007) reported that formal risk assessments had an average predictive accuracy equivalent to a relative operating characteristic (commonly referred to as "ROC") area of .62 for spousal assault recidivism. Among domestic violence risk assessments, actuarial tools tended to perform better, especially the Ontario Domestic Assault Risk Assessment and the Domestic Violence Risk Appraisal Guide (see chap. 4), and there was no evidence that adding clinical intuition improved prediction—in fact, the trend was in opposite direction (Hanson et al., 2007). Several nonactuarial schemes exhibited no statistically significant predictive accuracy.

---

statistically significant correlations with other rationally constructed domestic violence risk assessments, including our own jurisdiction's Domestic Violence Supplementary Report (DVSR) checklist for police (Ontario Ministry of the Solicitor General, 2000), the Danger Assessment (DA; J. C. Campbell, 1986, 2007), and the Spousal Assault Risk Assessment (SARA; Kropp et al., 1999). We scored these schemes as closely as we could to their instructions, although we conducted no victim interviews for the study. We scored them using correctional records for items that required more than frontline information (e.g., evidence of mental health problems, psychopathy), although these items were not considered for the ODARA.

Concurrent validity was not sufficient evidence of accuracy. The form of validity most relevant to a risk assessment is predictive accuracy: the extent to which the assessment predicts the outcome it was designed to predict. It turned out that each of the other assessments we tested predicted wife assault recidivism, but the ODARA was significantly more accurate. Figure 3.2 compares the ODARA scores of recidivists and nonrecidivists. Few cases scored 5 or above, which meant that these scores had to be collapsed into two categories (5–6 and 7–13) in order to yield reliable estimates of recidivism. This figure is similar to the example given in Figure 2.1, where the black bars represent those cases who recidivated. A slightly different way to present the same results is with only one bar instead of two for each category. In this case, the height of each bar shows the proportion of all cases in each category that met the criteria for wife assault recidivism. Figure 3.3 shows the proportion of recidivists in each ODARA category for two samples: the 589 construction

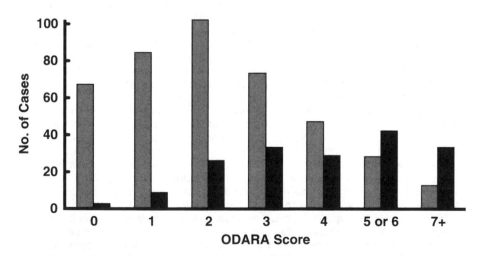

Figure 3.2. Ontario Domestic Assault Risk Assessment (ODARA) scores of recidivists (black bars) and nonrecidivists (gray bars) in the ODARA construction sample. Data from Hilton et al. (2004).

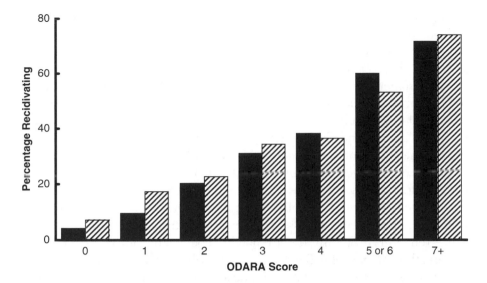

Figure 3.3. Percentage of perpetrators recidivating according to Ontario Domestic Assault Risk Assessment (ODARA) score in the ODARA construction sample (black bars) and cross-validation samples (cross-hatched bars). ODARA construction sample data from Hilton et al. (2004); cross-validation data from Hilton, Harris, Rice, Houghton, and Eke (2008) and Hilton and Harris (2009b).

sample cases (in black bars) and the remaining cases in our research (in cross-hatched bars).

Cross-Validations

We tested the validity of the ODARA in the sample of 100 cases we had earlier set aside for cross-validation; the ODARA significantly predicted wife assault recidivism in this sample, too, with a relative operating characteristic (ROC) area of .72, a large effect (Hilton et al., 2004). In two subsequent tests using entirely new cases, the predictive validity of the ODARA was reconfirmed. We were able to conduct a cross-validation when we tested the relative accuracy of our in-depth assessment (Hilton & Harris, 2007; Hilton, Harris, Rice, Houghton, & Eke, 2008). In that study, we found further evidence for its statistical association with the frequency and severity of wife assault recidivism (see chap. 4, this volume). The third cross-validation involved cases that had no in-depth assessment information available (Hilton & Harris, 2009b). This time, we experimented with different research designs and found that the ODARA yielded ROCs of up to .80 when equal-sized groups of known wife assault recidivists and nonrecidivists (with no known subsequent violence) were compared. The total number of cases in all three studies was more than 1,420.

Across all our samples, 32% of men recidivated, and the ODARA yielded an ROC area of .71, corresponding to a large effect size and a correlation of $r = .36$ (for explanations of correlation, accuracy statistics, and effect sizes, see chap. 2, this volume; Rice & Harris, 2005). ODARA category yielded smaller but statistically significant ($p < .001$) correlations with the total number of recidivistic offenses, the total amount of injury caused, the severity of new assaults, and the seriousness of criminal charges at recidivism ($rs = .26, .22, .30,$ and $.20$, respectively). As well, the available data pertaining to time at risk indicated that recidivists with higher ODARA scores reoffended sooner ($r = .26$; Hilton et al., 2004). The precision of measurement (that is, how close, on average, a single obtained score is to the "true" score) is calculated using interrater reliability and the standard error of measurement (SEM, which is equal to the standard deviation multiplied by the square root of 1 – reliability). The interrater reliability coefficient for the ODARA was .90, and the SEM for ODARA category across all cases was .54. The 95% confidence interval (see Exhibit 2.2) around an obtained score was 1.06. That is, an individual result would be expected to be misclassified (i.e., deviate from the true score) by more than one category in only 5% of cases.

APPLYING THE ONTARIO DOMESTIC ASSAULT RISK ASSESSMENT

The next step was to create a manual describing the eligibility criteria for scoring the ODARA and how to score each item as closely as possible to the way in which it was coded in the research (Appendix A). As simple as this might sound, the process went through many drafts as we sought to respond to users' questions and correct for misinterpretations. One version of the manual, produced by our OPP colleague Tracy Lowe-Wetmore, was designed for law enforcement use and attempted to express the research coding criteria in language familiar to frontline police officers. Some important aspects of the manual were a prorating table to allow scoring when there is missing information (Appendix A); an experience table, a tabulated version of Figure 3.3 that permits statements about an individual's risk of wife assault recidivism in both absolute and relative terms (Appendix B); and an example risk assessment report summary (Appendix B). The manual improved scoring accuracy among police officers (Hilton, Harris, Rice, Eke, & Lowe-Wetmore, 2007; see also chap. 5, this volume).

A more subtle issue pertained to whether we would recommend any factors to be added to ODARA scores to determine risk. Potential users expected us to recommend the ODARA score as but one aspect of a risk assessment and to allow other salient aspects of the case to be considered as well. However, in the absence of more in-depth information (e.g., psychological characteristics, juvenile history; see chap. 4, this volume), we hold that the ODARA should be used as the sole index of wife assault recidivism risk. We accord no role to users' impressions, intuitions, imputation of special or unusual risk factors, or incorporation of items from other risk assessment tools (e.g., cruelty to animals, perpetrator justifies his violence). Although these variables might be related to risk, there is no empirical basis for incorporating users' intuitive impressions of them or for their value in improving the predictive accuracy of an ODARA score. Professionals may feel that additional factors cause them to be particularly concerned about a perpetrator regardless of his ODARA score; yet the ODARA item Victim Concern (as stated by the women who have the closest knowledge of the perpetrators' violence) was positively related to all other ODARA items, and statistically significantly so with all but Prior Nondomestic Incidents. The variable most strongly associated with Victim Concern was Threat to Harm or Kill at the Index Assault, $r = .26, p < .001$. A related point is that some users feel uncomfortable including certain items, such as prior offenses that did not result in criminal conviction (see Exhibit 6.1 in chap. 6) or the victim's substance abuse (which can reduce access to crisis services; e.g., Kernic & Bonomi, 2007). Permitting users to modify, adjust, or set aside the ODARA score would introduce an unknown degree of error. Thus, we reiterate that we recommend against adjusting the ODARA score or blending it with professional opinion.

When the ODARA is scored as specified, assessors can use the experience table to make individual assessments of the risk of wife assault recidivism. The norms are from the combined construction and validation cases. The last column indicates the proportion of wife assaulters obtaining each ODARA score who met the research criteria for wife assault recidivism in an average follow-up of nearly 5 years. The other columns provide more useful information, especially if an assessor needs to make a decision about a different time period. The proportion columns indicate the rank order applicable to individuals with the obtained score, regardless of time. That is, the worst scoring 7% of domestic violence perpetrators are the same individuals regardless of the time period of interest. The proportion scoring lower, sometimes with the addition of the proportion obtaining the same score, is called the *percentile rank*.

As an example of how this relative information can be used to make decisions, consider the police chief of a hypothetical small city whose officers handle 1,400 wife assault occurrences each year. The police cells can hold four men accused of wife assault at any one time, and the bail court takes an average of 2 days to deal with an accused (i.e., to release on bail or remand to the county jail). The police chief can instruct the city's police officers that all men who are charged with wife assault and who score 3 or greater on the ODARA will, as a matter of departmental policy, be detained for a bail hearing. Under normal circumstances, those scoring 2 or lower shall be released with a summons or promise to appear. The police chief can also inform the city council that an estimated two more cells would allow the ODARA cutoff score to be reduced by 1 point, providing an additional estimated amount of public protection.

Many decisions about perpetrator custody are made just once in any particular case and would have to be determined on the basis of a single scoring. That this score might have changed since a previous offense can have no bearing on such decisions until such time as research shows that prior ODARA scores can improve predictive accuracy from the ODARA scored at the time of the index assault. We have been able to show, meanwhile, that police were more likely to arrest or charge higher risk wife assaulters in our construction sample and that arrest did not adversely affect recidivism (Hilton, Harris, & Rice, 2007). In relatively low risk cases, arrest appeared to have a small benefit, delaying the time until recidivism occurred. This is one example of how actuarial risk assessment can be used not only to make decisions about offender management, but also to evaluate how well a system is managing risk (for more detail, see chap. 6, this volume).

In this chapter, we have presented all the currently available empirical evidence of the ODARA's ability to discriminate wife assault recidivists from nonrecidivists. Indeed, in several tests of the prediction of wife assault, the ODARA has statistically significantly outperformed any other domestic violence risk instrument tested, including the DVSR, which was also created to be scored from police investigation records (Ontario Ministry of the Solicitor General, 2000), and the SARA and DA, which we scored from police and correctional records (Hilton et al., 2004; Hilton & Harris, 2009b; Hilton, Harris, et al., 2008). We have been able to improve on the ODARA only when using in-depth information not normally available in frontline police and victim service work. The next chapter describes this research.

SUMMARY OF MAIN POINTS

- The ODARA was developed on a representative sample of men who had a police record for wife assault (i.e., forceful physical contact with his female domestic partner or credible threat of death with weapon in hand in the victim's presence) before 1997.
- The ODARA was designed to predict a subsequent instance of wife assault.
- The ODARA contains 13 items, each of which is scored dichotomously and each of which adds incrementally to predictive accuracy.
- Our research shows that police officers can reliably score the ODARA with a scoring manual.

- When scored by a trained rater, an offender's score would be expected to be misclassified by more than one category in only 5% of cases.
- Scores on the ODARA are correlated with, but more strongly related to, wife assault recidivism than scores on other domestic violence risk assessments.
- The ODARA is a validated tool for assessing the risk of wife assault recidivism from police reports and criminal records.
- In data from construction and three cross-validations, the ODARA yielded a large effect size for predicting dichotomous outcome (ROC area of .71) and also predicted number of recidivistic offenses, time until first recidivism, total amount of injury caused, and severity of new assaults.

4

IN-DEPTH RISK ASSESSMENT AND THEORETICAL EXPLANATION

The Ontario Domestic Assault Risk Assessment (ODARA; Hilton et al., 2004) was developed for frontline police officers or victim counselors rather than for forensic clinicians and criminal justice professionals, who usually have access to in-depth case information. As we show in this chapter, certain in-depth information can substantially improve the identification of men at risk of wife assault recidivism. At the same time, information specific to domestic relationships does not necessarily add to the assessment of risk, and some predictors are actually related in the opposite direction to that often believed.

In this chapter, we make a case for adding measures of habitual antisociality to domestic violence risk assessment, where possible, to increase the accuracy, replicability, and utility of the assessment. We describe steps we took (and the directions we abandoned) as we developed the Domestic Violence Risk Appraisal Guide (DVRAG; Hilton, Harris, Rice, Houghton, & Eke, 2008). We also address some practical questions about when and how to use the DVRAG, whether to adjust scores after an intervention, and the ethics of risk assessment. Then we explore the implications of this work for explaining wife assault. Together, this research paints a picture very similar to what we know about violent offending in general.

THE VALUE OF IN-DEPTH INFORMATION

Clinicians often feel they can do the best job of predicting whether a perpetrator will reoffend if they have as much information about him as possible. Characteristics clinicians especially want to know include mental health status and psychiatric symptoms, parent–child attachment and childhood exposure to abuse, insight, stresses in the offender's life, and self-esteem. Many of these details, however, have turned out to be unrelated to violent recidivism or related in the direction opposite to that believed. Certain other kinds of clinical information, though, can increase the accuracy of risk assessments. Our search for an improved tool included identifying aspects of a perpetrator's life history that improve prediction.

As we described in chapter 3, the ODARA has predicted wife assault recidivism with a moderate or large effect size in several samples of men known to the police for an incident of violence against their female partners. Why, then, would we want to add harder-to-obtain case history variables? There are several answers to this question. When we constructed the ODARA, we considered only information that would normally be available to a police officer conducting a domestic investigation; thus, we did not include robust predictors like scores on the Hare Psychopathy Checklist—Revised (PCL–R; R. D. Hare, 2003; see also chap. 2, this volume) and the Violence Risk Appraisal Guide (VRAG; Harris, Rice, & Quinsey, 1993; Quinsey, Harris, Rice, & Cormier, 2006) and childhood behavior. Furthermore, we considered items from existing domestic violence risk assessments only if a frontline police officer could reasonably score them, and we had not examined whether the ODARA could be improved simply by incorporating it with another assessment. In some circumstances, the opportunity might arise to score more information. So we set about the task of identifying cases for which in-depth information would be available and began the search for improvements to the ODARA.

DEVELOPING AN IN-DEPTH RISK ASSESSMENT

Because we wanted to develop an actuarial risk assessment instrument, we relied on a follow-up study as we did when developing the ODARA (Hilton et al., 2004; see chap. 3, this volume). For the in-depth instrument, however, we took a different approach to selecting the sample and to choosing potential predictors. In this section, we describe the method we used to develop the DVRAG.

Selection of Cases for Study

We started our search for instruments or variables to improve on the ODARA by examining predictors in the original 589 cases used to construct the ODARA plus the first 100 cross-validation cases, for a total of 689 (from Hilton et al., 2004) cases. Several nonactuarial tools—scores on the Spousal Assault Risk Assessment (SARA; Kropp, Hart, Webster, & Eaves, 1999), the Danger Assessment (DA; J. C. Campbell, 1986, 2007) and the Domestic Violence Supplementary Report (DVSR; Ontario Ministry of the Solicitor General, 2000)—predicted wife assault recidivism, and each was correlated with the ODARA (Hilton et al., 2004; see also chap. 3, this volume). Many, but not all, of the 689 cases had an extensive correctional file that contained enough information to score existing in-depth tools completely. The SARA in particular includes personality disorder, attitudes, and childhood exposure to violence. When we had in-depth information, we relied on it (rather than only the police reports) to score these other assessments. In the remaining cases, however, we had only brief descriptions of the index assault, prior incidents, and criminal history; we were missing the information to score some items on these assessments, and so our earlier tests of predictors to include in the frontline risk assessment did not include such items.

We embarked on a new study to examine how well these tools, or other variables obtained from more in-depth information, would perform when we had adequate information to score all cases (Hilton, Harris, et al., 2008). To be confident that we had adequate information, and consequently to give each tool the best chance of predicting the outcome, we chose from our 1,400 cases those that had some form of a risk–needs assessment on the corrections file. We ascertained that 303 of the original 689 cases had this information, usually in a presentence report. This meant there were 303 cases in the DVRAG development sample and that the resulting in-depth risk assessment would apply to cases in which there had been the opportunity for a professional forensic or correctional assessment.

Restricting the sample this way had some effects on the expected predictive accuracy of all the tools we tested. It tended to limit the number of cases with relatively low ODARA scores and thus the cases least likely to recidivate, which would be expected to reduce the correlation between all assessments and recidivism. To illustrate this effect, imagine you were computing the correlation between height and weight. In the adult population, this correlation is positive, which means that as height increases, so does weight. The relationship is not perfect—there are people who are 5 feet 7 inches (1.7 meters) tall and weigh more than people who are 6 feet 0 inches (1.8 meters) tall, for example—but across the population of all shapes and sizes, height is a good predictor of weight. If we eliminated anyone under 5 feet 2 inches (1.6 meters) from consideration, an adequate sample size would still likely yield an association between height and weight, but without the shortest (and usually the lightest) adults contributing data, the correlation would be somewhat reduced.

So it was with the correlations among the assessments and recidivism in our sample when we limited it to cases that had a correctional assessment on record. The percentage of cases scoring in the lowest two ODARA categories was cut to about a third of what we saw in the ODARA construction sample, and the percentage in the highest two categories doubled. Not surprisingly, the 303 cases had higher scores on average (e.g., the mean ODARA score was now 4.1 compared with 2.9, and there were similar increases in the SARA and DA scores) and a higher recidivism rate (i.e., nearly 50% compared with 30%). As a result, the correlations between risk assessment scores and outcomes and the relative operating characteristic (ROC) curve obtained were lower in these 303 cases than in the ODARA construction sample.

This lower accuracy of the ODARA in the correctional cases is a reflection of the fact that the police and criminal justice system detain those perpetrators who are more likely to recidivate (as described in chap. 6, this volume). Our goal when we developed the DVRAG was to find an instrument that would improve on the accuracy of the ODARA in the limited sample of offenders for whom in-depth information was available. The sample had proportionately more cases scoring relatively high on the risk measures than the original ODARA construction sample and so had the potential to yield an instrument that would permit greater discrimination at the higher end of risk; this advantage came, however, at the cost of reduced utility at the lower end.

Selection of Predictors and Outcomes

We had to make some rational decisions about the variables we would consider. We could have started from scratch and thrown every variable we were able to code into the mix. We already knew, though, that the ODARA items optimized prediction in the absence of in-depth information. Our approach, then, was to see what made an incremental contribution to the prediction of wife assault recidivism once the ODARA was already part of the assessment system. This approach meant we could avoid creating an entirely new tool and take advantage of existing assessments that were likely to be in routine use in correctional and forensic assessment. We considered the DA and SARA, as well as a newly published tool, the Domestic Violence Screening Instrument (DVSI; K. R. Williams & Houghton, 2004). We also considered the Hare PCL–R, an obvious choice because of its well-established association with violent recidivism (as reviewed in Harris, Skilling, & Rice, 2001; see also Leistico, Salekin, DeCoster, & Rogers, 2007).

The VRAG (Quinsey, Harris, et al., 2006) was another obvious choice. We had already found the VRAG to be a good predictor of violent recidivism among serious wife assaulters (half of whom were subsequently convicted and entered the correctional system; Hilton, Harris, & Rice, 2001). The VRAG's ability to distinguish between recidivists and nonrecidivists has proved robust, with replications now spanning several outcomes and populations. At the time of this writing, there were more than 40 studies replicating its ability to predict violent or criminal recidivism in Canada, Europe, and the United States (Blair, Marcus, & Boccaccini, 2008; M. Campbell, French, & Gendreau, 2007; Hanson & Morton-Bourgon, 2007; http://www.mhcp-research.com). These replications have yielded an average ROC area of .72, which is considered a large predictive effect according to standard criteria (Cohen's $d > 0.8$; Rice & Harris, 2005). Assessment is optimal when no VRAG items are deleted or replaced (Harris & Rice, 2003). Unfortunately, two of its items cannot vary in a sample of wife assaulters: (a) female victim of the index offense and (b) having never been in a marital or equivalent relationship. The DVRAG development sample raised a further challenge because we had insufficient evidence to indicate that any perpetrator met the criteria for a diagnosis of schizophrenia. The result is that what we actually tested was a nine-item modification of the VRAG.

Next, we made the decision to select the best predictors of not only whether recidivism would occur but also the frequency and severity of recidivism (defined later). These other outcomes might be just as important to sentencing decisions, to parole and supervision, or to a potential victim. In general, our actuarial risk assessments that were constructed with dichotomous (yes/no) recidivism as an outcome have turned out to be positively correlated with the severity of violence and how soon a new offense occurred (see chap. 3, this volume, for details on these statistics for the ODARA). When we developed the DVRAG, we took steps to ensure the selection of components associated with these other outcomes. To some observers, the only outcome of interest is the severity of the assault, especially domestic murder; however, we did not want to exclude from our concern those women who are saved from otherwise certain death by timely and expert medical intervention or men who perpetrate emotional terrorism on their families punctuated by occasional physical violence.

There were also empirical reasons to consider other outcomes. In the correctional sample, we anticipated a greater likelihood of recidivism, so examining other aspects of recidivism would help us discriminate among them. Continuous measures, such as a severity scale or the number of recidivistic incidents, can also afford greater precision of measurement than a yes/no dichotomy of recidivism. When we developed the DVRAG, then, we examined assessments that could improve prediction of several aspects of recidivism. These five outcome measures all showed moderate to large correlations with each other (Hilton, Harris, et al., 2008):

1. any new wife assault incident (a dichotomous measure);
2. number of incidents meeting the criteria for wife assault recidivism (a continuous measure);
3. number of recidivistic incidents involving severe violence—that is, incidents meeting the criteria for wife assault recidivism

in which the perpetrator committed acts ranging from punching or kicking to using a knife or gun (a continuous measure);

4. total score on the victim injury scale, from 1 = *no injury* to 5 = *wounds from a weapon*, summed across all the new incidents of wife assault (a continuous measure); and

5. total score on the Cormier–Lang Criminal History scale, which assigns a numeric value to the severity and frequency of criminal charges (Quinsey, Harris, et al., 2006), summed across all the new incidents of wife assault (a continuous measure).

A risk assessment that predicted whether an offense would occur but did not also predict the number and severity of such offenses could be confusing and difficult to apply in the context of the risk, needs, and responsivity principles of offender intervention (described in chap. 1, this volume). Another outcome that interests the criminal justice system, in our experience, is how soon a perpetrator might commit a new offense (e.g., if granted a conditional release, will he reoffend during this period?). In general, our actuarial risk assessments, although constructed with dichotomous (yes/no) recidivism as an outcome, have turned out to be positively correlated with how soon a new offense occurred. In chapter 3, we described these statistics for the ODARA, as well as the limitations of our original measure of perpetrators' time at risk to recidivate. When we developed the DVRAG, we took steps to ensure the selection of items that were associated with several outcomes, including the number of recidivistic incidents within a follow-up of specified time, which is logically related to time at risk. At the same time, we manually checked all our available records on time spent in custody for an improved estimate of opportunity to reoffend.

What Improves Prediction Over and Above the Ontario Domestic Assault Risk Assessment?

In our study of the 303 cases with in-depth information available, 49% of the men committed wife assault recidivism, and the ODARA was correlated with dichotomous wife assault recidivism ($r = .27$; Hilton, Harris, et al., 2008; for explanations of correlation, accuracy statistics, and effect sizes, see chap. 2 of this volume; Rice & Harris, 2005). All of the other assessments we tested were also associated with wife assault recidivism in the sample of 303 cases; correlations ranged from .18 (DVSI) to .25 (PCL–R total score). None, however, made an incremental contribution to the prediction of dichotomous recidivism once the ODARA was already considered. Using linear regression techniques, we found that the PCL–R score significantly improved predictive accuracy for the number of recidivistic incidents, the number involving severe violence, and the total victim injury resulting from recidivism. PCL–R score did not improve the prediction of the Cormier–Lang score for recidivism; the DVSI score did (even though it had the smallest correlation with dichotomous recidivism), perhaps because several of its items pertain to offenses incurring charges and convictions. From this procedure, we picked the PCL–R to add to the ODARA because it was the most highly correlated with wife assault recidivism and the most consistent contributor to improved prediction of the remaining outcome measures. Of interest to victim services, PCL–R was also correlated with the item Victim Concern, $r = .21$, $p < .01$.

As described earlier, we based all scoring on correctional and criminal justice records and did not interview perpetrators or other informants. Of course, these records themselves often contained material from such interviews. This file-based method is commonly used to study interrater reliability and predictive accuracy (e.g., Kropp & Hart, 2000), even though interviews may be recommended for the tools in practice. Any limitations on predictive accuracy that this method might impose would apply equally to the PCL–R, yet its predictive accuracy was clearly superior to the other tools. We also note that this research method indicates the predictive accuracy of these instruments when scored from the file only; it leaves unexplored the question of whether the addition of interviews improves predictive accuracy.

Definition and Cross-Validation of the In-Depth Assessment

We considered several ways to combine the ODARA and the PCL–R to create a new instrument. We wanted something that would be easy for assessors to fit in with their normal assessment, so we tried simply adding the two scores together. The combined score, however, gave undue weight to the PCL–R, whose potential scores run from 0 to 40, compared with the ODARA, whose maximum possible score is 13. We also considered a decision tree approach, in which the ODARA score would be calculated first and the PCL–R scores within each ODARA category would be associated with a particular rate of recidivism. The tree, however, would have required so many potential ODARA/PCL–R categories as to be unwieldy to use and impossible to construct reliably without thousands of cases.

Our search for a valid and parsimonious combination of assessments led us back to a system that weights each item, with a positive or negative score, based on how much the item's presence changes the likelihood of recidivism compared with the base rate (the Nuffield weighting system, as used in Harris et al., 1993). That is, we calculated weights (+ or −) for each ODARA item and for PCL–R score according to the contribution (and direction) of each item to the prediction of dichotomous recidivism in the DVRAG development sample of 303 cases. For each item, values that resulted in no change from the base rate of recidivism were assigned a weight of zero.

We did not base the item weights on the other outcomes (e.g., frequency, severity), but our choice of the PCL–R on the basis of on its ability to improve prediction of these outcomes ensured that the eventual in-depth assessment would predict those outcomes, too. In fact, the DVRAG was a significant improvement over the ODARA in the development sample of 303 cases for every outcome measure (Hilton, Harris, Rice et al., 2008). The ROC area for dichotomous recidivism was .71 ($d = 0.78$), compared with .67 ($d = 0.62$) for the ODARA in this sample. The DVRAG was also associated with shorter time at risk ($r = -.23$), similar to the ODARA in this sample ($r = -.21$).

In 346 new cases, all with in-depth assessment information from a corrections file, the DVRAG had an ROC area of .70 ($d = 0.75$), a moderate effect size. In this cross-validation sample, the correlations for the continuous outcome measures ranged from the Cormier–Lang score ($r = .29$) to the number of incidents and victim injury (both $rs = .40$), all moderate effect sizes (Rice & Harris, 2005). That is, the cross-validation showed that DVRAG score is related not only to how likely it is that a man will assault his partner again but also to how many assaults there will be, known to police, within a given time frame; how many will involve severe violence; how much injury will result; and how serious the resulting criminal charges will be.

Possible scores on the DVRAG range from −10 to +41. We have provided the scoring instructions and a scoring sheet that allows simultaneous scoring of the ODARA and DVRAG in Appendix C.

Our next task was to define the DVRAG categories. The DVRAG has a wide range of scores compared with the ODARA, where each score could easily be considered a category, except for higher scores, which were too uncommon to yield stable risk estimates without some collapsing across scores. The DVRAG is more like the VRAG, whose scores are divided into categories on the basis of an equal range of scores, except for the highest risk category containing a range of scores at which 100% of cases reoffended. We observed that the 3% of cases in our combined sample of 649 wife assault cases with the highest DVRAG scores all reoffended, leading us to place these scores into the top category and an equivalent number of cases into the lowest category. The remaining categories were created to capture about 20% of the sample each.

Figure 4.1 shows the proportion of men who recidivated within each DVRAG category. As with the ODARA (see Figure 3.3), recidivism increases with each increase in DVRAG category. The DVRAG also identifies a category with 100% recidivism and a second category that corresponds to recidivism rates over 70%, thus affording more discrimination among the highest risk cases. The norms (Appendix D) show that the lowest DVRAG category comes with an expected recidivism rate of 14%, compared with 7% for the lowest category on the ODARA. Thus, the DVRAG may be a poorer instrument than the ODARA for relatively low risk samples.

In sum, we examined the predictive power of several risk assessments to improve on the ODARA, but the PCL–R, a diagnostic tool for psychopathy, was superior because of its ability to predict both the occurrence and con-

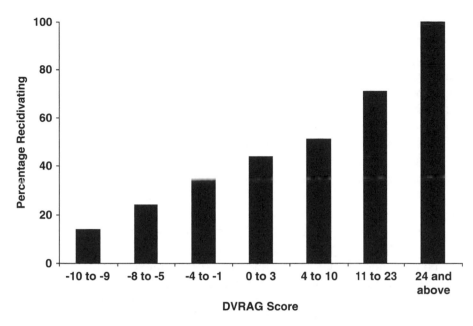

Figure 4.1. Percentage of perpetrators recidivating as a function of Domestic Violence Risk Appraisal Guide (DVRAG) score in the combined DVRAG construction and validation samples. Data from Hilton, Harris, Rice, Houghton, and Eke (2008).

tinuous measures of wife assault recidivism. A linear combination of the ODARA items and PCL–R score significantly improved prediction over the ODARA score alone. The result was an actuarial risk assessment suitable for use when in-depth file information is available, especially when discrimination among relatively high risk cases is desired. We named the in-depth risk assessment the Domestic Violence Risk Assessment Guide not only because of its connection to the VRAG and its related assessment for predicting violence by sex offenders, the Sex Offender Risk Appraisal Guide (Quinsey, Harris, et al., 2006), but also to reflect their similar empirical development, including statistical selection of the strongest, unique predictors. Of both practical and theoretical interest, all include measures of criminal history and the PCL–R.

ONTARIO DOMESTIC ASSAULT RISK ASSESSMENT–DOMESTIC VIOLENCE RISK APPRAISAL GUIDE SYSTEM

The DVRAG is not designed to make the ODARA obsolete, nor is it intended to be one more tool that a professional might score in an attempt to gather "more" risk information before making a judgment about risk. Rather, the ODARA and DVRAG together form a system of risk assessment. It is conceivable, even desirable, that the ODARA would be scored at the time of the perpetrator's first contact with the criminal justice system, usually during or shortly after police contact. The ODARA results could be sent to central police information centers, and the score and its interpretation might be posted along with other alerts and cautions. During a subsequent presentence or forensic assessment, a probation officer or mental health professional would build on the information in the ODARA by scoring the DVRAG using available in-depth information. Our research indicates that correctional and forensic decision makers typically handle higher scoring cases on average than do frontline assessors, and the additional discrimination among higher scores that the DVRAG affords can aid decisions about sentencing, security, release, intervention, and so on. The DVRAG can also be used in these contexts to allocate resources according to risk: broader and more intense interventions for higher risk perpetrators, less secure and intense supervision for lower risk perpetrators, and so on. Our recommendations for implementing a policy of assessment, communication, and forensic decisions using the ODARA and DVRAG systematically are covered in more detail in chapter 6.

Obtaining Psychopathy Checklist—Revised Scores

We advise use of the DVRAG whenever sufficient information is available for a reliable and accurate PCL–R score because the DVRAG improves prediction of recidivism over and above the ODARA in these cases. We recommend scoring it whenever there is sufficient information about childhood behavior and adult adjustment to score the PCL–R from the case file or, at a minimum, an existing PCL–R score provided by another professional. The diagnostic and predictive power of the PCL–R renders insupportable any claim that it is too inconvenient or time consuming to score in correctional or forensic institutions.

Qualified professionals can use the PCL–R as a psychological assessment to diagnose psychopathy (R. D. Hare, 2003). As an item contributing to risk assessment, the PCL–R scored either from both file and perpetrator interview or from the file alone predicts violent recidivism, including wife assault recidivism (Quinsey, Harris, et al., 2006). Our research team routinely uses file information alone to score all variables, including PCL–R, and we have a well-established record of demonstrating that this method produces good predictive accuracy. To use PCL–R score as a DVRAG item, it should have been scored by assessors who can demonstrate good interrater reliability (i.e., correlation coefficients of at least $r = .80$). Other items cannot substitute for the PCL–R (Exhibit 4.1).

Obtaining a good PCL–R score can be time consuming, especially in places such as child protection agencies or community treatment programs where no one has been trained to assess psychopathy. In such cases, we rec-

EXHIBIT 4.1
Substituting Items on the Domestic Violence Risk Appraisal Guide

Occasionally, we are asked whether a similar item can be substituted for an item for which details are missing. In the Violence Risk Appraisal Guide (Quinsey, Harris, Rice, & Cormier, 2006), a body of research allowed us to support the substitution of the Psychopathy Checklist—Youth Version (PCL–YV; Neumann, Kosson, Forth, & Hare, 2006) or the Childhood and Adolescent Taxon Scale (CATS; Quinsey, Harris, et al., 2006) for the Psychopathy Checklist—Revised (PCL–R; R. D. Hare, 1991, 2003). The Ontario Domestic Risk Assault Assessment (ODARA) research studied only adults, though, making the PCL–YV inapplicable. Although our analysis of the limited available data showed that the CATS bore a small, positive statistical association with wife assault recidivism, we did not have extensive information on childhood and adolescent behavior problems, and in practice the Domestic Violence Risk Appraisal Guide (DVRAG; Hilton, Harris, Rice, Houghton, & Eke, 2008) would be scored only when there is sufficient in-depth information to score the PCL–R.

The Psychopathy Checklist: Screening Version (PCL:SV; Hart, Cox, & Hare, 1995) contains no items related to preadolescence but still does not obviate the need to gather in-depth offender information. Furthermore, our research did not examine its validity as a DVRAG item.

Sometimes assessors can think of alternative item criteria that are similar to the specified scoring criteria. For example, a perpetrator might have recently immigrated from a jurisdiction where wife assault would not incur a police record, so an assessor might wish to substitute a victim-reported assault for a police record of domestic assault. Or a victim might have a physical disability that limits her mobility, which could create a barrier to support. We cannot endorse substitutions in this manner. Although we empathize with assessors in such situations, no research to date demonstrates that such modifications carry the same predictive accuracy as the items they replace.

---

ommend weighing the costs and benefits of a more accurate risk assessment based on the initial ODARA score. In the combined samples of 649 cases, we found that over 50% of cases scoring in the lowest or second lowest ODARA categories (i.e., scores of 0 or 1) remained in the lowest or second lowest categories, respectively, when scored on the DVRAG. At ODARA scores of 2 or more, there was more dispersion of DVRAG scores, indicating that adding PCL–R conferred relatively more information about risk of recidivism. For ODARA scores of 7 or more, few cases (14%) were identified as being lower risk by the DVRAG, but a quarter of these cases were distinguished as being in the highest risk category. We suggest that assessors in these circumstances score the ODARA first and, whenever the ODARA indicates a score of 2 or more, consider whether their services can be optimized by obtaining a reliable PCL–R score to enable scoring the DVRAG.

Interpreting Domestic Violence Risk Appraisal Guide Scores and Categories

The DVRAG is an actuarial risk assessment and therefore should be scored with close attention to the item criteria (Appendix C) and interpreted with reference to the experience table (Appendix D). The "percent scoring lower" column of the experience table can be used to indicate a perpetrator's rank order—that is, how he compares with other known perpetrators with respect to risk for recidivism. The "percent recidivating" column (which corresponds to Figure 4.1) can be used to indicate the perpetrator's probability of recidivism. Assessors should remember, though, that the operational definition of recidivism is new incidents of wife assault appearing in a police report within an average follow-up of nearly 5 years (or an estimated 4.3 years of opportunity); different definitions or time frames would change these probabilities, and not necessarily uniformly across all groups.

Sometimes assessors are reluctant to treat individuals as members of a group. Once individuals have been grouped according to their shared characteristics, some commentators believe that the group characteristics no longer apply to the individuals that form the group. This belief is a misunderstanding of the ecological fallacy (see chap. 2, this volume). In actuarial risk assessment, a larger group (in the case of the DVRAG, wife assaulters with an in-depth correctional file) has been subdivided into smaller groups (or risk categories) that are alike with respect to characteristics associated with risk at the individual level. An individual's likelihood of recidivism may be directly inferred from the rate of recidivism of the group of individuals that form his respective risk category. It is not appropriate for an assessor to arrive at an actuarial likelihood of, for example, 51% and then seek further to determine whether the individual perpetrator is in the half that will incur a police report for a new incident of wife assault or the half that will not. The empirical process of developing the actuarial risk assessment has already identified the variables that optimally subdivide the population into risk categories and eliminated many others that do not permit further valid subdivision. Seeking further information to characterize individual risk (based on idiosyncratic factors) actually yields a modification of unknown, but almost certainly poorer, reliability and validity. Such practice cannot be supported.

Are Individual Scores Reliable?

We established excellent interrater reliability of DVRAG scoring among research coders (Hilton, Harris, et al., 2008). Ensuring agreement among assessors, or between assessors and published case examples (such as those provided in Appendix E), may offer greater quality assurance than simply attending some number of hours of training. Although establishing interrater reliability is important in high-stakes decision making, the standard error of measurement (SEM) is even more important. As discussed in chapter 3, SEM is the average relationship between an observed and true score and is a function of reliability and variability. The SEM for the DVRAG indicated that on average, an offender would have less than a .05 probability of misclassification by more than one category.

Should Scores Be Altered?

It can be tempting to adjust an individual perpetrator's actuarial score on the basis of idiosyncratic information, strong disapproval of his offenses, opinions about changes in his antisocial tendencies, or hypotheses about differences between him and the original construction and validation populations or to modify the scoring criteria on the basis of case information that is intuitively similar to the item definition. Doing so, however, is another practice that yields a modified risk assessment that has unknown, but very probably poorer, reliability and validity; such practice is not supported by any empirical data.

This restriction applies even when a perpetrator has undergone domestic violence treatment. Treatment efficacy is addressed in chapter 6, but here we note that there have been few scientifically rigorous evaluations of treatment, and the relatively weak literature so far indicates small or minimal effects at best on wife assault recidivism (e.g., Babcock, Green, & Robie, 2004; Feder & Wilson, 2005). We believe it will eventually be possible to reduce recidivism by providing offender treatment, but clinical work still requires much development. The work described in this book will, we hope, move the domestic violence field closer toward apportioning intervention resources according to risk. In the next section, we offer a small contribution to the task of identifying criminogenic needs among wife assaulters.

DOMESTIC-SPECIFIC PREDICTION AND EXPLANATION OF WIFE ASSAULT

One might expect that domestic-specific variables would be most helpful to discerning domestic-specific recidivism. However, we found that this was not so. When we first ventured into the field of violence prediction among wife assaulters specifically, we wondered whether a risk assessment specifically for wife assault was needed at all. We had just found that the VRAG gave a large effect size for the prediction of violent recidivism by serious wife assaulters (Hilton et al., 2001). We have also found that the VRAG and PCL–R predict well in the DVRAG development and construction samples when the outcome is wife assault specifically. The predictive accuracy of the domestic violence assessment tools (DA, SARA, and DVSI) was substantially lower than that of the nondomestic assessments, with ROC areas of .56 to .61 and correlations with the continuous outcomes small (under .30) at best.

We were not the first to discover the relatively modest ability of domestic-specific risk assessments to distinguish between recidivists and nonrecidivists in a sample of wife assaulters. Grann and Wedin (2002), in a 1-year follow-up of men convicted of domestic violence or homicide, found that total score on the SARA predicted subsequent convictions for violence, sexual assault, threats, or no-contact violations against an intimate partner, with an ROC area of .59; in the same time frame, however, the PCL–R achieved an ROC area of .71 and the VRAG of .75, both significantly more accurate than the domestic-specific assessment (i.e., falling above the upper 95% confidence limit). Since then, a meta-analysis of 19 studies examining predictive accuracy of domestic violence or general violence risk assessment tools found that the latter yielded higher effect sizes than the former (Hanson, Helmus, & Bourgon, 2007; see Exhibit 3.3), raising the question as to whether domestic-specific assessments offer any value above general violence risk assessments. In our view, this finding is partly due to the nonactuarial nature of the domestic-specific tools.

When we developed the DVRAG, we wanted to be sure that we gave domestic-specific variables every chance to be selected as predictors. So we also examined, in addition to total scores on the DA, SARA, and DVSI, individual items from these assessments that were not already covered by the DVRAG items. Many of the items we tested concerned prior assaults, conditional releases or no-contact orders, substance abuse, threats, victim fear, or assault during pregnancy, all of which are DVRAG items. Others measured aspects of jealousy, stalking, psychological abuse, sexual abuse, escalation of violence, violence toward pets or property, separation of the partners, weapon use in prior domestic incidents, victim support persons, and the perpetrator's suicidal history. We tested nearly 50 other variables that were included in these assessments or elsewhere in our coding manual because we or other professionals had thought them promising. Some had been considered in the ODARA construction but failed the statistical selection. This time, we tested whether any of these variables was correlated with dichotomous wife assault recidivism in the combined samples of 649 cases used to develop and cross-validate the DVRAG. Three items from the SARA did predict recidivism: recent employment problems; personality disorder with anger, impulsivity, or behavioral instability; and extreme minimization or denial of assault history. However, they were highly correlated with PCL–R score and did not improve prediction of wife assault recidivism over the DVRAG.

Only one other variable—stalking the index victim by following her—had a small, significant correlation with recidivism, $r = .08$; however, once all the DVRAG items were accounted for, stalking did not add any predictive validity. Stalking has received much public and legal attention during the past decade, and emerging evidence suggests that stalking is a risky circumstance in itself (e.g., Mohandie, Meloy, McGowan, & Williams, 2006). To date, though, we have not been able to conclude that stalking contributes uniquely to risk of wife assault recidivism over the ODARA or DVRAG. Not all the characteristics typical of wife assaulters or severe assaulters predict recidivism. Childhood variables are commonly thought to be associated with wife assault risk, and the research literature does indicate that men who report childhood exposure to violence or other abuse are also more likely to assault their partners (e.g., Ehrensaft et al., 2003; Hines & Saudino, 2002), but these variables have not so far been found to predict recidivism (e.g., Hanson & Wallace-Capretta, 2004). These variables were present in at least 200 cases in our DVRAG samples, but they were not related to wife assault recidivism.

Could there be some worthwhile variables that we have overlooked, pertaining either to the domestic relationship or to victim characteristics that were not measured on our coding form? Analogously among sex offenders, domain specific variables, such as measures of sexual deviance and the age and sex of victims, have consistently been shown to distinguish recidivists and nonrecidivists. The DVRAG includes some items that look very specific to the domestic relationship and the victim, such as the victim having children from a prior relationship, the perpetrator assaulting her while she was pregnant, and barriers to victim support. Although we cannot rule out that future research might discover a new predictor or a new way to measure a variable that captures unique predictive power, we have been very thorough in our search for domestic-specific prediction using the extensive literature on the correlates of domestic violence. So we are not optimistic that many will be found; we believe measures of general antisociality will make the most robust contribution to domestic violence risk assessment.

THE PREDICTIVE POWER OF GENERAL ANTISOCIALITY

After developing the DVRAG, we were so impressed with the performance of the PCL–R and the nine-item modification of the VRAG that we explored further tests of the predictive power of general antisociality. This search involved statistical analysis beyond the techniques we have described so far in this book. For readers without a background in statistics, we will describe these steps using as little statistical nomenclature as possible.

A Search for Any Remaining Predictive Power

First, we examined any remaining variables that were coded as present in at least 200 cases and that were associated with wife assault recidivism. The few such variables had previously been shown to predict violent recidivism generally: procriminal attitudes, attitudes unfavorable to convention, and suspension or expulsion from elementary school. Only one improved on the DVRAG: having been arrested before the age of 16, which predicted recidivism in 3 of 15 tests (total victim injury in the combined sample of 649 and in the cross-validation sample alone and the Cormier–Lang score for recidivism in the cross-validation sample only; Hilton, Harris, et al., 2008).

Factor Analysis

Next, we conducted an exploratory factor analysis of all items from the ODARA, PCL–R, DA, SARA, and DVSI. Factor analysis is a multivariate statistical technique used to determine whether many variables can be boiled down to just a few common factors. The basic theory is that these few factors can explain why the variables are more or less correlated with each other. We used it to test whether there was a factor of domestic-specific items and a separate factor of antisocial behavior and whether antisociality might be more strongly related to wife assault recidivism among all 649 perpetrators.

We used a principal components factor analysis model with varimax rotation, which examines the data for the simplest relations among the items. We used all scores on every item of the five assessments in our study, replacing any missing items with the sample average. Four factors emerged (Table 4.1). The first factor comprised variables reflecting attitudes toward domestic violence, plus several emotional and interpersonal aspects of psychopathy that also group

TABLE 4.1

Exploratory Factor Analysis of Items From the ODARA, DA, SARA, DVSI, and PCL–R for the DVRAG Construction and Validation Samples

Factor 1[a]	Factor 2[b]	Factor 3[c]	Factor 4[d]
SARA attitudes	PCL–R versatility	DVSI restraining order violations	SARA weapons/ threat
SARA minimization	PCL–R revocation	DVSI restraining order at index	DA death threat
PCL–R lack of remorse	PCL–R irresponsibility	SARA index violation of no-contact order	ODARA threat
PCL–R shallow affect	PCL–R poor behavioral controls	DVSI domestic restraining orders	DVSI weapon
SARA personality disorder	PCL–R parasitic lifestyle	SARA past violation of no-contact order	DA forced sex
PCL–R impulsivity	PCL–R stimulation	SARA conditional release violation	
PCL–R conning	ODARA sentence	ODARA conditional release failure	
PCL–R callousness	ODARA conditional release failure	ODARA prior domestic incidents	
PCL–R grandiosity	PCL–R delinquency		
PCL–R lack of goals	ODARA substance abuse		
PCL–R glibness	DVSI prior assault arrests		
DA controlling			

Note. For all items, loadings ≥ .45. Empty cells indicate no further items with loadings ≥ .45. ODARA = Ontario Domestic Assault Risk Assessment (Hilton et al., 2004); DA = Danger Assessment (J. C. Campbell, 1986, 2007); SARA = Spousal Assault Risk Assessment (Kropp, Hart, Webster, & Eaves, 1999); DVSI = Domestic Violence Screening Instrument (K. R. Williams & Houghton, 2004); PCL–R = Psychopathy Checklist—Revised (R. D. Hare, 2003); DVRAG = Domestic Violence Risk Appraisal Guide (Hilton, Harris, Rice, Houghton, & Eke, 2008).
[a]r_{recid} = .10, $p < .05$, Wald = 7.17; variance explained = 15%. [b]r_{recid} = .28, $p < .001$, Wald = 48.18; variance explained = 5%. [c]r_{recid} = .11, $p < .01$, Wald = 8.27; variance explained = 5%. [d]r_{recid} = .07, $p > .05$, Wald = 4.15; variance explained = 4%.

together on the PCL–R. Other research, though, has indicated that these aspects of antisociality are not as strongly correlated with criminal recidivism (e.g., Harris et al., 2001; Leistico et al., 2007; Quinsey, Harris, et al., 2006; Salekin, Rogers, & Sewell, 1996), and this factor also had a small statistical association with wife assault recidivism (Table 4.1).

The second factor to emerge was the most strongly related to wife assault recidivism. It seems to identify antisocial lifestyle and criminal behavior, including substance abuse, prior arrests, and correctional sentences. Previous research has shown that the criminal lifestyle aspects of psychopathy best predict violent recidivism (e.g., Harris et al., 2001). We believe these measures of general antisocial lifestyle also appear to represent a discrete natural entity, known as a *taxon*, rather than a continuum (Harris, Rice, & Quinsey, 1994; Haslam, 2003; Skilling, Harris, Rice, & Quinsey, 2002; Vasey, Kotov, Frick, & Loney, 2005; but see Edens, Marcus, Lilienfeld, & Poythress, 2006). That is, it seems that a type of offender especially prone to general antisociality could be important in the explanation as to why wife assault occurs.

Variables concerning conditional release failures, particularly in relation to domestic assaults, loaded on a third factor, and threats, use of weapons, and sexual assault loaded on a fourth. Each explained, like the antisociality factor, about 5% of the total variance. Conditional release failures also had a small statistical association with recidivism, whereas the final factor did not.

General Criminal Recidivism

Our final step was to explore the ability of the Level of Service Inventory (LSI; Andrews & Bonta, 2001) to predict wife assault recidivism. The LSI is used to assess factors relating to a perpetrator's offending behavior as well as to identify offenders at risk for criminal recidivism in general. There is abundant evidence that the LSI is associated with general criminal recidivism (Andrews & Bonta, 2006) and some evidence that it is associated with domestic violence (Hendricks, Werner, Shipway, & Turinetti, 2006). Our in-depth cases almost always had a version of the LSI on file, as it is used routinely in the Ontario correctional system. Every LSI in our samples was scored in the field, usually by probation officers, with access to the files, the offenders, and sometimes a victim interview, too. In contrast, other assessments in our research were scored item by item by research assistants using only archival information. The relative completeness of information could bias the data in favor of the LSI, or it could be disadvantaged by variation in rater ability and experience. Because it was obtained in a systematically different way from the rest of our measures, we did not include it in our search for assessments to improve prediction over the ODARA.

In the whole sample of 649 cases, we used the first LSI scores recorded in the correctional files if (for recidivists) it was recorded before the calendar year of the first recidivistic incident. The mean LSI score in the resulting 406 cases was 9.88 ($SD = 6.61$), and it had a small predictive effect for wife assault recidivism, $r = .22$, $p < .001$. LSI score was most strongly correlated with the VRAG, $r = .69$. It was also strongly positively associated with the ODARA, PCL–R, and, not surprisingly, the DVRAG, with large correlation coefficients of .54 to .58, and it had smaller correlations (up to .34) with the remaining domestic violence risk assessments. In regression analyses, the LSI did not significantly improve on the predictive validity of the ODARA, DVRAG, PCL–R, or VRAG, but it did improve on the SARA, DVSI, and DA (according to Wald statistics that ranged from 8.24 to 14.19). Although these results have yet to be replicated when the LSI is scored in the same manner as the other assessments, it appeared that the nonactuarial domestic risk assessments could be improved by adding an established assessment of the risk of general criminal recidivism.

The corollary to this conclusion is that a risk assessment that predicts domestic violence recidivism well should also be able to predict general recidivism. In our research, we coded not only wife assault recidivism but also any new nonviolent incidents involving a partner and any incidents of violence, weapons use, or stalking involving nondomestic victims. We have found that the ODARA is just as strongly associated with all incidents of recidivism we coded from police files as it is with wife assault recidivism specifically. We also examined criminal charges for any type of offense (i.e., violent or nonviolent, domestic or nondomestic) after the index incident. Although the best predictor of charges for any violent recidivism was the nine-item modified VRAG, $r = .30$, the ODARA's predictive accuracy was comparable, $r = .27$. The best predictor of general recidivism, defined by criminal charges of any kind, was also the VRAG, $r = .37$, and the ODARA provided a small predictive effect, $r = .20$, $p < .001$.

Implications for Explanations of Wife Assault

The results we have described in this section show how strong general antisociality variables are in predicting wife assault recidivism. There is a comparison here with the research into sexual recidivism among sex offenders, which is also well predicted by variables that predict violence in general (Hanson & Bussière, 1998; Hanson & Morton-Bourgon, 2007). The few domain-specific predictors among sex offenders are limited to laboratory assessment of deviant sexual interests and past sex offenses, with essentially no additional contribution of having been a victim of sexual abuse, sociodemographic characteristics, individual personal variables, interpersonal stress, or developmental concerns unrelated to general antisociality. Furthermore, Seto (2005) found that actuarial risk assessments that account for general antisociality and sexual deviance could not be improved on by other sex offender risk assessments that sample the same domains. In our own research with sex offenders, we have found that early, frequent, and coercive sexual behavior is a fundamental feature of psychopathy (Harris, Rice, Hilton, Lalumière, & Quinsey, 2007), so it is not surprising that general antisociality plays an important explanatory role in wife assault.

We can also speculate that some variables that appear specific to the domestic domain are actually cues of general antisociality. For example, the number of children that the perpetrator and victim have might be associated with wife assault recidivism to the extent that their presence increases stress and conflict. On the other hand, it is characteristic of antisocial men to have multiple short-term marriages, and they tend to start having sex and producing offspring at an earlier age than other men (as reviewed in Harris, Rice, et al., 2007; Lalumière, Harris, Quinsey, & Rice, 2005). In a study we conducted with 177 adolescents, we found that students reported more violence in dating relationships in which they also reported having had sex (see also Roberts, Auinger, & Klein, 2006). Thus, both the number of children and violence against partners could be aspects of antisociality. As another example, attitudes toward violence loaded in our factor analysis on a common factor with personality characteristics describing psychopathy, so perhaps these attitudes are not unique to domestic violence, but merely an aspect of more general attitudes. Perhaps general antisociality might account for *who* commits wife assault, but *when* it happens might depend on more specific factors such as sexual jealousy and proprietary behavior (e.g., Smuts, 1992; M. Wilson & Daly, 1996) and proximal triggers such as conflict over a woman's contact with an ex-partner over child custody matters (e.g., Koziol-McLain et al., 2007).

THE ROLE OF EXPLANATION IN PREDICTION AND INTERVENTION

If one knew for certain why some men commit wife assault, it would be easier to predict wife assault recidivism. For example, meteorologists know that when a mass of warm, moist air collides with a cold front, the moist air is forced upward and that this rising, in combination with the contact with colder air, causes the temperature to drop in the moist air. Cooler air can hold less dissolved moisture, so condensation in the moist air falls as precipitation. This knowledge of the causes of some rainfall makes it easier to forecast. By definition, correct and complete explanations of phenomena accurately predict those phenomena. The pitfalls of an incorrect or incomplete explanation are obvious: Recall the erroneous explanation of London's cholera outbreaks discussed in chapter 2. We believe that the poor performance of clinical judgment and the small (or negligible) treatment effects demonstrate that our field has not yet developed truly correct and complete explanations of violence or of wife assault in particular. Therefore, the most accurate risk assessment must rely on actuarial predictors, regardless of their explanatory power.

In chapter 1, we observed that offender interventions must identify and target criminogenic needs; that is, they must attempt to change characteristics or behaviors that are causally related to violent behavior. Identifying the causes of domestic violence is therefore key to designing and evaluating interventions. The domestic violence literature has a number of heuristic ideas, and attempts have been made to integrate modest and moderate correlations into multilayer explanations (Harris & Hilton, 2001), but no one (including us) has a fully articulated causal theory of wife assault with adequate explanatory power. Our hypothesis is that a complete explanation of the most frequent and severe violence against women, including intimate partners, will have to include general tendencies toward antisocial behavior and psychopathy in particular. The strong association between PCL–R score (measured up to and including the time of the index) and violent outcome (occurring after the index) supports this hypothesis. It would be prudent, therefore, to reserve the most intensive interventions for men who have high scores on the PCL–R and, by extension, the DVRAG.

Community treatment programs appear unlikely to recruit men with psychopathic traits, leading some observers to comment that routine measurement of psychopathy is hard to justify in such settings (Huss & Langhinrichsen-Rohling, 2006). In mental health settings, few clinicians, even forensic clinicians, use psychopathy to assess risk (Elbogen, Huss, Tompkins, & Scalora, 2005). Yet psychopaths' abilities to charm, deceive, manipulate, and lie raise the real possibility that if not properly identified, they will avoid treatment, attend treatment for shorter periods, or apply minimal effort (e.g., Spidel et al., 2007; Tanasichuk & Wormith, 2008). For this reason alone, we recommend routine assessment of risk in domestic violence treatment programs using the full DVRAG where possible. Psychopathy predicts all criminal justice outcomes too strongly for a forensic treatment setting to fail to gather the in-depth information required to measure it.

THE FUTURE OF DOMESTIC VIOLENCE RISK ASSESSMENT

Over the past 10 years, we have seen an increase in prediction accuracy for violent recidivism in general, and we have anticipated that ROC areas for actuarial predictors alone could exceed .90 with improved research (Harris & Rice, 2003). So far, our research has not shown that wife assault recidivism can be predicted with the same accuracy as can general violence recidivism. There could be a limit set by the smaller target that researchers have to aim at: not just any criminal violence, nor just that involving women as victims, but that involving a female domestic partner. Previous research has also been limited by the tendency to use domestic-specific variables such as jealousy, escalation of domestic violence, relationship separation, and attitudes toward wife assault rather than more global measures of interpersonal style, criminal history, unstable lifestyle, and attitudes toward criminal behavior or convention.

The research described so far in this book constitutes the entire contribution of actuarial methods to wife assault risk assessment that we are aware of and represents a much shorter history than that of violence prediction in general. So much has happened in the latter field since Monahan's (1981) germinal monograph stating that clinicians' predictions of violence are correct no more than one time out of three that when we first read those words—as a student, a forensic clinician, and a research psychologist, respectively—we could not imagine that we would publish the first actuarial risk assessment for domestic violence nearly 25 years later.

From our current experience, however, we can see that publishing articles alone will do very little to improve the lives of women affected by domestic violence. In the next two chapters, we look at the need to integrate this knowledge into criminal justice policies and services for victims and to communicate the findings of violence risk assessment in a way that optimizes their chances of being understood and influencing vital decisions about offender intervention.

SUMMARY OF MAIN POINTS

- We tested several other assessments of violence risk and general antisociality among ODARA construction sample cases with in-depth information, and the PCL–R (a well-established measure of psychopathy) produced the most consistent improvement in prediction.
- Risk assessments that predominantly consider variables specific to domestic violence do not identify the most dangerous offenders as accurately as risk assessments that predominantly consider variables related to general antisociality.
- The DVRAG provides an algorithm for combining the ODARA items with the PCL–R score using weights based on the DVRAG construction sample.
- On average, an offender would have a less than 5% probability of misclassification by more than one DVRAG category when scored by a trained rater.
- Adjusting the DVRAG score on the basis of any idiosyncratic information, including whether the perpetrator has undergone

treatment, is not supported by empirical data and is therefore not recommended.

- The DVRAG was designed to predict victim injury and the severity of assaults, not just the likelihood of recidivism, and yields a moderate effect size for all these measures.
- Assessors who can obtain a reliable PCL–R score should use the DVRAG except for cases falling into the lowest categories on the ODARA.
- This research adds to existing evidence that general antisociality influences and explains a wide range of antisocial and violent behavior.
- A complete and certainly correct explanation of wife assault would be extremely valuable in assessing perpetrators' risk, but such an explanation does not yet exist. In the meantime, actuarial methods are the most scientifically appropriate approach to risk assessment.
- The ODARA/DVRAG system is currently the only actuarial assessment for the risk of domestic violence recidivism.
- Offender intervention programs should routinely assess psychopathy and consider general antisocial behavior as a treatment target.

5

RISK COMMUNICATION

The murder of Arlene May by Randy Iles while he was on conditional release (see Introduction to this volume) was a tragic lesson in failed risk communication. This case was but one high-profile case that occurred in our jurisdiction; each province, state, or country has its own examples.

In the aftermath of the May–Iles murder–suicide, there was much public discussion about the criminal justice system's apparent inability to assess and communicate the danger Randy Iles posed throughout the period leading up to the fatalities, especially during his court appearances. No actuarial risk assessment for domestic violence was available at that time, but Iles did have an extensive criminal history, including threats of violence. The courts, police services, and even a shelter Arlene May visited did have risk-relevant information, but their efforts to share and act on that information were insufficient, ineffectual, and—perhaps most important—uncoordinated. In our opinion, an actuarial risk score placed on court and criminal records and shared between a shelter and the police could have served as a fulcrum for a coordinated response by the community and as a trigger for more intensive intervention.

A statement of actuarial risk is essentially one form of risk communication. Other common forms of risk communication include a warning that violence is imminent, a psychological report identifying a violent client's treatment needs, a probation officer's report summarizing an offender's history as indicating low risk, a mental health tribunal's decision that a forensic patient can be managed under minimum security, a parole board's refusal to grant an inmate early release, and a woman's report to police that she fears her ex-husband will kill her. A different, dramatic example of risk communication was seen in the case of Ralph Hadley.

Ralph and Gillian Hadley married in 1997. Her two children lived with them, and they had a child together in June 1999. Ralph was charged with criminal negligence causing bodily harm in an incident involving Gillian's son; this charge was withdrawn in December 1999, conditional on an order to keep the peace. The next month, during an argument between the estranged couple, Ralph assaulted Gillian and was consequently charged with assault and breach of the peace bond. Ralph was released again on bail, but he continued to contact Gillian despite a no-contact order. When Gillian complained to the police on February 23, 2000, about Ralph's repeated attempts to contact her, he was charged with this breach and with criminal harassment and again released on bail with a new no-contact order. A police officer filed a brief stating that Ralph would "absolutely reoffend." A pretrial hearing on all outstanding charges took place in June 2000, after 10 costly adjournments in the provincial court. On June 20, 2000, Ralph broke into the matrimonial home, where Gillian was living. After a dramatic chase in front of the house, during which neighbors managed to rescue the baby, Ralph fatally shot first her and then himself. The court reconvened on June 30 to withdraw all charges (Brown, 2001; Cross, 2002; FACT Ontario, 2000).

Communication of risk, as this example makes clear, is not as straightforward as providing an assessment report. In this chapter, we present evidence that actuarial risk assessment results can be communicated effectively, leading to good forensic decisions. Most of this work has been conducted with respect to general violence, but we will identify the implications for the communication of domestic violence risk and guide readers through a model for reporting results on the Ontario Domestic Assault Risk Assessment (ODARA; Hilton et al., 2004) and the Domestic Violence Risk Appraisal Guide (DVRAG; Hilton, Harris, Rice, Houghton, & Eke, 2008).

Some observers have argued that accurately assessing violence risk is of little help to the task of managing violent offenders (e.g., Heilbrun, 1997; Kropp, 2008b). The reasoning is that if clinicians work to alter risk factors, then violence will be reduced. In fact, there is little evidence favoring wife assault treatment and currently no scientific research guiding idiosyncratic, case-specific approaches to risk management. We therefore believe it is irresponsible to eschew violence risk assessment using tools with measured levels of prediction accuracy in favor of untested assumptions that risk management will have its desired effects.

We further believe that any attempt to manage offenders implies a prediction about recidivism. For example, bail courts, parole boards, and forensic tribunals all must primarily consider the risk of harm should an offender be released; it would be unconscionable to release offenders to the community without regard to the risk of new acts of violence. Furthermore, the wide variety of agencies providing offender interventions in institutions and the community cannot reasonably deliver and coordinate such services without some way to determine who gets how much of which interventions, which is a way to agree on and communicate about each offender's risk. Failure of risk communication can result in different parts of the "system" working at odds with each other, such as a court requiring violent offenders to attend a community anger management program only to have that program deny treatment because ongoing substance abuse is one of its exclusion criteria. Even with an established communication system, we have seen actuarial risk assessment reports overlooked by clinicians who have their own (usually unvalidated) methods of evaluating potential violence. It is our fervent hope that the ODARA and DVRAG will not be merely assessments that are scored and filed but tools for communication within and across criminal justice, offender intervention, and victim services.

"ASK THE EXPERT": WHAT DO FORENSIC PROFESSIONALS PREFER TO HEAR?

A popular way to determine the best approach to a task is to ask the people who are already doing it. When we began to study risk communication, the few existing studies had surveyed forensic clinicians about what they did. Heilbrun, Philipson, Berman, and Warren (1999) reported that only 1 of 55 clinicians used numerical ways to communicate violence risk. Half the respondents explained that they did not use probabilities because they did not believe the research literature justified them. Others said there was no suitable assessment or that numbers could be more misleading and open to misinterpretation than nonnumerical statements. Heilbrun and his colleagues then asked 59 other clinicians to compare eight different forms of risk communication (only five of which contained a conclusion about violence risk). The least popular option was "Express risk relative to norm or base rate for that population," and the most favored was "Describe recent and present behavior, give clinical impressions based on history, current behavior, mental status, and dynamics, and make a prediction" (Heilbrun, Philipson, et al., 1999, pp. 401–402). In subsequent surveys, simply identifying risk factors and specifying risk-reducing interventions were most popular among clinicians (Heilbrun et al., 2004; Heilbrun, O'Neill, Strohman, Bowman, & Philipson, 2000). On average, the next most popular forms of risk communication were characterizing violence risk as high, moderate, or low or simply describing clinical features presumed to be relevant to risk. Thus, clinical description was preferred over any statement of the probability of violence.

It seemed that forensic clinicians, at least toward the end of the last century, endorsed clinical and intuitive approaches to both the evaluation of and communication about violence risk. The most common reasons for rejecting numerical statements, moreover, were negative and subjective: "I don't feel that precise" and "I don't know how to go from base rates to single cases" (Heilbrun, Philipson, et al., 1999, p. 403). Heilbrun and his colleagues observed that the research literature already had demonstrated valid numerical approaches and suggested that clinicians were actually reluctant to adopt them out of feelings of self-importance, attachment to invalid theoretical perspectives of human behavior, the belief that statistics are dehumanizing, dislike of computers, misconceptions about the relative accuracy of statistical prediction, and fears of being replaced by a technical innovation. In other words, actuarial risk assessment touched an emotional sore spot or foundered on clinicians' innumeracy, which had nothing to do with the scientific or empirical adequacy of the actuarial research.

We also think it possible that clinicians favored nonnumerical categories (e.g., low, moderate, or high risk) because they wanted to communicate comparative risk. Comparative risk (as in rank order or percentile) is more useful than absolute probability of violence because it permits more discrimination and does not fluctuate according to the particular operational definition of the outcome or the follow-up time of interest. Ironically, comparative risk appears less well understood than absolute probability, and clinicians frequently confuse the two (e.g., Hilton, Harris, Rawson, & Beach, 2005; Slovic & Monahan; 1995; see also Schwarz, 1999).

WHAT SHOULD EFFECTIVE RISK COMMUNICATION LOOK LIKE?

Another way to decide the best way to communicate risk is to measure the effect of various methods. Inherent here is that there is an optimal outcome, or a performance standard, by which the proficiency of decision making can be evaluated: Objectively high-risk cases should receive greater supervision (or generally more intensive intervention) than lower risk cases. All else being equal, by this definition, the greater the difference between the use of secure custody for offenders of highest versus lowest risk, the greater the forensic decision-making proficiency. Risk communication that results in the most proficient decisions is, we argue, the most effective communication. The difference between risk-related decisions for cases of objectively different risk provides a standard against which to measure the effect of risk communication (and other aspects of a system's performance).

Effect of Actuarial Risk Communication on Forensic Decisions

Our study of decisions by an autonomous tribunal that determined the security placement of offenders held in forensic hospitals was originally conceived as a review of current practices in order to narrow down variables for a subsequent experiment, but it became an interesting story in itself (Hilton & Simmons, 2001). The relevant legislation required the tribunal to base decisions on "the need to protect the public from dangerous persons, the mental condition of the accused, the reintegration of the accused into society and the other needs of the accused" (Hilton & Simmons, 2001, p. 396). Tribunals have a range of available options, from detention in maximum security to discharge to the community with or without conditions.

The principal concern of our study was the extent to which actuarial risk scores influenced clinicians' recommendations to the tribunal and the tribunal's subsequent decisions. Previous studies concluded that such forensic tribunals were essentially "rubber-stamping" recommendations made by psychiatrists, although there was little relationship between clinical judgments and recidivism (Konečni & Ebbesen, 1984, p. 12; Quinsey & Ambtman, 1978; Quinsey, Khanna, & Malcolm, 1998). We therefore expected recommendations by clinicians, and psychiatrists in particular, to influence the tribunal strongly, but we also expected that scores on the Violence Risk Appraisal Guide (VRAG; Quinsey, Harris, Rice, & Cormier, 2006) would influence them both. At the time, actuarial violence risk assessment was fairly new, and the single other study on the subject reported that tribunals did not routinely use such information (Taylor, Goldberg, Leese, Butwell, & Reed, 1999). Our expectations, however, were based on the fact that the VRAG had been developed in the study institution, and VRAG scores for individual patients had been available for almost a decade. We had repeatedly made the case that actuarial scores should form the basis of violence risk assessment. The institution and government officials had supported the VRAG's creation and implementation, forensic services had been reorganized in accord with empirical research (Rice & Harris, 1988), and the administration had mandated evidence-based practice.

We collected data on review decisions made since 1992, when the VRAG was first admitted in tribunal hearings. That same year, trained staff began completing the VRAG so that by 1997, 90% of patients had a VRAG report on file soon after admission. The report provided the information considered for each offender's score on each item and a statement of the percentile rank, category (1 to 9), and probability of violent recidivism within a stated time frame (7 or 10 years) similar to that in Appendix D for the DVRAG. Mental health tribunals tended to be quite conservative, most resulting in no disposition change; therefore, we oversampled release decisions to bring the proportion of released cases to about a third.

It is important to note that in this study of risk-related decision proficiency, we were not evaluating the validity of actuarial or clinical assessment. VRAG scores were already established as an objective index of risk; the empirical question was whether clinical opinion and tribunal decision would be related to VRAG scores. If there was no VRAG score available to the tribunal hearing, it was obtained or scored later. The VRAG reports that were available entailed one form of risk communication, and we expected that their availability would improve decision-making proficiency by increasing the association between VRAG score and the tribunal decisions.

We found a very large association between tribunal decisions and opinions given by psychiatrists in oral testimony and by the clinical team in a written report. We were wrong, though, in our expectation that decisions would be related to the VRAG score. The association between VRAG score and clinical opinion was essentially zero overall, and even a little worse when the score was known. When available, the VRAG score was the only thing that influenced tribunal decisions in addition to clinical opinion, but this effect was very small. Consequently, there was no difference in objective risk of violence between offenders who were detained in maximum security and those given a less secure disposition. Clearly, neither the tribunal's decisions nor the advice received from clinicians showed evidence of forensic decision-making proficiency (Hilton & Simmons, 2001). Jury decision making can be similarly influenced by clinical opinion testimony over more accurate actuarial assessment (e.g., Krauss & Lee, 2003).

Our results showed that the tribunal, far from juggling multiple and sometimes conflicting sources of information, simply shifted most decision-making responsibility to the psychiatrists who testified about the best placement for the patients. In more than 90% of cases, this testimony alone exactly corresponded with the tribunal decision. A statistical model of clinical opinion revealed that patients with more serious criminal histories, worse institutional management problems over the previous year, and less compliance with or response to psychiatric drugs and who were less physically attractive were least likely to garner a favorable recommendation from clinicians. Most of these characteristics are, in fact, irrelevant to the tribunal's primary mandate, but ours was not the first study to show that such factors influence forensic decisions (see Esses & Webster, 1988; MacCoun, 1990). On the basis of our experience on multidisciplinary clinical teams and our conversations with clinicians who testified at the tribunals, we concluded that the actuarial risk communication was unsuccessful and that psychiatrists perceived it as irrelevant. Their attempts to balance the actuarial risk information with traditional, unaided clinical intuition instead succeeded in obliterating the effect of the actuarial communication.

Consequently, recidivism among those released was significantly related to VRAG score but not to clinical opinion. Based on observed rates of violent recidivism for VRAG scores (Quinsey, Harris, et al., 2006), the expected rate of violent recidivism over the ensuing decade for offenders released in this study was nearly twice that achieved by release decisions strictly governed by actuarial scores. Thus, effective risk communication could have cut the danger to society in half without an increase in the number or proportion of patients detained.

We recently repeated this study and found some improvement—a modest statistical association between violence risk and clinicians' advice to the tribunal—but no significant improvement in the proficiency of tribunal decisions (McKee, Harris, & Rice, 2007). Clinicians continued to be influenced by factors known to be unrelated to violence risk, but there was evidence to suggest that risk communication based on actuarial scores had improved. Other researchers have also found a small but positive association between Psychopathy Checklist—Revised (PCL–R; R. D. Hare, 2003) scores and judicial decisions regarding release of forensic patients in a U.S. jurisdiction (Manguno-Mire, Thompson, Bertman-Pate, Burnett, & Thompson, 2007). In the next section, we examine what methods of communication can increase the influence of actuarial risk on forensic decisions.

Communicating Risk Factors and Probability of Recidivism

In these experimental studies, we examined hypothetical forensic decisions about violent offenders in general. Our research participants were forensic clinicians with experience making decisions about the risk of violence in general but not much experience making decisions about the risk of domestic violence in particular; at the time, neither the ODARA nor the DVRAG had been published.

Our first question was simply whether clinicians would use the VRAG to decide an offender's level of security more when the actuarial risk score was clearly communicated, compared with only risk-relevant case information or with only risk-irrelevant case information. As in previous studies of forensic decision making, we limited the case information to a single paragraph plus a summary communication about the availability and results of "an actuarial risk assessment." Clinicians typically have much more information available (Carter & Hilton, 2007) but appear not to make use of it all in their decision making (Quinsey & Ambtman, 1979). Furthermore, Mamuza (2001) reported that more accurate estimates of risk were elicited when relevant information was presented in a way that maximized its salience. In our study, each forensic clinician read two short case summaries of men described as maximum security forensic patients with either a 24% or 64% probability of violent recidivism within 10 years of opportunity based on VRAG scores (Hilton et al., 2005). VRAG score was either explicitly stated or only implicitly available from the risk-relevant case information. We used a 2 (24% vs.

64% actuarial estimate) × 2 (risk-relevant vs. risk-irrelevant case information) × 2 (actuarial summary statement present vs. not present) factorial design. Clinicians estimated the likelihood of violent recidivism and compared it with that of other maximum security offenders.

One might imagine that communicating the risk information twice— once in the risk-relevant case material and again in the actuarial summary— would increase the effectiveness of risk communication. In fact, the effect was to increase the estimated risk, such that decisions were more conservative than accurate. Thus, contrary to the clinical lore that more information means more proficient decisions, essentially repeating the same information in the case summary reduced clinicians' accuracy, perhaps because they did not recognize that the risk-relevant information was subsumed by the actuarial summary statement. This finding gives us a clue as to why clinicians who feel that actuarial risk assessment is just one part of the clinical picture end up making decisions that effectively ignore objective violence risk.

Communicating Actuarial Risk Along With Forensic Professionals' Preferred Information

In that 2005 study, we used only a brief paragraph to describe the case, far less information than is typically available in a risk appraisal report, let alone a complete case file (Hilton et al., 2005). In the Heilbrun studies described earlier in this chapter, respondents said they wanted to know about the current clinical presentation and potentially treatable offender characteristics. In a small survey, we sent reports of relatively low- and high-scoring VRAG cases to forensic psychologists and psychiatrists in Ontario (Carter & Hilton, 2007). One third of the reports were simply risk-relevant summary paragraphs followed by an actuarial risk summary statement, one third had a more complete risk assessment report that detailed the psychosocial history from which the VRAG was scored, and one third had the summary paragraph and VRAG statement embedded in a general psychological report that encompassed personality and neurological assessments irrelevant to violence risk. The relatively low scoring case was stated in all reports to have a 10% likelihood of violent recidivism within 10 years of opportunity. This case was rated as "low risk" by more than 80% of clinicians who read the single paragraph or full risk assessment report but by fewer than 30% of those who read the full psychological report. Thus, the kind of clinical case information forensic professionals desired substantially influenced their perception of risk but by making it less accurate and excessively conservative.

Studies such as this suggest that the phrases "low risk" and "high risk" have no clear meaning even to professionals who use them daily. Forensic clinicians want information about comparative risk of violence but cannot distinguish it from absolute risk (i.e., probability of violent recidivism). In our next study, we examined whether we could more effectively communicate actuarial risk if we provided nonnumerical categories to add emphasis to probabilistic information (Hilton, Carter, Harris, & Sharpe, 2008). We found no such evidence, and there was substantial disagreement among forensic clinicians as to the numeric meaning properly associated with the terms *low*, *moderate*, and *high risk*. On average, participants indicated that low risk was 0% to 27% likelihood of violent recidivism, moderate risk was 28% to 68%, and high risk was 69% to 100%. Averages, however, hid a great deal of disagreement: More than a third of the range that was moderate on average (38% to 51%) was considered low by some participants and high by others.

We found a similar level of disagreement among ratings of the comparative risk, or rank order, that experienced forensic clinicians thought should correspond to the three categories. The actual numbers assigned to each comparative risk category were so similar to those for likelihood of violent recidivism that clinicians evidently did not understand them to be different metrics. Whereas probability of recidivism depends on the definition of recidivism and the time frame of interest, comparative risk depends on the population with which the offender is being compared (e.g., other violent offenders, the general population). Our research has found that forensic clinicians do not in practice distinguish between these fundamentally distinct concepts.

We have also found poor agreement on the meaning of low, moderate, and high risk when forensic clinicians rated groups of offenders. We gave each participant a brief description of a group of violent offenders described as having a 10% probability of violent recidivism (10th percentile), a 48% probability (65th percentile), or an 82% probability (93rd percentile). Then we presented a brief description of a second group always stated as having a 48% probability. The forensic clinician participants then rated the second group as low, moderate, or high risk. Although the second group did not vary in objective risk, these experienced participants judged them as high risk more often when the previous group had a 10% probability (Figure 5.1). There was also a tendency to judge them as low risk more often when the previous group was at the 93rd percentile (Hilton, Carter, et al., 2008).

Ours was not the first study to report the lack of consensus on the meaning of such nonnumerical terms. Grann and Pallvik (2002) found 56 different nonnumerical expressions of degrees of risk among 122 written forensic evaluations. Mills and Kroner (2006) reported that nonnumerical risk terms were interpreted inconsistently and yielded overestimations of risk even when base rate data were provided. In nonforensic medicine, physicians prefer to communicate using such terms but vary widely in their interpretation of them (Sedgwick & Hall, 2003; Shaw & Dear, 1990), often illogically. Bryant and Norman (1980) reported, for example, that even the words *certain* and *always* were not rated as indicating 100% likelihood. Medical patients, on the other hand, appear comparatively distrustful of nonnumerical terms

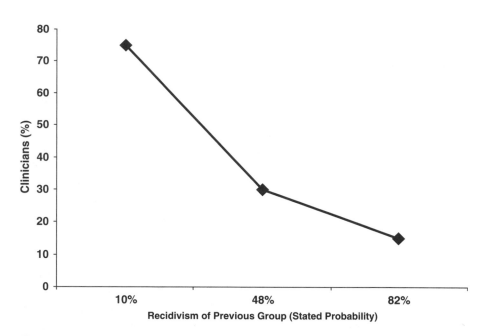

Figure 5.1. Percentage of forensic clinicians rating an offender group with a 48% probability of violent recidivism as high risk as a function of the stated risk of the previous group in a pair of descriptions. Data from Hilton, Carter, Harris, and Sharpe (2008).

(Gurmankin, Baron, & Armstrong, 2004). Psychological research generally indicates that nonnumerical judgments show poor agreement and are invalidly influenced by context (e.g., Karelitz & Budescu, 2004), and our research described here indicates that experienced forensic clinicians' decisions are no exception.

Reliability and Interpretation of Risk

When we conduct our research based on file coding, we seek interrater reliability correlations of at least .80 on continuous measures and have found reliabilities of at least .90 for the ODARA scored by research assistants, police officers, or training participants (using a somewhat conservative correlation model; see chap. 6, this volume). Excellent agreement has been reported for the numerical components of risk assessment schemes for both domestic assault and general violence (i.e., total item scores and number of risk factors present), but much lower agreement has been reported for nonnumerical risk judgment (Douglas, Ogloff, & Hart, 2003; Douglas, Yeomans, & Boer, 2005). For example, Kropp and Hart (2000) reported that interrater reliability on 86 cases scored from institutional files by a case manager and independently by a graduate researcher was .63 for the judgment, compared with .84 for the total score. A coefficient of .63 on a variable that, according to Kropp and Hart's Table 9, had a mean of 2.25 (where 1 = *low* and 3 = *high*) and a standard deviation of 0.79 indicates a standard error of measurement (SEM; see chap. 3, this volume) of .48, leading to a 95% confidence interval of .94 around an obtained score. Thus, a judgment of moderate (2) could reliably exclude neither low nor high as the true risk.

The obvious problem for both research and practice is that if an instrument cannot be scored reliably, then it cannot reliably yield an accurate assessment of the risk of violence when used in practice. The less obvious problem with poor reliability is that assessors and decision makers cannot effectively communicate and manage risk because they do not agree on the risk posed by an individual offender, a problem that is exacerbated by lack of awareness of the amount of disagreement.

Why do forensic clinicians resist actuarial methods and adhere to informal ways of evaluating and communicating about risk? Our research shows that clinicians can understand and use actuarial information about violence risk, particularly probabilistic estimates. In fact, keeping actuarial information from them seems to result in more conservative and less proficient decisions. Although probabilities and numerical information in general might not be clinicians' preferred form of risk communication, we are optimistic that forensic decision makers, if not the clinicians themselves, can come to understand and proficiently use actuarial information about risk, just as people began to prefer probability statements about weather (A. H. Murphy, 1991).

We argue, furthermore, that this change is necessary. In the studies we have described in this chapter, the best forensic decisions—those that make the greatest distinction in security placement between actuarially higher and lower risk patients—were made in the context of numerical (probabilistic) statements about violence risk. Absence of actuarial risk information led to poorer decisions. Nonnumerical categories yielded poor reliability among assessors, were vulnerable to confusion between absolute and comparative risk, and exhibited unjustifiable biases due to context effects. Actuarial risk information is likely to result in greater fairness to the offenders themselves and can be accomplished without extra costs to the forensic system.

COMMUNICATING THE RISK OF DOMESTIC VIOLENCE: WHO, WHAT, WHERE, WHEN, AND WHY

We believe that the ODARA, and more generally the system of risk assessment represented by the ODARA and DVRAG together, demonstrates that using an actuarial risk assessment need not be daunting. Our work with the Ontario Provincial Police resulted in a one-page report suitable for submitting in a prosecution (or defense) brief. One side of the page summarizes each ODARA item, its score, and the evidence on which it was based (e.g., the date of a criminal record check, an occurrence incident number, the witness name and statement date). The other side contains a summary of the research on which the interpretation was based, the perpetrator's raw and adjusted score, and statistical interpretation using tables provided in Appendixes A and B of this volume. Our recommended method of risk communication does require numerical terms to optimize accuracy, consistency, fairness, and cost-effectiveness. Forensic professionals, despite their objections to and discomfort with numbers, can understand them and make better decisions by using them. Victims, too, can use actuarial information, and we suggest a graphic approach for frontline victim service users (Appendix F).

The "Five Ws" of newspaper reporting remind the communicator to pack the most important information (in decreasing order of importance) into the opening paragraph of a story. When reporting on violence risk assessment, it is first necessary to state *who* is the subject of the assessment—in the case of the ODARA or DVRAG, the male perpetrator. Although the ODARA can be conducted as part of a clinical interview with a female victim of assault (as we describe later in this chapter), the calculated risk is that posed by the perpetrator, not that necessarily faced by the victim. In the ODARA construction sample, most recidivists did in fact assault the same women as in the index assault, but some victimized a different partner.

What is defined as recidivism (i.e., physical violence); the probability of its occurrence in this case and the rank of the score within a stated population must also be reported. Both the ODARA and DVRAG research defined recidivism according to police reports and criminal records. Reliance on official recidivism increases the utility of these tools throughout the criminal justice system. For cases without police involvement, though, official recidivism could substantially underestimate the actual rates of assault. As an analogy, convicted sex offenders admit to more offenses than come to the attention of police (e.g., Harris & Rice, 2007).

On the basis of the research described in this chapter, we believe a statement of the probability of recidivism will improve risk communication. Also, a statement of comparative risk is essential to help decision makers understand where a perpetrator stands in relation to others with respect to risk. For brief oral communication (e.g., in case conferences or interagency referrals), these two facts could suffice. Actuarial risk assessment permits one to make conclusive statements about the probability of reoffending based on the perpetrator's similarity to a group of offenders for whom the violent outcome was known. By the same token, the statement must always be connected to the known group. Thus, "men in this range of scores had approximately a 70% likelihood of recidivism" is preferred to "this offender is 70% likely to recidivate," even though these statements are formally equivalent.

We explained actuarial methods and their application to risk assessment in chapter 2. Occasionally we encounter the misconception, however, that an actuarial instrument would be inadequate because it fails to address all known risk factors (Exhibit 2.1). Thus, some assessors, especially mental health clinicians, are tempted to regard an actuarial score as just "one piece" of the total information required to assess risk and think they should modify the actuarial score using aspects of clinical presentation or intuition about other things. Some schemes encourage such empirically unsupported judgments (as we describe in chap. 2). Empirically derived actuarial approaches add items only if they increase the predictive validity of the instrument over and above items already included. Even lengthy descriptions of the material used to score the items are of questionable value because they seem to result in more conservative decisions, as though more information means higher risk. A similar concern arises with the question of whether to communicate risks in a positive or negative frame (e.g., Kahneman & Tversky, 2000), as strengths or weaknesses. Many of the problems of invalid interpretation might best be resolved by incorporating actuarial scores explicitly into policy (see chap. 6, this volume; McKee et al., 2007).

Where reminds us to state that the violence is expected to occur in a domestic relationship—specifically, against a female partner. *When* must also be stated in terms of the known follow-up period. Base rates of recidivism depend on the duration of the follow-up. If a decision concerned the lifetime likelihood of recidivism, probabilities based on a follow-up of only five years would underestimate the outcome of interest. Recidivism rates for actuarial categories cannot be directly extrapolated; for example, perpetrators in the highest risk categories are likely to show proportionately greater increases in risk as follow-up duration is increased. For decisions concerning shorter terms, the observed probabilities overestimate the outcome. It is difficult to imagine, however, circumstances in which a decision maker is truly only concerned with a short time span and that what happens later is legitimately of no concern.

Why could refer to the information on which the assessment is based. For example, the ODARA would usually be based on a police investigation report, including the statements made by the victim, perpetrator, and witnesses and the documentation indicating the perpetrator's criminal history. The results of an ODARA clinical interview based only on the victim's report (we recommend a police record check whenever possible) should be communicated to the victim as "according to your responses" or "based on the information you have provided." In addition to using the documented police and criminal history to score the DVRAG, it is necessary to compile a psychosocial history (e.g., Quinsey, Harris, et al., 2006), possibly supplemented by an offender interview, in order to score the PCL–R. All sources of information (including the referral) should be stated in the report. Written reports also typically list the ODARA or DVRAG items.

It is also typical when reporting in-depth risk assessment to describe each item and note whether it contributed positively or negatively to the score. Our research indicates that including details about items in the assessment (as well as details about things not on the instrument) could lead to more conservative decisions, perhaps because decision makers feel that there is more information to support a conservative decision or to perform a post-actuarial adjustment (e.g., Krauss, 2004) incorporating items not part of the risk assessment. On the other hand, listing the items promotes transparency and accountability of the assessment and assessor (e.g., Mills, Kroner, & Hemmati, 2007). A remedy for this dilemma is to link actuarial scores more strictly to actual decisions via a formal system that instantiates the decision policy (McKee et al., 2007).

It has been noted that both prediction and theoretical explanation are needed for effective management of offenders (Kroner, 2005; see also chap. 4, this volume). But the two activities must not be confused. Theoretical explanations are not necessarily part of risk assessment and, in our experience, detract from the effectiveness of risk communication. In training sessions, for example, we often are asked to give causal explanations for ODARA items, and we enjoy a healthy debate (even among ourselves) as to why such things as a woman having children to care for increases the risk that her partner will assault again. When clinicians feel they understand the causal connection, however, they also feel authorized to incorporate conceptually similar issues into the scoring. For example, one clinician reasoned that having young children makes it harder to access services, which explains why it is an ODARA item, and thus that a victim's physical disability requiring wheelchair use should also garner a point on the ODARA. Although physically challenged women are vulnerable to abuse (e.g., 2005; M. M. Cohen, Forte, DuMont, Hyman, & Romans, 2005; Coker, Smith, & Fadden; but see Brownridge, 2006), there were too few such cases in our research to indicate that it increased risk, so adding a point for disability is not valid.

Similarly, reasoning that gambling problems are equivalent to substance abuse (because they both indicate problems of impulse control), and adding a point for gambling addiction, is invalid. Subtracting a point because a perpetrator agrees to abstain from alcohol is not defensible (see chap. 6). Likewise, nonactuarial approaches that encourage assessors to adjust scores on the basis of their opinions about what has caused or might cause violence cannot be considered empirically valid. Adjusting formal risk assessments on the basis of the causes of violence will be empirically valid only when those causes have been demonstrated to relate to recidivism incrementally over other predictors.

RISK COMMUNICATION WITH FEMALE VICTIMS
OF DOMESTIC VIOLENCE

Our ideal for use of the ODARA/DVRAG risk assessment system is that it be accessible to everyone involved in the integrated community response to domestic violence. We do not believe that the ODARA is a tool for only the police to score, even if they do share the results with victims. We have endeavored to provide the ODARA more directly to assaulted women, primarily through agencies that provide services for women, children, and families. In particular, Norah Holder, the former director of the Sexual/Domestic Assault Program at the Orillia Soldiers' Memorial Hospital, helped us transform a research-based list of criteria into a series of questions that could be used as an interview with a female client while maintaining the integrity of the scoring criteria (Hilton, Harris, & Holder, 2008). The program nurses were the first to use the ODARA with recently assaulted women and provided valuable feedback, including the suggestion of using pie charts rather than statistical tables for interpreting scores. With the ODARA thus easily accessible to the victim service sector, we have had the privilege of partnering with a number of clinics and shelters that supported our goals of establishing a tool for both criminal justice and clinical use. The clinics were part of a provincial network supported by the Ontario government to provide emergency medical and nursing care and assessment, crisis counseling, forensic evidence collection, and referral services to adults and children who have been recently assaulted, including risk assessment and safety planning with victims of assault by partners. From 111 women who participated in a study at these clinics, we gained valuable information about characteristics of the ODARA when scored by victim interview.

For more than three quarters of these women, the index assault was not the first time their partner had assaulted them. In two thirds of cases, the perpetrator's ODARA score, according to the information the women provided, was 7 or more; that is, in the highest risk category for recidivism. Women's direct knowledge of the perpetrator's behavior might be expected to produce higher scores than results based on police records. On the other hand, perhaps the higher scores were due to the fact that the men were truly higher risk. Actuarial risk is higher among repeat offenders, and the clinic sample had experienced particularly serious assaults. Statistically, ODARA interview scores showed a more or less normal distribution, and the items were correlated with each other, giving evidence of internal consistency, as in the construction research. Also, the scores were associated with other variables in ways similar to the original research; for example, higher scores were observed in cases with stalking or prior injury. These results provided some validation of the ODARA interview in terms of consistent psychometric properties and concurrent validity.

Most women suffered cuts and bruises, but others were stabbed, strangled, or sexually assaulted. Most injuries were in the hand or arm and face, consistent with a woman trying to protect herself from an attack to the upper body, but many other, sometimes serious injuries occurred at other sites. Over half of these women rated the risk of violence by the perpetrator in the next year as 10 on a scale of 0 (*no chance*) to 10 (*sure to happen*). This rating is the highest reported in the literature (cf. Cattaneo & Goodman, 2003; Weisz, Tolman, & Saunders, 2000). Despite this, only a small minority of the women had current police involvement or had gone to a shelter, and those who had were not necessarily those with worse injuries or greater risk of reassault (according to ODARA scores). The low rates of concurrent service use suggested that the partner assault clinics served a unique clientele. Most women relied on an informal support network, primarily their female friends and female biological relatives (Table 5.1). Social networks could help protect victims, but friendships may be particularly vulnerable to disruption by perpetrators (e.g., Coohey, 2007). Participants were significantly more likely to contact professionals rather than police, providing further grounds for making the ODARA available outside of police services.

Partner assault clinic staff have told us that they appreciate being able to show clients the graphic interpretation materials (Appendix F) rather than just expressing their own professional opinion to their clients and that the women view it as an objective assessment that has direct relevance to their personal safety. Such feedback encourages us in our goal of making the ODARA/DVRAG system available to the entire community responding to domestic violence, and especially to frontline services for assaulted women.

ESTABLISHING NORMS FOR THE ONTARIO DOMESTIC ASSAULT RISK ASSESSMENT AND THE DOMESTIC VIOLENCE RISK APPRAISAL GUIDE: WHAT DO THEY PREDICT?

Appendixes B and D offer information pertaining to individual perpetrators: the proportion of men with the same score who met the criteria for wife assault recidivism in our databases and where such cases stand with respect to the risk of wife assault recidivism in relation to all others in the same databases (the percentile rank). As described in detail in chapter 4, it is also important to our work that ODARA and DVRAG scores are related to other ways of quantifying wife assault recidivism. Thus, with respect to how soon recidivism occurs and its severity, as indexed by the amount of subsequent injury to victims, the seriousness of the assaults, and the gravity of criminal charges, scores on the ODARA and DVRAG yielded the largest associations among several structured assessments evaluated. Consequently, the claim that actuarial tools merely assess the risk of minor events occurring (cf. Litwack, Zapf, Groscup,

TABLE 5.1

Sources of Help Reported by Participants in the Partner Assault Clinic Study

Source of help	%
Female friends	60
Female biological relatives (e.g., sister, mother, daughter)	55
Professionals (e.g., clergy, therapist, lawyer)	32
Male biological relatives (e.g., father, brother, son)	30
Male friends	26
Police	21
Other relatives	17
In law relatives	14
No one	9

Note. Data from Hilton, Harris, and Holder (2008).

& Hart, 2006) is incorrect. The evidence we described in chapter 4 indicates that the perpetrators identified as highest risk, and thus highest priority for incarceration, intensive supervision, or indeed any intervention, on the basis of their likelihood of wife assault recidivism, are the same as those who would be most accurately identified on the basis of their likelihood of seriously injuring a partner. Selecting wife assaulters for intervention on the basis of the DVRAG scores represents the optimal method for doing so.

Some users have asked why we have not produced norms that indicate, for example, what proportion of those who score more than 10 on the ODARA will cause a serious injury requiring hospitalization resulting in a criminal charge for at least aggravated assault within 8 months. Proficient risk-related polices do not usually require this kind of normative information, and it is not obvious how it could improve the apportioning of resources. We hope readers will recognize that this sort of fine-grained customization is untenable and does little to further the purpose of designing the ODARA/DVRAG system to enable a shared metric for communicating risk across criminal justice, offender intervention, and victim service sectors. If readers do need such customization, they could develop local norms using their own cases; the requisite data can be accumulated simply by adding ODARA/DVRAG scores to existing offender databases.

In this context, we note that some commentators (Hart, Michie, & Cooke, 2007) have criticized developers of actuarial tools for producing too much in the way of norms. These critics, using an unusual estimation procedure (E. B. Wilson, 1927) for confidence intervals, have said that the dichotomous likelihoods of recidivism for persons all obtaining the same score (or range of scores) are "worthless" when applied to a single person. They used confidence intervals to calculate the precision of a single score, but confidence intervals refer to multiple measurements (see Exhibit 2.2). Another statistic, the standard error of measurement, is needed to calculate the margin of error associated with an individual's true score (which is an aspect of reliability). Needless to say, we disagree with this complaint and have detailed our counterposition elsewhere (Harris & Rice, 2007; http:// www.mhcp-research.com/hmcrespond.pdf). Nevertheless, we do agree that it would not be appropriate to produce norms for actuarial tools that imply greater precision than is necessary for the execution of effective public policy.

Regardless of our advice about what should and should not be included in a risk assessment report, merely producing the report is not effective risk communication, even within a policy that directs decisions to be based on actuarial risk. The crucial test is whether the use, reporting, and implementation of a validated domestic violence risk assessment produce a measurable improvement in the allocation of resources—custody, conditional release, offender intervention, or victim protection services—and ultimately reduce harm. We recommend that the probability of a specified outcome within a given time frame and the comparative risk of the perpetrator within a known population of wife assaulters be the minimum information in a risk assessment summary. For optimal communication, this summary should be accompanied by a statement of the appropriate actions according to that risk, and these actions should be determined by empirically informed policy, as we describe in chapter 6.

SUMMARY OF MAIN POINTS

- Risk communication is more than scoring a risk assessment and submitting the report.
- In forensic practice, actuarial risk is often overlooked, resulting in the detention of offenders who are no more likely to violently recidivate than those who are released.
- Health professionals prefer risk to be communicated in terms of clinical impressions and nonnumerical categories such as "low risk" or "high risk," but a variety of studies show no reliable meaning of these nonnumerical terms.
- Forensic professionals can understand actuarial risk assessment results and base decisions on them, although too much information can result in more conservative decisions.
- Violence risk communication should include the probability of recidivism for the risk category in which the perpetrator falls, the definition of recidivism (including behavior, time frame, and victim definition), and an explanation of the comparative risk.
- The ODARA can be scored from a clinical interview with the victim, but a police check should also be performed whenever possible; when a police check is not possible, the assessor communicating the results to the victim should make it clear that they are based on her responses.

6

IMPLEMENTING ACTUARIAL
RISK ASSESSMENT

In previous chapters, we showed that the Ontario Domestic Assault Risk Assessment (ODARA) predicts recidivism by domestically violent men in Ontario who had at least one incident of wife assault in police records. In this chapter, we consider how that knowledge has been, and could be, applied in the criminal justice system to increase both the safety of women and fairness to perpetrators. When we developed the Violence Risk Appraisal Guide (VRAG) in the early 1990s, we (Harris, Rice, & Quinsey, 1993) might have thought that publishing an article in the peer-reviewed literature demonstrating the first actuarial tool to predict violent recidivism among serious male offenders, and then providing that information to clinical administrators and policymakers, would suffice to ensure that it would soon be adopted in the forensic hospital and criminal justice systems. We hoped, moreover, that a measurable improvement in public safety would thereby result.

We soon learned that doing the research was only the first and easiest part. Getting our new instrument into use even in our own hospital and province would be much more daunting. Although government officials did create policies mandating use of the VRAG, these policies lapsed once the particular individuals moved to other positions. Some of the greatest opposition to the VRAG came from colleagues at our own facility, perhaps because of the apparent human tendency to consider "experts" to be people who come from far afield. Another reason was that our facility is predominantly guided by a medical model. There is a preference among some mental health clinicians to reject actuarial tools (that can be completed by research assistants or psychosocial historians) in favor of professional judgment (as we described in chap. 5 of this volume).

In Canada, correctional systems are not so overtly medical, and greater efforts are made to ensure that offender assessment and programming are evidence based. A higher proportion of staff have training in standardized assessments. In fact, wherever we have traveled, we have found that actuarial risk assessments are most likely to be adopted in correctional systems. Correctional Services Canada, for example, has adopted several actuarial tools at its assessment centers, including the VRAG and a related tool for the prediction of violent recidivism by sex offenders, the Sex Offender Risk Appraisal Guide (SORAG; Quinsey, Harris, Rice, & Cormier, 2006). The correctional system's use of actuarial assessment might be due in part to its greater scrutiny and accountability (as well as feedback about actual recidivism).

We tried to use our experience in fostering widespread acceptance of the VRAG to facilitate acceptance of the ODARA and the Domestic Violence Risk Appraisal Guide (DVRAG). With the VRAG, we had the advantage of support of senior government officials who adopted our advice regarding mandating use of the VRAG. In the case of the research that led to the ODARA, this support came from the Ontario Provincial Police (OPP), and in particular from a senior officer, Kate Lines, who was involved with an interministerial committee responding to the inquest into the May–Iles murder–suicide described in the Introduction to this volume. She was committed to the aims of this research and gained the full support of the OPP Behavioural Sciences and Analysis Section. She also succeeded in hiring three new threat analysis officers with primary responsibility for developing officer training and implementation of the ODARA.

Together, Mental Health Centre Penetanguishene researchers and OPP threat analysts created instructional materials for frontline officers and provided information sessions to government ministers, officials, and judicial decision makers. The result was a risk assessment developed in collaboration with the very personnel and organization that would lead its use and implementation. The OPP took responsibility for training police officers and participated extensively in a pilot project that aimed to have the ODARA become required evidence at bail hearings of men charged with domestic assault. Although this project encountered problems (described later), it worked very well at the police level, and the officers continue to use the instrument. Getting the ODARA scored as soon as possible on eligible cases is an essential first step in the successful use of the ODARA/DVRAG system.

GETTING THE ONTARIO DOMESTIC ASSAULT RISK ASSESSMENT SCORED

Whereas the VRAG has a sophisticated scoring system requiring attention to detail and careful addition and subtraction, we made the ODARA items simple dichotomies that could be tallied easily. Also in contrast to the VRAG, we created a single-sheet scoring form and interpretation materials developed with feedback from users. The VRAG has several items that require access to detailed life history and mental health information, but we considered information for inclusion in the ODARA only if it could be readily obtained during frontline police investigations (see chap. 3), and in our training materials we tried to ensure that potential ODARA users were informed as to why each item was on the assessment (and others were not).

We designed a training program so the ODARA could be used with integrity; an actuarial tool that could not be reliably scored by its intended users would be of little practical value. Our first tests of interrater agreement showed that the ODARA was reliably scored by a variety of professionals. Specifically, interrater reliability coefficients were at least .90 for trained research assistants, who did the coding, and for police officers, who were given the scoring sheet but had no specific training on how to score the ODARA (Hilton et al., 2004). To promote integrity of the instrument in practical use, we then created and evaluated a detailed instruction booklet (Hilton, Harris, Rice, Eke, & Lowe-Wetmore, 2007). We also developed training sessions, applying the educational principles of repetition of material, association of material with existing knowledge, and repeated testing. Trainees' feedback at each session was used to improve future content.

At the time of writing, we have conducted nearly three dozen training sessions for potential users of the ODARA with attendees from victim services such as shelters and hospital partner assault clinics, as well as child protection workers, counselors and clinicians, and correctional and law enforcement officers. At least two of us led all evaluated sessions. Evaluation was based on two case videos rather than live role-plays, primarily because videos were standardized stimuli that provided exactly the same information each time they were presented, permitting us to compare trainees' scores across all the training sessions. We created the scripts for these videos on the basis of randomly selected cases from the ODARA research, but we elaborated on the information in the police reports and we changed names, locations, and other details to create a simulated clinical interview with the female victim. The scripts were performed by members of our research department or the local community and were digitally recorded at the Mental Health Centre Penetanguishene.

One video interview was set in a hospital clinic within hours of an assault. The client had obviously been treated for a cut to the face and was portrayed as being resigned to the violence recurring at some point in the future. This victim had, according to the police report, consumed two alcoholic drinks before the index assault and had also struck the perpetrator. The perpetrator had a history of domestic and nondomestic violence, a prior correctional sentence, and a violation of conditional release and exhibited substance abuse. The case yielded an ODARA score of 9. The other video interview was set in a shelter. The client was a nondrinker, had not assaulted the perpetrator, and planned to end the relationship; this case scored 3.

The interviews proceeded quite quickly, and questions were omitted if they could be answered using responses to previous questions. To make them more challenging, some ambiguous responses were deliberately not probed so that the relevant items had to be treated as missing. These challenges made the videos excellent for discussing the scoring criteria and permitted us to discriminate between scoring accuracy before and after the training. Trainees scored the cases independently after viewing the video once only. When trainees scored the first video, we had not yet drawn their attention to the scoring criteria. When they scored the second video, they had been exposed to a detailed presentation of all the scoring criteria and scored a practice case video together. A total of 201 trainees completed the evaluation and showed a statistical improvement in their scoring after the training. Before training, their average scores were incorrect by 1.2 points, and after training, the mean error was down to 0.7 (Hilton, Harris, Rice, Eke, & Lowe-Wetmore, 2007). One case appeared easier to score than the other one. Fortunately, we had alternated the order of videos at each training session in an experimental procedure called *counterbalancing*. It turned out that trainees scored them equally well by the end of training.

Subsequently, we tested how much the apparent training effect was simply due to practice—that is, whether the experience of scoring one case makes it easier to score another. We asked 61 new trainees to score the two cases one right after the other; this test demonstrated no significant improvement (Hilton, Harris, Rice, Eke, & Lowe-Wetmore, 2007). We have given certificates to all trainees who scored 10 standard cases with an interrater reliability of .75 using a more exacting estimate, single measures intraclass correlation requiring absolute agreement on ODARA category; based on several hundred trainees, the actual average intraclass correlation is more than .90.

We can conclude that although developing an actuarial tool is laborious, the tool can be relatively simple to score and can require only a brief training session. If cases are scored entirely from written documentation and without pressure of time, the way our research coders did, perfect scoring can be obtained using the scoring instructions alone. Many assessments, however, are not conducted under ideal circumstances. Also, a 1-point error could affect interpretation of risk, especially at scores below 5, so training—consisting of detailed instruction in the scoring criteria and practice with feedback—is advisable if an actuarial assessment is to be used to aid decision making. Although we have not evaluated how well potential users of the ODARA or DVRAG score these instruments after reading the material in this book, we have included all the elements of our training that are possible to provide in written form: literature reviews to help the reader integrate the new knowledge with existing knowledge, the research background and performance statistics of the ODARA, detailed scoring instructions, our responses to frequently asked questions, and practice cases with feedback.

GETTING THE DOMESTIC VIOLENCE RISK APPRAISAL GUIDE SCORED

Scoring and using the DVRAG entail a different set of challenges. The DVRAG requires considerably more clinical information about the offender and more time to score than does the ODARA, especially because it includes the Psychopathy Checklist—Revised (PCL–R; R. D. Hare, 2003). The PCL–R is a psychological test that is used to identify psychopathy, and it is robustly associated with violence risk. Psychologists in the Canadian correctional systems are generally familiar with the PCL–R and are accustomed to scoring it from information available in offenders' correctional records along with a structured interview or from file information alone.

Our experience with the VRAG revealed that some forensic clinicians erroneously believed that risk assessment is incomplete without supplementing actuarial data with idiosyncratic case characteristics, clinical observations about the offender's presentation, or the assessor's opinion about the value of an actuarial score. Elbogen, Huss, Tomkins, and Scalora (2005) described a similar situation and found evidence for the "availability heuristic," whereby decision makers discount relevant information, attending to clinical information rather than PCL–R score. Because they contain the PCL–R score, both the DVRAG and VRAG allow an important role for clinical expertise. That expertise, however, is properly limited to scoring the instrument and not to clinical judgments about risk factors or their combination.

Although the DVRAG requires time and other resources to score, we maintain that assessors should not overlook actuarial tools or override or adjust them on the basis of clinical judgment regarding unique features of the individual. From our studies of decisions made in our jurisdiction (described in chap. 5, this volume), it is evident that clinicians compromise public safety when they exercise personal discretion or fail to adopt empirical risk assessment methods.

USING ACTUARIAL INSTRUMENTS IN COURTS
AND OTHER LEGAL FORUMS

The VRAG and SORAG have been admitted into evidence by courts in Canada and the United States and have rarely been ruled inadmissible. In general, courts have been remarkably receptive to actuarial tools (Monahan, 2006). We are aware, though, of few evaluations as to whether introducing actuarial evidence has actually affected dispositions or, more importantly, subsequent violence by a cohort of offenders. It is noteworthy that our actuarial tools have been used almost exclusively by the prosecution. We are aware of very few occasions on which the defense has sought to introduce actuarial evidence. It seems logical that the VRAG, for example, would be useful in showing that a client was of relatively low risk. The DVRAG is very new and has not been used in court to our knowledge at the time of writing. The ODARA, in contrast, has been admitted in several jurisdictions. To the best of our knowledge, there have been few problems in using the ODARA in higher courts, but we have experienced some difficulties when the prosecution wished to present expert testimony to support its use in bail court.

The bail courts in Ontario, Canada, are unusual in that they are presided over by lay justices of the peace and yield so many denials that the remand population in the province's correctional institutions exceeds that of sentenced offenders (Doob, 2006). Government officials stipulated that the lay justices could be offered no training on domestic violence risk assessment because such training would infringe on judicial independence. The government had previously endorsed police use of the OPP-developed Domestic Violence Supplementary Report (Ontario Ministry of the Solicitor General, 2000) as recommended practice across the province and did not want to create a new policy about the ODARA. Officials decided that all aspects of adoption must be borne exclusively by case law, supported by expert testimony in bail court (an unusual event). They hoped for an eventual appeal to a higher court that would produce a binding ruling mandating the use of the ODARA in bail court. They required expert testimony from us, rather than investigating officers or the OPP's own experts, but they excluded us from strategic planning, located the project in bail courts hundreds of miles apart, and argued that the ODARA scoring criteria should be changed to exclude criminal behavior that did not result in conviction (Exhibit 6.1). After 2 years, negotiations to support a similar project in our local area were curtailed when government officials declared the reliance on expert testimony to have failed.

During this attempt, meanwhile, police officers scored the ODARA in hundreds of cases, and decisions about whether to detain perpetrators for a bail hearing were made more strongly in accord with actuarial risk than we observed before the ODARA was available (Hilton, Harris, & Rice, 2007).

Effects of Altering the Scoring Criteria

During our 2 years working with government lawyers who were striving to achieve a higher court ruling that the Ontario Domestic Assault Risk Assessment (ODARA) must be admitted into bail hearings, we were asked to reanalyze our data in a variety of ways to suit legal arguments. We were very reluctant to do so, believing that piecemeal analysis was counter to the scientific method and to our own professional obligations. One argument that had been made quite forcefully in bail court, however, was that the court could not consider information about prior criminal behavior unless it had resulted in a criminal conviction. Our reasoned response to the notion that risk assessment should be based only on criminal convictions is presented in chapter 7 of this volume. It was also suggested, moreover, that changing the scoring criteria would not alter the scientific basis of the ODARA and would, at worst, result in an underestimation of risk among perpetrators who committed violent acts for which they were not convicted. What follows is an explanation of how surprisingly damaging it can be to alter the scoring criteria.

Predictive Validity

We calculated the predictive validity of a modification of the ODARA using the convictions-only criterion to score the items Prior Domestic Incident, Prior Nondomestic Incident, Conditional Release Failure, and Violence Against Others. An offender whose criminal conduct did not result in a conviction was given a score of zero on these items. The modified score was positively but not statistically correlated with subsequent conviction for wife assault ($r = .08$, $p > .05$). The ODARA score (computed as originally specified) fared better and was significantly and positively associated with recidivism leading to criminal conviction ($r = .10$, $p < .05$).

Validity of a risk assessment refers to error rates. Errors include both false negatives (failing to identify a true recidivist) and false positives (incorrectly identifying a nonrecidivist as a recidivist). A scoring modification that worsened accuracy would almost inevitably increase errors of both kinds, thus needlessly overestimating the risk presented by some offenders and underestimating the risk presented by others. Furthermore, modified ODARA norms calculated by including only men who were convicted for their index offense would arguably not be applicable to nonconvicted men, including perpetrators awaiting adjudication of the index assault.

Prorating: A Valid Alternative to Altering the Scoring Criteria

In our analyses, a model that prorated (i.e., using Table A.1 to adjust the ODARA score) for criminal conduct that met our criteria for the items Prior Domestic Incident, Prior Nondomestic Incident, Conditional Release Failure, and Violence Against Others but for which a conviction was not obtained performed slightly better than the modified ODARA described above ($r = .10$, $p < .05$). This result is consistent with analyses conducted to develop the prorating table. When considering only domestic violence convictions as the outcome, prorating was also significantly and positively associated with recidivism. We continue to recommend, however, that if an investigating officer concludes that reports of past violent or criminal behavior are true, criminal conviction notwithstanding, the relevant ODARA items be scored 1.

ODARA scores were also associated with denial of bail, suggesting that the bail court pilot led to improved risk-related decisions. Furthermore, although one small-town police service and prosecution office declined to participate in the pilot implementation (and another claimed that it had no eligible cases), the ODARA was used with good results in Ottawa, Canada's capital city, and it continues to be used and presented in bail courts today. This success has contributed to decisions by jurisdictions outside Ontario to adopt the ODARA across the criminal justice system, from policing to presentence assessments and probation supervision.

Embedding Actuarial Tools in Policy

A lesson we learned from the bail court pilot project (as well as experience with the VRAG) is that the use of actuarial tools must be embedded in policy to maximize the likelihood that they will be used (Harris & Rice, 2007; McKee, Harris, & Rice, 2007). We also believe that a policy to use actuarial tools to make decisions and allocate resources can increase fairness to offenders. For example, busy professionals are inclined to perform a clinical judgment first and then use actuarials in cases they deem high risk; if the actuarial contradicts the intuition, they may ignore this actuarial evidence. In court this could mean that although all assessments are disclosed, the prosecutor continues to present a case as high risk even though it falls in one of the lower actuarial categories. As a result, a perpetrator might receive a more restrictive intervention than he would under a system that based allocation of resources on actuarial risk.

There are many examples of public policy initiatives improving the health and safety of citizens. Two good examples in Canada pertain to tobacco (L. W. Green et al., 2006; Hammond, Fong, Zanna, Thrasher, & Borland, 2006; Pechmann, Dixon, & Layne, 1998) and seat belts (Boase, Jonah, & Dawson, 2004; Houston & Richardson, 2005; A. F. Williams, Wells, & Reinfurt, 2004). Tobacco use in Canada has fallen significantly over the past few decades, and public policy initiatives are at least partly responsible. Similarly, seat belt use has increased and injuries caused by failure to use them have declined, at least partly because of public policies. The success of these initiatives seems to have depended on (a) clear specification of the outcome desired and ways to measure it, (b) education about the harms of tobacco and benefits of seat belts, and (c) changes in laws and in their enforcement.

Examples of How Policy Decisions Can Affect Criminal Justice Outcomes

In this section, we examine policy decisions that attempted to spur change in the area of wife assault and then examine how actuarial or formulaic tools have been used in public policy.

Mandatory Arrest for Wife Assault

In the 1980s in Canada and the United States, mounting pressure from battered women's groups and a changing political climate resulted in proarrest legislation (Hilton & Harris, 2009a). Many police services initiated mandatory arrest for cases with reasonable and probable grounds to believe that an assault had taken place. There is evidence that such policies did indeed increase arrests (Jaffe et al., 1993) and that partner assault yielded criminal justice responses comparable to those for other violent crimes despite extensive attrition of cases at every stage (Dutton, 1988). Also, women now report proportionately more assaults to the police than they did in the 1970s (Logan, Walker, Jordan, & Leukefeld, 2006). Furthermore, most women who call the police under the mandatory arrest policies express satisfaction and report less subsequent violence (Apsler, Cummins, & Carl, 2003, Buzawa & Buzawa, 2003; Jaffe, Hastings, Reitzel, & Austin, 2003), even though arrest is far from universally applied (e.g., Hilton, Harris, & Rice, 2007) and victims of wife assault are reported to be less satisfied with every level of the criminal justice response than are female victims of other assaults (e.g., Byrne, Kilpatrick, Howley, & Beatty, 1999).

On the other hand, evaluations of the effect of arrest on domestic assault recidivism have yielded mixed results (Hilton & Harris, 2009a). Sherman and Berk (1984) found that arrest significantly reduced subsequent violence (whether measured by victim reports or by official records) compared with separating the couple or giving advice. In subsequent studies, the effects of arrest varied according to follow-up time, source of outcome data (victim report vs. official record), perpetrator employment, postarrest counseling, and other factors (Berk, Campbell, Klap, & Western, 1992; Miller, 2003; Pate & Hamilton, 1992; Sherman et al., 1992). Other studies found no support for arrest (Dunford, Huizinga, & Elliott, 1990; Hirschel & Hutchison, 1996). When data from all five of these studies were combined, arrest was found to produce a slight reduction in partner violence (Maxwell, Garner, & Fagan, 2001).

We evaluated the effect of arrest relative to several perpetrator and incident variables expected to be correlated with arrest, particularly prearrest actuarial risk for wife assault recidivism as measured by the ODARA (Hilton, Harris, & Rice, 2007). We found that police were more likely to arrest men who were higher in prearrest risk, even though police were unaware of perpetrators' ODARA scores (the ODARA was scored later by research assistants). Police were also more likely to arrest men who had committed more serious assaults. In more recent research, physical assault, victim fear, no-contact order violations, substance abuse, and previous domestic incidents were among the variables that increased the likelihood of police judging domestic offenders to be at risk and pressing criminal charges (Trujillo & Ross, 2008), and more postarrest interventions were used in cases judged to be higher risk (Belfrage, 2008; Kropp, 2008a), confirming our impression that arrest is associated with prearrest risk of recidivism. In our study, arrested men were more likely to commit a new assault in the 5-year follow-up, but this effect was entirely attributable to the fact that police arrested men already at relatively high risk of recidivism. When we entered the ODARA score first into a regression analysis, arrest added nothing to the prediction of recidivism. We also estimated how much time the men were at risk to reoffend. We found that among men with average or lower ODARA scores, arrested men spent more time without assaulting a partner again than did men not arrested. Among men with higher ODARA scores, we found no such effect. For lower risk men at least, then, arrest might have delayed recidivism. In summary, we are cautiously optimistic that arresting and pressing charges for partner violence has some beneficial effect; whether any benefit can be attributed to the current widespread policy of arrest per se or whether apparent effects depend on some subsequent criminal justice intervention has yet to be determined.

No-Drop Prosecution Policies for Wife Assault Cases

In addition to mandatory arrest policies, there have been some attempts to limit discretion in the prosecution of wife assault. Although there have been claims that no-drop policies reduce violence, we are aware of only one attempted experimental study (Ford & Regoli, 1993). In the no-drop condition, some cases were dropped despite the policy because the victim failed to appear in court or refused to testify. In the drop-permitted condition, however, nearly half of the cases were dropped, mostly at the victim's request—a strong statistical difference. Six months after the prosecution process, victims who had been permitted to drop charges reported a marginally lower violence rate. Although Ford and Regoli (1993) concluded that permitting victims to drop charges reduced the risk of violence, our inspection of the data reveals that the better outcome was entirely due to cases where the victim did not drop the charges (see also Hilton & Harris, 2009a). Those victims who did drop when permitted experienced more violence than the no-drop cases. These results lead to the paradoxical conclusion that permitting victims to drop charges was more effective than a strict no-drop policy, but only when victims chose not to drop the charges. As with mandatory arrest, the no-drop condition was not always implemented. The study revealed that much discretion is exercised in prosecution and illustrates the complexity of evaluating criminal justice policies.

The well-known Duluth project ensured that each criminal justice juncture had formal guidelines to limit discretion, including no-drop prosecution. The Duluth model was developed by a battered women's advocacy organization working together with criminal justice and nongovernmental agencies to develop and monitor a coordinated system (e.g., Pence, 2002; Pence & Shepard, 1999). Courts could order offenders into treatment. Probation officers placed offenders into risk categories on the basis of their abuse histories. Several other U.S. states adopted the Duluth model, and step-by-step instructions for similar protocols have been developed (Boles & Patterson, 1997). Meta-analysis of experimental studies yielded a small treatment effect, although the studies suffered from judicial overrides of randomization, high treatment dropout rates, and low follow-up response rates (Babcock, Green, & Robie, 2004; see Exhibit 6.2).

EXHIBIT 6.2
The Quandary of Batterer Treatment

Readers might notice an apparent contradiction in our position on treatment for domestically violent men. We advocate assigning perpetrators to treatment on the basis of their actuarial risk but make no suggestion that treatment reduces recidivism. In fact, in the original Ontario Domestic Assault Risk Assessment (ODARA) research, perpetrators who received treatment were significantly more likely to recidivate (Hilton & Harris, 2005), a finding paralleled by the inclusion of prior treatment as an item on the Domestic Violence Screening Instrument (K. R. Williams & Houghton, 2004), in which treatment raises the assessed risk. Why, then, recommend treatment for perpetrators of any level of risk?

For at least 25 years, many men accused or convicted of domestic violence have been obliged to participate in group therapy aimed at reducing their likelihood of such violence in the future. The assumption has been that men who attend therapy become less likely to recidivate. From an empirical and policy perspective, however, the important question is, Does being assigned to such therapy result in lower recidivism than the routine criminal justice processes alone? By generally accepted rules of scientific inference, the burden of evidence lies with the treatment and requires clear evidence of efficacy. Unfortunately, a minority of treatment programs attempt to collect recidivism data, and few claim to be engaged in any research (Dalton, 2007). In our own jurisdiction, the government funds group therapy for thousands of domestic violence perpetrators each year but has not evaluated whether it reduces domestic violence compared with routine criminal sanctions, an apparent contradiction in an era of fiscal austerity.

Random assignment of eligible perpetrators to treatment is the most informative evaluation design but strikes fear into the hearts of some policymakers: What if a man assigned at random to the control group later commits a serious assault? That is exactly what treatment is intended to avoid, so a deliberate decision to allow perpetrators not to attend treatment seems hard to defend. Indeed, evaluation reports of experimental designs indicate that they have been compromised by police or judges overriding random assignment (e.g., Babcock, Green, & Robie, 2004; see also Hilton, Harris, & Rice, 2007).

Other methodological problems pertain to who should count as a treated case: perpetrators assigned to treatment; those who begin it; those who attend all sessions; or those who, in the opinion of the therapists, are successful? What should the outcome be—therapists' ratings of successful completion, official recidivism, or victim reports of subsequent violence? Because the highest risk offenders are most likely to avoid treatment, quit, or be ejected (Hilton & Harris, 2005) and because therapist ratings have little or no association with recidivism (Barbaree, 2005; Gondolf & Wernik, 2008), intent-to-treat designs, in which everyone assigned to treatment, whether or not they attend, is counted in the treatment group are the most informative. A good evaluation would also track the outcome of all noncompleters. Because various biases might affect police and victim reports in different ways, program evaluators should gather both. Important decisions must still be made about what counts as success or nonrecidivism (Hilton & Harris, 2009b). The technical and political difficulties of evaluating treatment probably explain why there are so few sci-

(*continues*)

EXHIBIT 6.2
The Quandary of Batterer Treatment   *(Continued)*

entifically informative published findings. Even the good studies and meta-analyses that do exist may have little influence on policymakers and practitioners because of the complicated statistics used to report results (Gendreau & Smith, 2007).

Regarding the evidence, the news is good and bad. The good news is that there have been some empirical evaluations (Babcock et al., 2004; Feder & Wilson, 2005; see also Eckhardt, Murphy, Black, & Suhr, 2006; Hanson & Wallace-Capretta, 2004; Sartin, Hansen, & Huss, 2006; Shepard, 1992). The bad news is that almost all the studies that reported treatment effects compared completers with dropouts. Meta-analyses show small average effects at best, and most are very small effects with confidence intervals that include zero, precluding the conclusion of an overall treatment effect (e.g., Babcock et al., 2004; Feder & Wilson, 2005). The possibility must be faced that current treatments for wife assault do not reduce domestic violence overall. Perhaps some treatments reduce violence among some perpetrators while increasing it among others. Although we can measure the risk of violence quite accurately, we know much less about how to change it. This need not lead to pessimism: Accurate assessment and measurement typically precede effective intervention, often by a long time. In medicine, for example, physicians identified epilepsy and leprosy centuries before they developed effective treatments.

These disappointing results provoke some hypotheses about the shortcomings of existing therapies. Measures of general antisociality and criminality were much better predictors than were domain-specific domestic and relationship variables (discussed in chap. 4, this volume). Perhaps current therapies aimed at changing attitudes toward gender roles and marital conflict are simply targeting the wrong things (as has been observed for sex offender treatment; Hanson & Morton-Bourgon, 2005). Wife assaulters' criminogenic needs might differ little from those of other offenders for whom therapy aimed at enhancing insight (as opposed to building skills) is contraindicated (Andrews & Bonta, 2006). Treatment essentially puts a theory into practice, and the causal theories underpinning current batterer treatments are, at best, incomplete and possibly also incorrect (e.g., Dutton & Corvo, 2006, 2007; Dutton & Nicholls, 2005). We recommend the development and testing of new treatments based on other explanations (e.g., D. B. Stuart, 2005; M. Wilson & Daly, 1996). Furthermore, we strongly recommend that priority for treatment participation be in accordance with actuarially determined risk and that perpetrators of lowest risk be excluded.

Examples of Formulaic Systems in Public Policy: Immigration and Speeding

In the early 1960s, Canada's immigration practice involved considerable discretion on the part of immigration officers. One consequence was that applicants of European ancestry were favored over qualified applicants of non-European ancestry (Hiebert, 2006). Since 1967, however, Canada's immigration policy has used a mechanical, formulaic approach to selecting economic immigrants specifically designed to limit the discretionary powers of immigration officers (A. G. Green & Green, 2004). Currently, for example, a prospective immigrant requires at least 67 points out of a maximum of 100. An applicant can earn up to 25 points for education, 24 points for English and French language ability, 21 points for work experience, 10 points for age, 10 points for arranged employment, and 10 points for adaptability (Immican, 2003). The method of assigning points is objective (e.g., one of the components of "adaptability" is "You or your accompanying spouse or common-law partner has worked in Canada," which is given 5 points if answered "Worked full-time in Canada more than 1 year").

There is evidence that embedding the point system in policy has had considerable success. Immigration numbers have followed targets set by regulations, and the racial composition of immigrants has radically changed. However, there is less evidence that changes to the point system over the years have resulted in other objectives, such as an increase in skilled workers or improvement to the economy (A. G. Green & Green, 2004; Hiebert, 2006), at least in part because the policy did not include specific steps for achieving that outcome or for cooperation between provincial and federal policies (A. G. Green & Green, 2004). A formulaic system in Australia was designed to "select for success" and achieved its goals of reducing unemployment and welfare use and increasing salaries and job satisfaction among immigrants (Hawthorne, 2005).

The Province of Ontario has laws that set maximum speed limits on most of its roadways and fines for exceeding them that are formulaic in nature. For example, major highways have a speed limit of 100 km/hour. Fines are $2.50 per kilometer over the limit plus $5.00 for driving 1 to 19 kilometers over the limit, $3.75 per kilometer plus $5.00 for 20 to 35 kilometers over the limit, and so on. Drivers also incur demerit points according to the amount by which they exceed the speed limit. Nevertheless, road accidents are still a major cause of death, and speeding is one of the major contributors (Chen & Warburton, 2006). In a meta-analysis of police programs to reduce injury-causing accidents, photo radar was found to result in a 30% reduction (Blais & Dupont, 2005). Nevertheless, the program was extremely unpopular with the driving (and voting) public and was abandoned in Ontario following an election promise by an ultimately victorious political party (C. Wilson, 1995). Clearly, even policy enshrined in legislation and enforced cannot be guaranteed to have its desired positive effects without a considerable measure of public acceptance and cooperation at all levels.

Sentencing and Sexual Predator Evaluations in the United States

Attempts have been made in other jurisdictions to improve public safety by embedding the use of actuarial instruments in criminal justice policy. In one example, Krauss (2004) studied the effect of U.S. federal sentencing guidelines that were created in the 1980s to eliminate sentencing disparity. Under the guidelines, an offender's sentence was to be determined by first considering a calculation using a formulaic system based largely on an actuarial risk assessment, the Salient Factor Score, that had empirical support (Hoffman,

1994). Judges, however, were allowed to override the calculated sentence when they felt it appropriate based on factors not included in the formula. Using the 10-year postsentencing recidivism rates of 102 defendants, Krauss compared the proficiency of decisions rendered by the judges with decisions that the judges would have made if they had adhered to the formula. Although the formula was not significantly related to recidivism in this sample, the judicial departures not only failed to improve on but were actually significantly less proficient than the formula. Similar to the results of our studies described earlier in this chapter (Hilton & Simmons, 2001; McKee et al., 2007), judges, like forensic clinicians, were unable to improve on predictions of recidivism by adjusting them based on their professional intuition and, in fact, actually worsened them.

Krauss (2004) concluded that judicial discretion should be limited. His results imply that policies designed to reduce recidivism among released offenders ought to mandate the use of more accurate risk assessments and to disallow or at least minimize discretion to override the results of such tools. Unfortunately, as Krauss (2006) reported, the U.S. Supreme Court found the sentencing guidelines unconstitutional and ruled that they could be considered only advisory rather than mandatory. As the research indicates, this practice is unlikely to increase public safety beyond what would result with no federal sentencing guidelines at all.

Another attempt to improve public safety by embedding an actuarial tool in policy regarding offenders occurred in Virginia, which in 2003 became the first state to incorporate actuarial risk assessment into sexually violent predator (SVP) statutes. Accordingly, the Department of Corrections must identify all prisoners incarcerated for sexually violent offenses who obtain a score greater than 3 on the Rapid Risk Assessment for Sexual Offender Recidivism or a similar score on another designated validated instrument (Monahan, 2006). The actuarial has since been changed to the Static-99 (Virginia Secretary of Health and Human Resources, 2008). Although mandating actuarial tools in this manner is a positive step, there is no guarantee that the policy itself has any impact on who is actually committed as an SVP, aside from the fact that no lower risk offenders may be considered (e.g., *Miles v. Commonwealth of Virginia*, 2006).

The literatures on immigration, speeding, and sentencing suggest that policies do matter but are not usually sufficient to accomplish their stated goals (Cornelius & Rosenblum, 2005; Krauss, 2004; Reitz, 2002). Effective policy implementation requires methods to ensure adherence, ways to measure whether policies are having their intended effects, steps taken to redress ineffectiveness, and efforts made to gain cooperation and coordinate efforts among all stakeholders. We regard actuarial assessment as an important aspect of these additional steps, as we discuss in the following section.

EMBEDDING THE ONTARIO DOMESTIC ASSAULT RISK ASSESSMENT AND DOMESTIC VIOLENCE RISK APPRAISAL GUIDE IN CRIMINAL JUSTICE POLICY

As we have described in this chapter so far, changes in public policy can effect desired changes in specified outcomes. Success, however, is not guaranteed simply by the existence of a policy (or, for that matter, by the existence of an accurate, validated assessment). Rather, success depends on several additional factors, including (a) careful specification of the desired outcome, (b) precise and objectively stated policy, (c) cooperation and coordination among agencies implementing and enforcing the policy, (d) training of users in both the actuarial system and its application, and (e) methods for evaluating and revising policy implementation and outcome. Next we consider what such a criminal justice policy might look like for domestic assault.

Specification of the Desired Outcomes

The primary desired outcome of the policy would be reduced recidivism among perpetrators of domestic assault. Stated more specifically, the goal of the policy would be to reduce the occurrence, frequency, and severity of new cases of wife assault committed by men who have already come to the attention of law enforcement officials. We assume this ultimate public safety and victim protection goal would take priority over such desirable administrative or intermediate outcomes as having evidence deemed admissible at bail hearings, altering the proportion of detention spaces occupied by domestic offenders, improving victims' satisfaction with the court process, or increasing the number of domestic offenders attending treatment. As discussed earlier, because the ODARA and DVRAG have been shown to predict whether a perpetrator commits a new assault against a female domestic partner, as well as the frequency, severity, and rapidity of violent outcomes, they can also be used to evaluate some intermediate outcomes. For example, all other things being equal, perpetrators denied bail and detained for trial should have higher ODARA and DVRAG scores than those receiving conditional release. A lack of difference between bailed and detained cases (or a difference indicating that detained cases are lower risk) is evidence that bail decisions cause avoidable harm to victims, unnecessary detention of the accused, or both.

Specification of Policy

Similar to the way other actuarial tools have been embedded in policy, the ODARA could be specifically mandated by legislation at a number of junctures in the criminal justice system. For example, legislation could mandate that police complete an ODARA and submit the score to prosecutors in all cases of clear evidence of violence by a man against a current or former female domestic partner. Legislation could specify that the ODARA score be disclosed to both sides at any relevant bail hearing and that the court must, except in specified circumstances, grant bail for all cases below a certain score and deny it to all those above another score. The legislation should specify how much weight to put on the ODARA score and how much to put on other relevant considerations under the law (e.g., severity of the offense, victim impact). Specification makes the decision explicit and open to inspection and, accordingly, less subject to bias. A suitable cutoff can be selected using the statistical properties of the relative operating characteristic (best known by its abbreviation, "ROC") curve (Harris & Rice, 2007; Streiner & Cairney, 2007), the distribution of scores (to estimate how many cases in a jurisdiction would be affected), and the resources available to implement the policy. For example, if bail were to be denied to the 10% of men scoring highest on the ODARA, then bail statistics and the actuarial norms could be used to determine the appropriate cutoff score and the number of places in jail required to implement such a policy.

Legislation could specify that DVRAG score be a major determinant of criminal sentences. As with bail hearings, history shows that to be effective, the legislation would have to specify exactly how much weight to put on the actuarial instrument and the sentence length to be associated with each score on the instrument. Of course, sentencing in particular involves considerations other than risk, but to the extent that reduced recidivism is a goal of sentencing, the heavier the weight given for factors empirically related to risk, the more successful the policy will be. The weighting of various considerations, including actuarial scores, can be made explicit and formulaic (e.g., McKee et al., 2007). Correctional policy could mandate that wife assaulters with higher DVRAG scores receive more intensive interventions aimed at reducing recidivism. Knowledge about effective correctional service in general supports the view that more intensive interventions should be targeted to higher risk offenders (e.g., Andrews & Bonta, 2006).

Again, to be effective, the policy would have to specify how each score on the actuarial tool translated to the amount of specific intervention provided. For example, if it were decided that all those whose probability of reoffending within 2 years of opportunity was greater than 25% would be offered 100 hours of treatment designed to reduce subsequent wife assault, then actuarial norms could be used to estimate the resources required to implement the policy. As well, policies pertaining to parole and probation could specify that greater efforts be put into supervision and monitoring for men with higher DVRAG scores. The policies would need to specify how each score is translated to eligibility for parole or probation and the intensity of services for men on parole or probation. For example, if it were decided that 100 hours of court-mandated treatment would be assigned to all wife assaulters who had at least a 50% likelihood of reoffending within 2 years, actuarial norms could be used to anticipate the number who would qualify and the resources required to implement the policy.

Training of Users

Education about the actuarial tools and their application would be required for all those involved in providing services for perpetrators. The education would also include training to a certifiable standard for all those who would be required to administer the ODARA or DVRAG, as well as education about the limitations of each, when they should and should not be used, and so forth. At each criminal justice juncture, there would be formal guidelines about criminal justice and community interventions for perpetrators at each score on the actuarial assessment. Step-by-step instructions would be developed to cover situations involving more than one agency.

Although they have a common ultimate goal, there often seems to be a disjunction among criminal justice systems, offender interventions, and victim services. For example, we observed some conflict between those who wished to use offender intervention resources according to risk and those who wished to offer the same intervention to all perpetrators, especially therapy (Exhibit 6.2). When we have led ODARA training sessions for members from both sectors together, it has provided an opportunity to interact on neutral territory and to discuss issues of shared concern. It is not uncommon for shelter staff to express frustration with police, especially over lack of information about the progress of criminal charges. Police officers have responded by explaining their organizational constraints, including their equal exasperation over the lack of time that prosecutors spend on such cases. In one session, a heated argument was averted when one victim advocate observed, "In my jurisdiction, the police are wonderful."

Cooperation and Coordination Among Involved Agencies

Readers will note that one theme of this book is that the interests of all (including victims and perpetrators) are best served when everyone works together to address important problems. Specifically, we believe that when law enforcement officials, the courts, the correctional system, forensic clinicians, victim support workers, and the staff of shelters and hospitals all evaluate the risk represented by each of their cases using a common and accurate metric, the safest and most cost-effective course of action can be adopted. We opened this book with an example of a real case in which failure to arrive at a common understanding of a perpetrator's risk resulted in tragedy. We have also described research showing that leaving the task of arriving at this common understanding to informal or intuitive practices cannot suffice. To be sure, common and accurate appraisal of the risk of a case does not guarantee appropriate handling;

truly effective strategies to mitigate the risk are still required. Nevertheless, we hope we have been persuasive that this shared approach to risk assessment is an essential first step.

Readers will also have sensed that we are proud of our partnership with our colleagues in the OPP. This collaboration, despite real and fundamental differences in organizational culture and tradition between a government agency responsible for a large police service and another government agency responsible for health care, stands as a tangible example of the sort of cooperation and collaboration we aspire to. We recognize, though, that gaining cooperation among government agencies is easier said than done. In the bail court implementation described previously, everyone was publicly committed to the ODARA, yet this project clearly lacked the basic groundwork for a successful partnership. An apparently desirable goal can be readily subverted by agencies having conflicting interests. Real interagency cooperation requires leadership in arranging contingencies so that all involved share the same interests.

Evaluating and Revising Policy Implementation and Outcome

The final piece of an effective policy is a component evaluating its effectiveness in achieving stated goals. A statutory requirement for a review of a policy a few years after implementation was included in at least one other criminal justice policy we are aware of. In Canada, the Corrections and Conditional Release Act (1992) included a clause requiring a parliamentary review of the provisions and operation of the act. As part of this review, several research evaluations were conducted, and several modifications to the policy were made (Public Safety Canada, 2000). For a policy that mandated the use of the ODARA, the evaluation component would require, at a minimum, that records be kept of the numbers of domestic violence incidents attended by police, the proportion for whom ODARA scores were produced, and statistics about the ODARA scores of offenders detained by police, denied bail, sentenced, mandated to and actually attending treatment, denied parole, and so on.

Ideally, the policy's efficacy would be determined experimentally by randomly implementing the policy in some jurisdictions and not in others or randomly applying it to some offenders and not others. There are also ways to evaluate the effectiveness of the policy through less rigorous means by examining how closely ODARA or DVRAG scores are related to decisions using the same logic as in our studies of forensic and tribunal decisions (Hilton & Simmons, 2001; McKee et al., 2007; see also chap. 5, this volume). In the case of a policy regarding use of the ODARA, the correlation between a forensic decision and the ODARA score would be used to evaluate how well the decisions match those that would be made based on the risk principle of offender intervention.

An experimental evaluation method would also increase the likelihood that unintended negative outcomes would be detected. For example, legislation mandating use of the ODARA in court might produce the desirable and appropriate difference between perpetrators released and those detained. But if this result occurred at the cost of a great increase in custody spaces devoted to domestic violence perpetrators such that perpetrators with a higher risk of committing other violence, such as violent sexual assaulters, had to be released (because there was no place to detain them), an apparently effective domestic violence policy might be achieved at an unacceptable cost to other victims. Rigorous quantitative evaluation is the best way to detect such inadvertent side effects.

MOTIVATING POLICY DEVELOPMENT

We have described knowledge about effective policy and several relevant precedents involving the incorporation of actuarial or formulaic decision systems into policy. We were unsuccessful in getting government officials to make any policy pertaining to the use of the ODARA in bail courts in the first place; the officials preferred that adoption rest on case law alone. Some scholars have attempted to elucidate the principles associated with the successful adoption of innovations in society in general and public policy in particular (Dopson, Locock, Gabbay, Ferlie, & Fitzgerald, 2003). Briefly, evidence-based policy innovations are more likely to succeed when they have opinion leaders and peer champions who can muster passion and emotional commitment (in addition to logic and empirical evidence). They are also more likely to be successful when the policies are highly flexible, when they solve a problem or offer an advantage important to the organization, when material and human resources are not already overtaxed, and when adoption of the policy does not carry risks (Greenhalgh, Robert, Macfarlane, Bate, & Kyriakidou, 2004).

In our first attempt to have the ODARA adopted, government officials responsible for the courts had initially championed a different approach and were dissatisfied with our apparent inflexibility regarding ODARA scoring criteria. There were also severe resource limitations in that bail courts were falling ever further behind the government's commitment to bring cases to trial expeditiously. Prosecutors did not perceive a benefit in adding actuarial assessment to their duties, and there was a potential risk of liability should a perpetrator who scored in the highest actuarial category commit a very serious offense after the prosecutor had agreed to his release on bail. We currently aim our efforts at training and supporting champions within individual police services and victim services (perhaps peer pressure will eventually produce the desired outcome; Dopson et al., 2003). We believe that incorporating a validated actuarial risk assessment system into an empirically informed systemic response to domestic violence is the best defense against accusations of dereliction of duty should a tragedy occur.

In summary, embedding the ODARA/DVRAG system into criminal justice policy and the policies of other sectors responding to domestic violence will reduce the number of repeat assaults on women by their partners. Our review of other circumstances in which actuarial or formulaic systems have been embedded in policy or in which the effects of criminal justice policy decisions have been evaluated leads us to recommend several ways to ensure that the policy will yield its intended result. Although we realize that these ideas might seem radical, all are based on sound empirical data, and there have already been initial efforts to follow the steps outlined here in the domestic violence field.

SUMMARY OF MAIN POINTS

- Using lessons learned from the VRAG, we did several things to enhance the implementation of the ODARA/DVRAG system, such as being ready to respond to public events with a research-based solution and collaborating with the biggest potential user of the system in our province.
- The ODARA can be completed easily and accurately by police officers and other frontline users with minimal training; the DVRAG requires expertise to score the PCL–R.
- Courts have been receptive to actuarial tools, and at least one jurisdiction has mandated the use of an actuarial tool by statute.
- A pilot project designed to induce a higher court decision mandating use of the ODARA in Ontario's bail courts failed in this objective but did appear to increase the correlation of custodial decisions with ODARA score.
- Research with criminal justice and nonjustice policy implementation alike shows the importance of using formulaic tools for making decisions, enshrining the tools in policy and legislation, and enforcing the legislation.
- Victim safety and fairness to the accused can be enhanced by the use of a shared risk metric among victim services, the criminal justice system, and offender intervention programs.
- Policy should be evaluated in terms of reduction of violent recidivism and monitored with respect to the correlation of decisions with actuarial risk score.
- Interagency cooperation can be mired in conflicting interests. Involving key players and enlisting opinion leaders and peer champions from the outset, as well as ensuring shared goals, are essential for successful teamwork.

7

QUESTIONS AND ANSWERS ABOUT THE ONTARIO DOMESTIC ASSAULT RISK ASSESSMENT/DOMESTIC VIOLENCE RISK APPRAISAL GUIDE (ODARA/DVRAG) SYSTEM

As principal authors of the Ontario Domestic Assault Risk Assessment (ODARA; Hilton et al., 2004) and the Domestic Violence Risk Appraisal Guide (DVRAG; Hilton, Harris, Rice, Houghton, & Eke, 2008), we have provided dozens of training sessions for diverse groups of professionals and volunteers interested in using our actuarial assessments. We began with brief training for the police officers, nurses, and shelter workers who were our research partners and then expanded our effort by opening the training to others in response to requests for on-site programs across Canada and the United States. A certification program was also developed for those who could not attend training sessions. We have also assisted the U.S. state government of Maine and the Canadian provincial governments of New Brunswick, Nova Scotia, and Saskatchewan in efforts to train all community corrections and other criminal justice officials to use actuarial violence risk assessments.

In the course of providing training, we are asked many questions about the ODARA and DVRAG. We have had similar experiences with our actuarial risk assessment tools for general violence recidivism, the Violence Risk Appraisal Guide (VRAG) and the Sex Offender Risk Appraisal Guide (SORAG; Quinsey, Harris, Rice, & Cormier, 2006). Our responses to the most frequently asked questions about the ODARA/DVRAG system are reproduced here to help readers grappling with the same issues. For those who just want to know whether they have a case that meets the eligibility criteria, we provide an at-a-glance guide (Exhibit 7.1).

Professionals who say they base their risk assessments entirely on clinical judgment are becoming rarer, but it remains unclear how far actual practice has changed. More common is the temptation to interpret items more broadly than the scoring criteria allow. One example occurs when assessors wish to score Threat to Harm as present because the victim was afraid, even though the perpetrator did not make an overt threat. Another arises when assessors infer that the victim was fearful of future assaults because she left the perpetrator and suggest substituting this for an explicit statement made at the time of the index

EXHIBIT 7.1

Quick Guide to Eligibility Criteria and Use of the Ontario Domestic Assault Risk Assessment (ODARA) and Domestic Violence Risk Appraisal Guide (DVRAG)

Criterion	ODARA	DVRAG
Person to be assessed	Adult male who has lived with the victim (i.e., married, divorced, cohabiting, separated, or lived together for any length of time)	
Index assault criteria	Physical assault, including physical contact with the victim or a credible threat of death with a weapon in hand in the presence of the victim	
Timing of index assault	No time limitation: Use the most recent occurrence that meets the index assault criteria.	
Information sources	Police record and criminal history required; any victim interview should be supplemented with this information for most valid use.	Police record, criminal history, and forensic, clinical, or correctional assessment information sufficient for scoring the Psychopathy Checklist— Revised (PCL–R; R. D. Hare, 2003)
Population to which norms apply	Men who committed an index assault that appeared in police records (regardless of criminal charges)	Men who committed an index assault that appeared in police records (regardless of criminal charges) and who had in-depth case information in an assessment conducted during probation, parole, or incarceration for any offense
Conditions of use	Whenever sufficient information is available	Whenever a reliable PCL–R score is available and an ODARA score is either unavailable or at least 2

assault. Sometimes trainees wonder whether the ODARA or DVRAG is suitable for cases that seem unique or unusual. Occasionally they wonder about applicability to populations that might differ from that on which the assessments were developed. Still others are tempted to modify eligibility and scoring criteria to fit some procedure or case ruling from their jurisdiction. We include these questions here to assist readers implementing the ODARA/DVRAG system in clinical or forensic settings and facing similar circumstances.

For most questions we get, a short unqualified answer often suffices. So for each question in this chapter, we provide a brief response to satisfy readers just wanting such confirmation. A short supporting explanation then follows, usually reminding readers how the original research was done. Lastly, we provide more detailed information on some topics, much of which was developed during our expert witness experience.

APPLICATION TO ELIGIBLE CASES
AND RELEVANT POPULATIONS

Question

The data that were used to create the ODARA and DVRAG came from police records in one province of Canada. How can I be sure that the ODARA and DVRAG generalize to all the racial, ethnic, religious, socioeconomic, and geographic segments of my own jurisdiction?

Answer

Research has shown that the strongest predictors of violent behavior are the same regardless of demographic characteristics.

When we sampled cases for the ODARA and DVRAG construction research, we excluded no perpetrators on the basis of race, ethnicity, or socioeconomic status or similar variables. In fact, race, ethnicity, and religion data were not available in the police record systems we used. The data represented all areas policed by the Ontario Provincial Police across the province, plus approximately 50 municipalities with their own police services and First Nations (aboriginal) communities. Because of this sampling procedure, even though different social groups might exhibit different rates of violence overall, we are confident that the predictive value of the ODARA and DVRAG is generally applicable to male wife assaulters.

More Information

Research into criminal offenders generally indicates that the best predictors of violence are valid across demographic characteristics (see chap. 3, this volume). Cross-validations of the ODARA and DVRAG are consistent with this body of research. That is, the ODARA was not developed using samples from predominantly large urban areas, but its predictive value was confirmed in samples from the Greater Toronto Area, Canada's largest and most ethnically diverse metropolis. Our other research has generalized well outside of Canada (e.g., replications of the VRAG and SORAG), providing further grounds for using the ODARA and DVRAG with confidence in other jurisdictions.

Another aspect of this question might be whether some racial, ethnic, socioeconomic, or other minority group would be overrepresented in the highest categories of risk as a result of using an assessment that is "blind" to demographic characteristics. Our research with domestic offenders in a sentenced correctional sample found that aboriginal offenders obtained higher risk assessment scores (Popham & Hilton, 2006). It is also true that aboriginal offenders are overrepresented among arrested, convicted, and incarcerated offenders (Correctional Service of Canada, 2007; Trevethan, Moore, & Rastin, 2002). It is important to keep in mind that victims of violence almost always have the same demographic characteristics as the perpetrators, especially when it comes to domestic violence, and are no less in need (compared with members of other groups) of an adequate response to domestic violence. Actuarial risk assessment is the first step in apportioning effective and appropriate interventions.

Question

The victim obtained a civil court restraining order on the basis of an act of violence that was not reported to police. Police became involved later when the perpetrator violated the restraining order. Can the ODARA be scored in this case, with the index assault being the assault history described in the restraining order application?

Answer

Previously unreported assaults can be used as the index assault only when they have become the subject of a police investigation.

The index assault is the most recent incident known to the police in which the perpetrator engaged in violence against a female domestic partner. If it can be established that an assault occurred (i.e., physical contact with the victim or a credible threat of death with a weapon in hand in the presence of the victim) and this evidence is contained in the police report filed subsequently, then it is an eligible index assault.

We would consider an exception if the ODARA is scored entirely from victim interview, such as at a shelter or hospital or other service where a woman wants the information only for herself and she is familiar with the perpetrator's criminal history. In this case, the assessor should communicate that the results are based on the woman's responses, that the predictive validity of the ODARA using only a victim interview has not been established, and that the perpetrator's risk could be different were a police record check to reveal different information.

Question

The ODARA and DVRAG concern only men's violence against female domestic partners. Women can also be violent, and violence occurs in dating and same-sex relationships. Should I use another assessment that is for all kinds of relationship violence?

Answer

The ODARA was developed and tested only for male-to-female domestic assaults; as yet, no risk assessment has been validated for other kinds of relationship violence.

In our more recent research with female victims and with perpetrators in correctional treatment, we have included dating relationships and found no evidence that they are different in terms of the distribution of the ODARA or its predictive accuracy. However, we have not had a large enough sample of these cases to test the predictive accuracy in this subgroup.

We have tried to study female offenders and men and women in same-sex relationships using the same methods that we used to identify cases for the ODARA research, but we found too few cases in which the woman was the sole or primary aggressor and fewer than five cases of assault in same-sex relationships in a sample of more than 200. It is possible that the ODARA or DVRAG, or modifications thereof, might one day be demonstrated to predict recidivism by women or same-sex partners; however, such research has not yet been done.

More Information

The same limitation applies to nonactuarial domestic risk assessments; that is, no norms have been delineated for cases of violence in dating relationships, and no empirical evidence yet supports their use for female-to-male violence or gay and lesbian relationship violence. Moreover, the only alternative to using a validated instrument in a new population is using an unvalidated approach or unaided professional judgment. We are aware of jurisdictions using the ODARA in cases other than male assault against a female domestic partner, provided the remaining eligibility criteria are met. Recent research suggests that the predictors of recidivism by women are similar to those for men (at least for sexual violence; Freeman & Sandler, 2008). In the absence of evidence that the predictors of violent recidivism by men and women in the context of domestic relationships differ from the empirical predictors of violent recidivism by men and women more generally across contexts, we consider it acceptable to use the ODARA/DVRAG with a statement about validation in these circumstances.

Thus, in circumstances for which no formal domestic violence risk assessment has been validated, it is unclear whether professional judgment or the application of an actuarial assessment (with a caution about the validity not being established) is the more empirically and ethically appropriate course. In our opinion, using an actuarial assessment accompanied by a statement that the validity of the very specific application has not been established represents the most empirically and ethically appropriate course of action (when reserving judgment is not an option), because professional discretion or unaided clinical judgment have been shown to be poorer methods of risk assessment for circumstances in which empirical studies are available.

Question

I work with convicted wife assaulters on probation. The majority of my cases fall into the highest categories on the ODARA, so should I use some other assessment method?

Answer

The DVRAG is suitable for perpetrators with more in-depth clinical information and can discriminate among perpetrators with relatively high scores better than the ODARA.

We have found that the distribution of ODARA scores in the correctional population is skewed toward the higher end and that the criminal justice system tends to filter out lower risk perpetrators from the time of police contact through to court decisions. In the correctional sample used to develop the DVRAG, a quarter of the perpetrators who scored in the highest category on the ODARA fell into the highest category on the DVRAG, and they all exhibited wife assault recidivism. If you do not have a full criminal history or other information needed to score the Psychopathy Checklist—Revised (PCL–R; R. D. Hare, 2003), however, you should score the ODARA instead.

ONTARIO DOMESTIC ASSAULT RISK ASSESSMENT/DOMESTIC VIOLENCE RISK APPRAISAL GUIDE ITEMS

Question

Why does the ODARA give 2 points against the perpetrator for violent behavior toward people other than his partner and children (i.e., Prior

Nondomestic Incident and Violence Against Others)? What if he was arrested for assault years ago after he got drunk at a football game and got into a fight?

Answer

Violence in general is such a strong predictor of wife assault recidivism that having an identified incident of violence against others and having a police report for such violence each independently predicted wife assault recidivism.

An item was incorporated into the ODARA when the analyses indicated that it contributed to the prediction of wife assault recidivism even after all other items were taken into account. The statistical procedure that led to the creation of the ODARA identified two items measuring the use of nondomestic violence. The two items are not the same—both require an identifiable incident of violence, but only one requires a police report—but can pertain to the same incident if the perpetrator was violent and has a police record for this violence. In essence, the statistical selection procedure resulted in a system that weights general violence according to its ability to predict domestic violence recidivism.

More Information

Actuarial risk assessments often use weighted items. Some behaviors contribute more to the score than others because they are stronger predictors of violent recidivism. In the original ODARA construction research, we measured criminal behavior, especially violent behavior, in a variety of ways. The predictive strength of general violence resulted in two items reflecting this behavior being selected by statistical analysis because they independently predicted recidivism. That is, having a police record for nondomestic violence predicted domestic violence recidivism even when the occurrence of violence against others was already taken into account. In the DVRAG, the predictive strength of nondomestic violence is also reflected in the substantial weights given to these two items. It was not the only characteristic that was measured and coded in more than one way. For example, from a range of variables pertaining to children of the perpetrator or victim, both the total number of children and the children from one particular relationship independently predicted recidivism (whether or not children were present and witnessed the index incident).

Question

The ODARA is based on static variables. Should violence risk assessment not include both static and dynamic risk? For example, should abstention from alcohol be taken into account so that his risk score is lower?

Answer

There is no available evidence to indicate that changes occurring after the index assault predict recidivism over and above the items that are included on the ODARA.

In the violence risk assessment literature, there are currently a number of definitions for a *dynamic* variable. To the extent that dynamic means *changeable*, several ODARA items are dynamic. To the extent that dynamic means *a score based on a change in a characteristic from one time to a later time*, research has yet to identify any dynamic variables that reduce the risk of wife assault recidivism. Substance abuse is a characteristic that some researchers call dynamic, and there are some changeable elements of substance abuse, but there is no evidence yet that a change in substance abuse alters risk of wife assault. We do not take *dynamic* to mean something that might change in the future, something that a perpetrator promises to do, or a condition of release, and the ODARA score should not be altered because of such things.

More Information

A useful kind of dynamic risk factor would pertain to fluctuations that occurred during community supervision and that indicated related changes in the risk of imminent violence. Some preliminary work has shown promising results with the prediction of violent incidents among forensic psychiatric patients (Quinsey, Jones, Book, & Barr, 2006). We await cross-validation research and evidence that similar patterns hold for predicting imminent wife assault recidivism. Without this evidence, adjusting the ODARA or DVRAG score for events that occur during supervision introduces unacceptable intuitive judgment.

Question

The ODARA and DVRAG give too limited a picture of a perpetrator's risk. Adding more items and areas to explore would help me feel that I am covering all the important aspects of the case. Wouldn't a more comprehensive assessment be more accurate?

Answer

The ODARA and DVRAG include all the items that had unique predictive validity and were available in police reports and correctional files, respectively.

To maximize predictive accuracy, an assessment does not need to include every predictor, only the ones that afford incremental validity. Adding variables that are not as strongly related to recidivism to the assessment can reduce overall predictive accuracy and increase measurement error. When we developed the DVRAG, we tested many other variables, including some specific to domestic relationships, but we were unable to find any that improved on the predictive accuracy of the DVRAG (see chap. 4, this volume). There is already statistical redundancy among the valid ODARA and DVRAG items; adding more items without empirical validation will not improve their accuracy. The best protection against missing important risk information is to read all available documentation carefully, to adhere to the specific scoring criteria for each item, and to treat items as missing only when the available documentation indicates that an item might be present but the information is unclear or incomplete.

More Information

Not all the characteristics typical of wife assaulters predict recidivism. Some can actually be unhelpful as predictors. For example, wife assaulters are more likely than other men to self-report being a victim of child abuse or witnessing wife assault as a child. Follow-up studies by us as well as other researchers, however, show that violence in the family of origin does not predict recidivism. It is possible that further research will discover variables that improve on the ODARA/DVRAG system, but using other predictors to alter the ODARA or DVRAG score before that improvement is demonstrated is likely to lead to poorer prediction.

It must be admitted that most people, including academics and professionals, live by different rules of inference (based on personal validation). Our position seems rigid and even objectionable compared with other assessment schemes that encourage users to incorporate additional variables. The fact that childhood violence and other variables such as suicide threats or animal abuse are not part of the ODARA/DVRAG system can be a real stumbling block for people who are quite well informed about domestic violence. We are always searching for ways to help such earnest participants deal with the method of scientific inference we try to live by.

INTERPRETATION OF SCORES

Question

The average length of the follow-up study in the ODARA research was almost 5 years. What if I need to know the risk of recidivism in the next year?

Answer

The rank order indicates how a man compares with other known wife assaulters with respect to risk, regardless of the time frame of interest.

The ODARA research indicated that perpetrators with the highest ODARA scores tended to meet the criteria for wife assault recidivism the soonest. As well, ODARA scores were related to the number of subsequent wife assaults and their severity in terms of victim injury. In contrast, the actual likelihood of wife assault recidivism would be expected to be lower (especially for the lowest risk categories) than the norms indicate over a period of less than 5 years and higher (especially for the highest risk categories) during a longer period.

More Information

Not all acts of domestic violence come to the attention of the police; therefore, the estimated rates of recidivism given by the ODARA/DVRAG norms are conservative. However it is measured, though, the estimated likelihood of wife assault recidivism can be expected to change if the period of opportunity changes. A domestic violence perpetrator's risk relative to other such men, however, does not depend on the time period.

Although we have good evidence that ODARA score predicts how soon recidivism will occur, in most cases we did not know whether or how long the perpetrators were remanded in custody before trial, for the index assault or any other offenses, which renders unreliable any point estimate of the net elapsed time until recidivism. Our reasonable estimate of the upper limit of the timing of recidivism across the construction sample is approximately 15 months on average. Also, because the ODARA is correlated with the number of recidivistic offenses in a given time, then it is certainly also correlated with how soon the first offense will occur, on average. Thus, whether an assessor is concerned about the occurrence of any act of wife assault, the anticipated number of such acts, the likely resulting injury, or how soon recidivism might occur, the ODARA/DVRAG system provides relevant information.

Question

You say that an individual's risk summary statement must always refer to the group data. Does this mean that the risk only actually applies to the group, not an individual?

Answer

The actuarial risk of the group that an individual belongs to applies to the individual.

The study of violent outcomes among a group of individual perpetrators in follow-up research permits us to make statements about the probability that violent recidivism will be committed by members of that group—that is, by individuals who are similar on characteristics that afforded incremental validity to the prediction of outcomes in the studied group. In fact, even nonactuarial decisions routinely made by clinicians and other assessors require the assessor to make connections between individuals and a reference group. How, for example, can a diagnosis be made without reference to clinical data about patients with similar symptoms or to an assessment standardized on patient groups? To take exception to this reasoning is to commit what Grove and Meehl (1996) called the "aggregate/individual" or "nomothetic/ideographic" error. It is, in fact, appropriate to operate as though each member of a group with the same computed level of risk or recidivism shares the same likelihood of recidivism implied by the risk categories. This does not mean that a risk category with a 50% likelihood of recidivism leaves the assessor having to use clinical judgment to determine whether an individual perpetrator is in the 50% that will recidivate or the 50% that will not. It does mean that it is reasonable to operate as though all members of the subgroup exhibit the same level of risk.

More Information

The presence of recidivism is a categorical outcome; that is, its presence is something different from its absence. In contrast, frequency and severity of recidivism are continuous measures: one occurrence is more than zero, two occurrences are more than one, and so on. A risk assessment score is a continuous variable also; that is, a higher number represents a greater risk. However, to provide stable probabilities of recidivism, a range of scores is often broken into a category, and the probability of recidivism is given as the proportion of offenders with scores in that category who recidivated in follow-up research. In the DVRAG, for example, there is a wide range of scores, and all are collapsed into seven categories with a corresponding risk level. In the ODARA, because of the dichotomous scoring, there is a smaller range of scores and a higher proportion of cases with a given score, permitting stable estimates of recidivism for some particular scores; therefore, the five lowest categories contain only one score each.

Question

I am primarily concerned about domestic murder. The ODARA/DVRAG system is not designed to predict lethality, so should I use another assessment that is?

Answer

The ODARA and DVRAG were not designed to assess the risk of lethal domestic violence specifically, but higher scores do indicate more severe future assaults.

Rare outcomes such as lethal wife assault are much more difficult to predict than is overall domestic violence, and there is no actuarial risk assessment that has been developed on a follow-up study with domestic murder outcomes. Moreover, sometimes it is only a matter of timely and expert medical intervention that makes the difference between murder and an assault with a nonlethal outcome. We did not include trivial acts of aggression in our research; only incidents in which an act of violence occurred met the definition of wife assault recidivism. We believe that all the acts the ODARA and DVRAG are built to predict are of great public concern.

More Information

Predicting specific kinds of violence is more difficult than predicting violence overall. Although there are published assessments intended to assess the risk of lethal assault, none has been demonstrated to predict domestic murder in a follow-up study. The necessary data would require an extraordinarily large sample from a high-risk population. Meanwhile, we have found that the ODARA, scored from information documented before a lethal assault in a small number of cases, yielded average scores just under 7 for cases that did not have prior police reports of wife assault and 9 for cases with police histories (Eke, Hilton, Harris, Rice, & Houghton, 2008). We recommend using the ODARA/DVRAG system in all cases of wife assault. The higher the perpetrator's score, the more effort and resources ought to be devoted to developing and adhering to the victim's safety plan. When lethality is a particular concern, the strongest known correlates of lethal wife assault, such as the perpetrator's use of firearms, divorce or separation, the victim having a new male sexual partner, and the victim being of childbearing age or having a child from a sexual relationship other than with the perpetrator (J. C. Campbell 2007; J. C. Campbell, Glass, Sharps, Laughon, & Bloom, 2007; Shackelford, 2001; M. Wilson & Daly, 1993) might indicate the timing of serious violence. That is, actuarial scores indicate who is at greatest risk of violence, and these other factors could indicate when such violence might occur.

RESOURCES REQUIRED FOR SCORING THE ONTARIO DOMESTIC ASSAULT RISK ASSESSMENT/DOMESTIC VIOLENCE RISK APPRAISAL GUIDE

Question

The ODARA is just one more piece of paperwork in a domestic investigation and takes too long for a police officer to complete. The DVRAG demands evaluation of psychopathy, and we don't have time for that.

Answer

Officers can obtain information for scoring the ODARA during the routine victim interview and incident investigation.

The ODARA items were all selected from information available to police, so scoring should take only a few minutes once a domestic investigation is underway. When scoring the ODARA, be sure to use the dichotomous (yes/no) scoring method, not the item weights used for the DVRAG. The DVRAG contains the PCL–R score, a measure of psychopathy and probably the single most important psychological assessment for forensic evaluation. If the ODARA indicates a score of 2 or more and a reliable PCL–R score can be obtained, we recommend scoring the DVRAG; if not, a valid assessment of violence risk is given by the ODARA.

More Information

In our experience, some aspects of the way police and court services are organized (e.g., multiple policing authorities within a single geographic area, police and court services under different government ministries) can affect readiness to implement new approaches. Agencies that have surmounted these obstacles, though, have earned a reputation as leaders in the domestic violence field. Agency-wide training before implementation is also more efficient and better received than haphazard training of officers, lawyers, or judges only.

Some reluctance to adopt actuarial risk assessment may be rooted in the fear of being held accountable or criticized if a released perpetrator recidivates, whether before trial or after sentencing. For example, a document clearly stating that a perpetrator was in the worst 10% of the population of known wife assaulters could seem inculpating if that perpetrator were to reassault his partner while later released on bail or parole. The fact is that failures of conditional release happen all the time; actuarial risk assessments, though not perfect, can demonstrably reduce such errors. A knowledgeable court gives little weight to opinions not based on data. As the routine use of actuarial data in forensic decisions becomes more widespread and even legislated, reliance on professional opinion without data should become unacceptable. The benefits will be seen in the reduction of violence and victims, as well as in more efficient use of courts and prison beds.

Question

Why can't I score the ODARA or DVRAG from a perpetrator interview? He has no reason to lie about things like the number of children he has or things he knows I can check in his criminal record.

Answer

Official records should be used whenever possible to maximize the accuracy of an individual perpetrator's score.

We strongly advise obtaining a police record check to score the ODARA and using a full correctional or forensic clinical file to score the DVRAG. If you have no reliable information about the perpetrator's criminal history, the index assault, or the victim's circumstances (including children in the relationship), then you should seek more information before scoring the ODARA. Without sufficient information to score the PCL–R (including a full criminal history), you should seek more information before scoring the DVRAG or score the ODARA instead. The ODARA and DVRAG were created from research that used criminal record information; wherever possible, that is the way these tools should be applied in practice.

More Information

Lying is a diagnostic characteristic of psychopathy. Yet, some psychopaths do not seem to care what anyone thinks of them and are willing to say that they would use violence if it served their interests. It is not impossible that an interview or paper-and-pencil test for perpetrators could be developed that predicts domestic violence recidivism; however, this research has not been done. The research on which the ODARA and DVRAG are based depended not on perpetrator interviews but principally on other sources of information. Consequently, we cannot recommend that the ODARA and DVRAG be completed based on a perpetrator interview.

Question

Actuarial risk assessment is not perfect and takes more time than just asking the victim for her own prediction. Do victims not know the perpetrator's violence potential best?

Answer

Women's statements about their partner's potential for violence do predict recidivism well, but the other items on the ODARA and DVRAG improve on that prediction.

Women's ability to predict reassaults might come from their intimate knowledge of the perpetrator's behavior and the proximal predictors of his violence. This knowledge is not always available to other people and is difficult to capture in empirical research studies. We have demonstrated, however, that including victims' predictions on the ODARA improves on the predictive accuracy of both.

More Information

As we described in chapter 4, women's predictions are correlated with domestic violence in subsequent months and years. The statistical process we used to create the ODARA selected the victim's statement of concern because of its predictive accuracy over and above many other variables we tested. A woman's fear for her children especially might prompt her to leave an abusive relationship, which in turn may be a proximal risk factor for assault. There are limits, however, on the accuracy of victims' predictions. Sometimes women minimize the violence or are overly optimistic about their ability to end their relationship with the abusive partner.

COURT ISSUES

Question

The ODARA research used research assistants' judgments to ascertain whether violence occurred at the index assault and recidivism. Would it not be more applicable to the courts if the research had been based on criminal convictions?

Answer

The ODARA research was designed to develop a tool for violence risk assessment rather than to identify the variables that influence whether a perpetrator is convicted.

The ODARA/DVRAG system is designed to predict the occurrence of an assault that comes to the attention of the criminal justice system. Our cross-validations and the extensive literature on unreported crime suggest that the published norms will underestimate the true likelihood of another wife assault. Basing eligibility, item scoring, and recidivism only on convictions would result in poorer estimation. Furthermore, criminal justice system decisions, such as in bail court or dangerous offender hearings, are concerned with the commission of future offenses, not the likelihood of reconviction. There is an established precedent of admitting actuarial risk assessments such as the VRAG and SORAG into evidence; these assessments use criminal conduct reflected in a police report, arrest, charge, or conviction rather than a conviction alone because it is generally agreed that this measure is closer to the true rate of recidivism than that obtained by using conviction alone.

More Information

Conviction is a poor measure of violent outcome for several reasons. First, only a fraction of actual assaults come to the attention of the police. Second, in the United States, Canada, and other countries based on British legal tradition, there is a deliberate preference for erring in favor of the guilty rather than convicting the innocent (although wrongful convictions do occur). Third, our unpublished reanalysis of the ODARA construction data showed that requiring convictions as the evidence to score the criminal behavior predictor items on the ODARA and to define recidivism yielded poorer predictive accuracy. With respect to recidivism alone, 11% of those men who met the criteria for recidivism were known to have done so without being charged; the ODARA's predictive accuracy remained when data for these men were removed. We are not suggesting that research criteria for recidivism replace legal standards for culpability, only that police reports are at least as valid in identifying risk factors for violence as are legal standards for guilt.

A risk assessment is not intended to indicate guilt. Forensic decisions are often made based on a person's conduct regardless of criminal conviction; examples include roadside suspensions of drivers' licenses based on Breathalyzer readings or a police officer's opinion that a person is impaired, the granting of search warrants on evidence of criminal activity that might be uncovered, limitations imposed on personal liberty pertaining to possible terrorist activity, and preventive detention in cases of mentally disordered offenders. The VRAG and SORAG have been admitted as evidence many times at such preventive detention sentencing proceedings, even though their scores consider past criminal charges that have not resulted in conviction. Bail courts, especially, can deny bail if the accused man might commit a new offense while awaiting trial; the ODARA is directly relevant to this question. Meanwhile, for those whose sole concern is whether a perpetrator will be convicted of subsequent wife assault, we found that the ODARA also predicts criminal conviction for wife assault recidivism, the area under the relative operating curve (ROC) = .66, 95% confidence interval = .53 to .78, under very conservative conditions in which men who were not charged or whose charges were withdrawn or unresolved at the time of coding were counted as nonrecidivists.

Question

You have suggested that the ODARA can be used to help make decisions about bail. Would that not usurp the legally enshrined role of the court to make decisions?

Answer

The ODARA is a decision support tool that provides information about grounds that are important to the granting of bail, especially whether there is a substantial likelihood that the accused would commit another offense if released.

Bail courts in our jurisdiction must consider three grounds: the accused person's risk of failing to attend court for trial, his risk of committing another criminal offense while on bail, and his risk of harming himself or others while on bail. The ODARA provides information on the latter two grounds. We have not specified cutoff scores for denying bail. In any jurisdiction, a decision would have to be made about which scores are appropriate for requiring a bail hearing and any other conditional release decision on the basis of available resources, the acceptability of recidivism, and justice needs. In sum, we explicitly intended that the ODARA influence the court's decisions, but to assist with rather than to usurp the function of the bail court.

More Information

The particular issue of bail court is raised because the ODARA makes possible, for the first time, the use of actuarial risk assessment for domestic violence suitable for the time frame of bail court. In Canada, at least, it has been unusual to present actuarial risk information at bail hearings. Such information has a well-established history of being admitted to higher courts and given weight in sentencing decisions, as well as in parole board decisions and mental health tribunals. In bail court, police usually provide the primary evidence in the form of written reports submitted by the prosecution and viva voce testimony. Police services now routinely use some form of risk checklist, and with the increasing availability of actuarial tools, the routine admission of such evidence into bail court is inevitable.

Question

Several items are based on what the alleged victim reported at the time of the index assault. Should the ODARA score be revised when the alleged victim recants her allegation?

Answer

The ODARA score predicts recidivism using information available at the time of the index assault and should not be altered using events that occurred later.

The investigation that occurred within the first few hours after the index assault was reported to police was the basis for the ODARA research.

ODARA items were partly but not exclusively based on victim statements. Investigating officers would have interviewed other witnesses and gathered other evidence. Statements by the persons involved made in subsequent days and weeks were not used. Whether later events such as the victim recanting would predict subsequent wife assault is unknown; therefore, altering or setting aside the ODARA score based on later statements would not be justified.

THE APPORTIONING OF RESOURCES ACCORDING TO RISK

Question

Even the lowest risk categories on the ODARA and DVRAG have a nonzero likelihood of recidivism. This shows that all men are at some risk, so shouldn't they all be denied bail and all given the best treatment we have to offer?

Answer

There is variation among wife assaulters, with some more likely to recidivate than others. Giving the same intervention to all perpetrators could leave those who need more intervention at risk and could increase risk among those at lowest risk.

If any interventions have any realistic prospect of altering the likelihood of recidivism (and thus increasing victim safety), they must abide by the risk, need, and responsivity principles of offender intervention, as we described in chapter 1. First, intervention must be delivered in accordance with risk; those cases of highest risk must receive proportionately more intensive service. Interventions aimed at the lowest risk groups can cause the actual risk to worsen.

More Information

Interventions must target characteristics associated with recidivism. Substance abuse, antisocial conduct, and poor temper control, as examples, represent empirically supported targets for intervention. Low self-esteem, anxiety, and personal distress are examples of unsupported targets. Intervention aimed at the latter can increase the likelihood of violence. Effective interventions are generally learning based and attempt to teach participants new behaviors and skills. Such interventions have to be highly structured and systematized. As we described in chapter 1, therapies aimed at changing insight or attitudes, especially if they are delivered in an unstructured process in which therapists and participants do not abide by a formal curriculum, also have the real chance of increasing risk. Interventions also require a formal ongoing monitoring system to ensure that they follow the curriculum and properly adhere to the other principles, including gathering preintervention risk assessment and follow-up information on participants to inform program improvements.

Question

What if a perpetrator's ODARA or DVRAG score places him in a relatively low risk category but he has stated that he will kill his wife and children when he is released? Do I not have to override the actuarial score and use my discretion in this case?

Answer

A policy incorporating the duty to protect can be implemented without use of a clinical override.

The duty to protect a person who is the object of a specific and credible threat of violence imposes a legal and moral obligation to act, regardless of the probability of recidivism. It should not be a matter of clinical discretion but rather a matter of policy to detain perpetrators who make specific threats of violence regardless of their actuarial risk. A policy can be implemented that not only states the default level of intervention at certain ODARA or DVRAG scores but also provides for custody or close supervision in cases in which a perpetrator makes a direct threat. This approach is quite different from using one's judgment to alter a risk score or deviate from an interpretation based on the experience table.

More Information

A valid risk assessment supports the first principle of offender intervention, but it is not the only consideration. It is reasonable, as a matter of policy rather than an aspect of risk assessment, that no one is conditionally released who threatens further violence. It is customary in many jurisdictions for the bail court to require a promise of good behavior before an accused person is released. In our view, forensic clinicians should consider similar requirements not because such statements tell us anything about risk, but because they make explicit our expectations about how everyone should behave. As another example, policy could specify that symptoms of mental disorder may be grounds for intervention, even though they are not ODARA or DVRAG items and even though research has demonstrated that such symptoms do not indicate increased risk of violent recidivism (e.g., Monahan et al., 2001; Quinsey, Harris, et al., 2006). Psychiatric treatment might be an appropriate and humane intervention in such cases, even when the perpetrator scores relatively low on an actuarial risk assessment; however, secure forensic hospitalization might be unnecessary.

BROADER CONCERNS

Question

The ODARA and DVRAG are entirely empirically based and atheoretical. Would risk assessment not be more useful if it helped to explain wife assault?

Answer

The task for risk assessment is simply to identify which men are most likely to assault their partners again in the future.

Often in training sessions we are asked why a particular item is on the ODARA. The correct answer is, of course, "because it predicts wife assault recidivism." But why and how it predicts recidivism is often the topic of much discussion. Theoretical explanations can be both fascinating and useful for designing interventions such as treatment; however, prediction can be done quite successfully without any reference to causal pathways. Some characteristics that distinguish men who assault their partners from men who do not might also predict recidivism or help identify serious wife assaulters from among less severe offenders. Alcohol use is one variable that might be both a predictor and an explanatory factor in wife assault. There is no necessary overlap, however, and the confusion between prediction and explanation can lead to the temptation to adjust items because one thinks one knows why they predict.

More Information

In considering this question, it is important to understand what is meant by *theory*. In one sense, a theory is a hunch, guess, or hypothesis about relationships. Police have made much practical use of the hypothesis that fingerprints are unique without having to know the genetic and prenatal environmental reasons for their uniqueness. Indeed, knowing why fingerprints are unique has not led to more accurate identifications than were achieved before. In the same way, useful risk assessment instruments have been developed primarily by including variables that have been found to be empirically related to recidivism, without necessarily knowing why. Current actuarial systems, though not themselves explanations of crime and violence, must be consistent with such explanations because they predict relevant outcomes. In contrast, because unaided clinical judgment is weakly or not related to recidivism, one may legitimately conclude that it is not generally based on a valid explanation of wife assault. The empirical superiority of actuarial over clinical intuition implies that clinicians should, for the purposes of risk assessment at least, abandon intuitions and preferences if risk-related decisions are to be optimally accurate.

Question

Violence against women is a product of a sexist society, and risk assessment just individualizes the problem. Do we not need a more fundamental change?

Answer

Although sexist attitudes and institutions can compound the problem of violence against women, individual differences do exist in men's proclivity for violent behavior.

The function of a risk assessment is to identify those men who are most likely to assault their partners again or to do so more severely. This information can then be used to reduce the occurrence of violence through selective incapacitation, increased supervision, or more intensive intervention. The same information can also be used to advise victims of the potential for repeated violence by their partners or ex-partners and to advocate for increased protection and support for these women and their families. We believe that actuarial risk assessment is one tool in a multifaceted approach to violence against women, one that can be used at the same time as changing societal factors.

OBJECTIONS TO ACTUARIAL ASSESSMENT

In our experience, most of the questions and concerns exemplified in these 20 examples are motivated by a genuine desire to do as good a job as possible. Most questioners just want a thorough understanding in order to protect potential future victims while avoiding unnecessary restriction of persons accused or convicted of domestic violence. On the other hand, after 2 decades of experience, we have to concede that there are sometimes more profound issues involved. First, we believe that each person's human nature entails a strong and irresistible expectation that the behavior of other humans is understandable and predictable. This "theory of mind" is fundamental to such a social species and has meant that unlike most other species, humans exhibit highly advanced levels of mutual cooperation, sophisticated social structures, and complex and abstract communication. All of this would be impossible without the human psychological capacity to appreciate others' perspective and anticipate their responses. In our view, however, the benefits of theory-of-mind capabilities do come at a cost: People have difficulty believing they need any help figuring out why others act as they do and especially what they will do next. People readily accept that scientific methods could result in better medicines, aircraft, and refrigerators than they could create themselves. But it is much harder to accept that science has anything special to offer interpersonal domains such as personnel selection, education, or mental health.

A second fundamental matter has to do with sociopolitical ideas about criminal behavior. At one end of this spectrum, crime is the result of poverty, racial discrimination, and social and educational disadvantage, and the solution to crime is the remediation of social injustice. By this view, if an offender is equipped with the ability to make his way in a world where people are prepared to give him an even break, crime and recidivism are solved. Similarly, simple social learning accounts of antisocial conduct imply that negative experiences and bad company are the principal causes of crime and that criminality is easily reduced by therapies that teach new ways of thinking and problem solving. It seems that these worldviews are sometimes threatened by actuarial risk assessment tools, and our research findings are politically and morally troubling to those who hold these views. This view is encouraged by some poorly conducted research and commentaries illustrating a misunderstanding of statistical arguments.

At the other end of this political spectrum is the feeling that a violent offender is a person apart who should be removed from the rest of society. The idea that the root causes of serious crime are internal and individual supports preventive detention statutes, sex offender registries, long and indefinite sentences, and even capital punishment. This view is threatened by evidence that offenders vary in their risk of violent recidivism and that not all victims of violent crime suffer permanent and irreparable harm. Because the bases of these opposing viewpoints are moral and personal, scientific arguments and findings often fail to persuade their adherents that the scientific research on wife assault currently supports a moderate position, whereby all resources in the criminal justice and community response to domestic violence should be distributed according to risk of violent recidivism.

Where we have proffered advice in this book, our bias is in favor of the empirical evidence pertaining to the prediction of violent recidivism and of wife assault recidivism in particular. Scientific studies, although not perfect, repeatedly show that accurate (and professionally competent) decisions about the risk of subsequent violence cannot be made without certain pieces of information, especially details of the perpetrator's criminal record, his history of substance abuse, and details of the offense. It is because of the robust association between these variables and recidivism, and not because of our professional judgment, that these variables were selected by the statistical analysis procedures that we used to construct the ODARA. In the case of in-depth forensic risk assessment, measuring psychopathy permits greater accuracy in risk assessment than is possible without measuring it. Not allocating the resources needed to obtain such information inexorably means accepting unnecessary revictimization, incarceration, or both. Instead, criminal justice, offender treatment, and victim services should permit—or preferably ensure through policy—this information to be the main determinant of the extent and type of intervention. The ODARA/DVRAG system is a tool for doing so.

APPENDIX A: SCORING CRITERIA FOR THE ONTARIO DOMESTIC ASSAULT RISK ASSESSMENT (ODARA)

This appendix provides instructions on how to score the ODARA items and how to adjust scores when information for one or more items is unclear or incomplete and answers some common questions about item scoring. First, we show readers how to identify the assault on which to base the ODARA scoring, specify the outcome that the ODARA predicts, and describe the information needed to score the ODARA.

IDENTIFYING THE INDEX ASSAULT

To adhere most closely to the method used in the research that resulted in the ODARA, the index assault for any assessment should be the most recent incident known to the police in which the man engaged in violence against a female domestic partner. The index assault requires physical contact with the victim or a credible threat of death with a weapon in hand in her presence. A *domestic partner* is defined as a woman that the perpetrator is or was married to, is or was in a common-law relationship with, or lives or did live with for any length of time. Criminal charges do not have to be laid for a domestic incident to qualify as the index assault. In our research, though, we had to be confident on the basis of evidence in the police report that the man perpetrated at least one act of physical contact with the victim or made a credible threat of death with a weapon in hand in the presence of the victim.

We excluded questionable incidents that research assistants did not agree on; often, an earlier incident that clearly met the eligibility criteria could be found. In practice, therefore, if the most recent incident does not clearly involve violence against a female partner, an earlier incident meeting the eligibility criteria can be used as the index assault.

Assessors should count each police occurrence report as one incident. For a cluster of assaults reported at one time to the police, the most recent eligible assault that is separated from prior assaults by at least 24 hours is the index assault; multiple eligible assaults within 24 hours count as one index assault. This cluster rule also applies to identifying prior domestic and non-domestic incidents.

Portions of this appendix have been adapted from "Ontario Domestic Assault Risk Assessment General Scoring Criteria" (2005) with permission.

DEFINING *RECIDIVISM*

During the research, only postindex incidents in which an act of violence occurred met our definition of domestic violence recidivism. In a small minority of cases, the criminal record indicated a charge of assault against a partner, but we did not have the police occurrence report to determine the specific acts of violence; these charges met the definition of domestic violence recidivism.

The criteria we used to code postindex acts of violence were broadly based on the physical violence subscale of the Conflict Tactics Scales (CTS; Straus, 1979) or the Conflict Tactics Scales Revised (CTS2; Straus, Hamby, Boney-McCoy, & Sugarman, 1996). We included any of the following acts as violence: held her down, threw something at her that could hurt, twisted her arm or hair, pushed or shoved her, grabbed her (includes pulled and dragged her), slapped her (includes struck her), inflicted other minor violence (e.g., shook her), punched her with fist or hit her with something that could hurt, choked her (includes grabbed her by neck or throat, put her in a headlock), slammed her against wall; "beat her up," burned or scalded her on purpose, kicked her, used a knife or gun on her (i.e., actual or attempted contact with the victim's body; includes discharging a gun while pointing it at the victim or threat of physical harm with weapon in hand), and inflicted other severe violence (e.g., picked her up and threw her, head-butted her, pushed her down the stairs, bit her).

In addition, we included as violence any use of force (by any means) to coerce the victim into having sexual contact when she did not want to. The same criteria for violence are used to code prior domestic and nondomestic violence.

GATHERING NECESSARY INFORMATION

Sometimes little information is available about the most recent incident, and assessors should seek more information before identifying the index assault. The perpetrator's prior police record or criminal history is essential information, and anyone conducting an assessment for use in criminal justice or offender intervention purposes should postpone scoring the ODARA until this information is obtained. It is also advisable to interview the victim or obtain documentation from a victim interview, especially about her children. The absence of information is not normally a reason to select a different incident as the index assault, and it is always a reason to consider the feasibility of obtaining more documentation about the case.

ITEM SCORING

Some ODARA items are scored with reference to events occurring at the index assault. Others are scored on the basis of events occurring before the index assault. Information pertaining to events that occurred on a separate occasion after the index assault is never used to score the ODARA. Each ODARA item is scored 0 or 1, and the total score is the sum of the item scores. Thus, the range of possible scores on the ODARA is 0 to 13.

1. Prior Domestic Incident

For the purposes of scoring the ODARA, a *domestic incident* is defined as one in which the man being assessed assaulted his current or previous female cohabiting partner and/or her children and the assault is recorded in a police occurrence report or criminal record.

Scoring Criteria

All of the following must be present:

- an act of violence (as defined above) carried out by the man being assessed
- *and* an incident that occurred on a separate occasion before the index assault
- *and* police involvement or a subsequent report made to the police.

If any one of these criteria is absent, then score 0 for the item, even if every other criterion is present. These criteria are all required.

At *least one* of the following must be present:

- a victim who is a current or previous female domestic partner of the man being assessed
- *and/or* a victim who is the child of the man's current or previous female domestic partner.

Either of these criteria must be present to score 1 for the item. They do not both have to be present. If neither of these criteria is met, then score 0 for the item.

Do not include

- the index assault;
- incidents involving only pets or property;
- or incidents involving only strangers, acquaintances, friends, parents, siblings, other family members, or police officers.

Frequently Asked Question

Question. The perpetrator came to the attention of police for the first time on the night that the index assault occurred. During the investigation, the victim reported two other assaults, one occurring the same afternoon and one occurring the week before. Do these other assaults count as prior domestic incidents, or are they all part of the index assault?

Answer. The assault that took place the week before can be used to score Prior Domestic Incident, provided that the assault is documented in the police record as a discrete incident occurring on a specific date. The cluster rule applies here (see the section above on Identifying the Index Assault).

2. Prior Nondomestic Incident

For the purposes of scoring the ODARA, a *nondomestic incident* is defined as one in which the man being assessed assaulted any person other than his current or previous female cohabiting partner or her children and the assault is recorded in a police occurrence report or criminal record.

Scoring Criteria

All of the following must be present:

- an act of violence (as defined above) carried out by the man being assessed
- *and* an incident that occurred on a separate occasion before the index assault
- *and* police involvement or subsequent report made to the police
- *and* a victim who is any person other than a current or previous female domestic partner of the man being assessed or her children.

If any one of these criteria is absent, then score 0 for the item, even if every other criterion is present. These criteria are all required.

Do not include

- the index assault,
- incidents involving only pets or property,
- or incidents involving only a current or previous female domestic partner of the man being assessed or her children.

Frequently Asked Question

Question. The perpetrator assaulted his mother, who lives in a basement suite. Does this incident count as domestic or nondomestic?

Answer. An assault on the perpetrator's mother, or any other member of his family of origin, counts as nondomestic for the purposes of scoring the ODARA.

3. Prior Custodial Sentence of 30 Days or More

A custodial sentence includes only the final disposition handed down by the court for a criminal offense. It is not necessary for the man to have served the entire sentence to score 1 for this item.

Scoring Criteria

All of the following must be present:

- a sentence handed down before the index assault
- *and* a sentence resulting in incarceration
- *and* a sentence of 30 days or more
- *and* actual admission to training school, jail, federal correctional facility, or provincial or state correctional facility.

If any one of these criteria is absent, then score 0 for the item, even if every other criterion is present. These criteria are all required.

The sentence need not have been served for a domestic incident; sentences for a nondomestic incident or any other criminal conviction should be included. Sentences that are served for any continuous or intermittent period should be included, as well as sentences that were not entirely (but at least partially) served in custody, as long as the total number of days in the disposition handed down by the court was at least 30.

Do not include

- the sentence handed down for the index assault,
- time spent in a police holding cell,
- or time spent in custody awaiting trial unless the sentence is stated as including time served (which may be a statutory requirement in some jurisdictions).

Frequently Asked Questions

Question. The perpetrator's criminal record shows a conditional or suspended sentence of 12 months. In essence, the sentence was to a custodial institution, and it was over 30 days. Can I use this sentence to score Prior Custodial Sentence?

Answer. No. The criterion of actual admission into custody must be met. Do not count sentences that are served entirely in the community.

Question. The perpetrator was held in custody for 6 months before sentencing and then received a sentence of "1 day plus time served." Can I use this sentence to score Prior Custodial Sentence?

Answer. Yes. If this disposition were specified as 1 day and 6 months or documented as "1 day and 6 months (time served)," then the total sentence is more than 30 days. It is the sentence that counts, not the number of days spent in custody after the sentence was handed down. If, however, the remand time is not specified in the sentence (e.g., the disposition is documented as "1 day"), then the criteria for Prior Custodial Sentence are not met.

Question. In my jurisdiction, a sentence to probation has an explicit custodial sentence attached to it that is invoked for a breach of probation. If I see that a perpetrator has been on probation, should I score this information under Prior Custodial Sentence?

Answer. If the underlying sentence was for at least 30 days *and* was not explicitly a suspended sentence *and* resulted in custody, then yes. If any of these three conditions is not met, then the criteria for Prior Custodial Sentence are not met.

4. Failure on Prior Conditional Release

Conditional release includes administrative release, bail, conditional discharge, parole, probation, promise to appear, suspended sentence, or any other occasion on which the man was at liberty in the community under supervision or other requirement ordered by a criminal court; it also includes no-contact, protection, or restraining orders imposed by a criminal or civil court. Some examples of conditional release failures are committing a new criminal offense, failing to appear for court, failing to attend an appointment with a probation officer, drinking when prohibited, having firearms when prohibited, coming to a person's home or workplace when prohibited, and contacting a person when prohibited.

Scoring Criteria

At *least one* of the following must be present:

- any known violation of the terms of conditional release, whether or not he was arrested or charged for it
- *and/or* a violation occurring at the time of the index assault or on a separate occasion before the index assault
- *and/or* a charge for a criminal offense committed while on a conditional release ordered by a criminal court.

Any one of these criteria must be present to score 1 for the item. Not all of the criteria have to be present. If none of these criteria are met, then score 0 for the item.

Do not include

- conditional releases that he obeyed
- or conditional release failures that occurred on a separate occasion after the index assault.

Frequently Asked Questions

Question. The perpetrator's criminal record shows a conditional or suspended sentence of 12 months and a subsequent revocation of that sentence, resulting in some of that time (less than 30 days) served in a correctional institution. Should I score this information under Failure on Prior Conditional Release or Prior Custodial Sentence?

Answer. Both. He met the criteria for a known violation of the terms of conditional release *and* had a sentence of 30 days or more that resulted in actual admission to custody.

Question. The perpetrator had a condition to abstain from alcohol while on probation, but he lapsed and got drunk while watching a game on TV at a friend's house. Because he was remorseful, agreed not to go to that friend's house again, and continued participating in his substance abuse treatment group, the probation officer documented the alcohol use but did not pursue charges for a breach of probation. Does this count as a Failure on Prior Conditional Release?

Answer. Yes. The perpetrator met the criteria for a known violation of the terms of conditional release. Criminal charges or revocation of conditional release are not required.

5. Threat to Harm or Kill at the Index Assault

For the purposes of scoring this item, a *threat* must clearly pertain to physical harm to a person. Normally this indication is in the form of a specific verbal threat to harm a person physically. In a criminal record, evidence of a threat meeting the criteria for this item would be found in a charge of threatening, criminal threatening, uttering a threat, or terrorizing. Evidence of a physical gesture that is commonly recognized as a threat to harm a person physically can also be used to score this item.

Scoring Criteria

All of the following must be present:

- a threat to harm any person physically
- *and* a threat made during the index assault, whether or not carried out.

These criteria are both required.

At least one of the following must be present:

- a threat made against any person, including police officers
- *and/or* a criminal charge of threatening, uttering threats, or terrorizing.

Either of these criteria must be present to score 1 for the item. They do not both have to be present. If neither of these criteria is met, then score 0 for the item.

Do not include

- threats of emotional harm, financial harm, legal action, or custody dispute;
- threats against pets or property;
- threats to harm or kill himself;
- or threats made on a separate occasion from the index assault.

Frequently Asked Questions

Question. The perpetrator saw the victim talking to another man at a party. Without saying anything, he glared at her in a way that she knew meant he was going to assault her. On their way home, he pulled the car off the road and committed the index assault. Can I use this information to score Threat to Harm or Kill at the Index Assault?

Answer. No. Covert acts, or acts of omission, that are not commonly recognized as a threat cannot be used to score this item, even though the victim may feel that harm is imminent. The same is true for other behavior intended to scare a person without an overt threat. Although we recognize that a victim may feel threatened by some actions by the perpetrator that cannot be classified as overt threats, in the ODARA development research, only acts that were clearly described as threats to harm a person physically were coded as threats. Similarly, in practice, there needs to be clear and objective evidence of a threat; a verbal threat is the clearest example.

Question. The perpetrator sexually assaulted the victim while holding a knife in his hand. She complied because she was afraid he would use the knife if she refused. Can I use this information to score Threat to Harm or Kill at the Index Assault?

Answer. No. An assault with a weapon is not sufficient evidence that the criteria for a threat were met.

Question. The perpetrator had sent the victim threatening letters and was previously charged with criminal harassment. He was stalking her near her workplace when the index assault occurred. Can I use this information to score Threat to Harm or Kill at the Index Assault?

Answer. No. Stalking and prior threats are not sufficient evidence that the criteria for a threat were met at the index assault.

6. Confinement of the Partner at the Index Assault

For the purposes of scoring this item, *confinement* is defined as any act carried out to physically prevent the victim from leaving the scene of the incident. In most cases, confinement would be scored on the basis of evidence that the perpetrator kept the victim in a room with the exit barred. In a criminal record, evidence to score this item would be found in a charge of forcible confinement or kidnapping arising from the index assault, provided the victim is known to be the female domestic partner.

In some cases, other acts by the perpetrator that deprived the victim of the ability to leave the scene of the incident can be used to score this item. These less common examples of confinement include holding on to or pinning down the victim when she tried to escape, purposefully standing between the victim and the escape route when she tried to escape, removing or destroying the victim's clothing when she tried to escape by going outdoors, and forcibly removing keys to a vehicle or damaging a vehicle while she is trying to escape in it.

Scoring Criteria

All of the following must be present:

- confinement of the female partner who is the victim of the index assault
- *and* an act by which the man being assessed physically prevented, or attempted to prevent, the victim from leaving the location
- *and* confinement carried out during the index assault, whether or not the victim eventually left the scene.

If any one of these criteria is absent, then score 0 for the item, even if every other criterion is present. These criteria are all required.

Do not include

- the perpetrator threatening harm to the victim if she leaves,
- ripping out the telephone or cutting the telephone lines,
- or committing acts of confinement on a separate occasion from the index assault.

Frequently Asked Questions

Question. The perpetrator pinned the victim to the wall and punched her. She was not able to move or escape while this assault took place. Does that count as confinement?

Answer. No. Evidence of restraint in the course of an assault, such as holding the victim down to assault her, is not sufficient to conclude that an act of confinement has taken place. The primary evidence should be physical confinement in a locked room or other place from which the victim cannot escape. If escape is physically possible, a required element for this item is the victim's attempt to escape.

Question. The perpetrator was charged with criminal restraint arising from the index assault. Can I use this information to score Confinement of the Partner at the Index Assault?

Answer. Because the definition of criminal restraint varies across jurisdictions, more information is required. If the restraint was committed as an attempt to restrict the victim's liberty or physical ability to leave the location *and* the restraint was committed by use of force rather than by threat or deception, then yes. If either of these two conditions is not met, then the criteria for Confinement of the Partner at the Index Assault are not met.

7. Victim Concern

This item captures the victim's prediction of future assaults against herself or her children. Any statement made by the victim that indicates concern, fear, worry, or certainty pertaining to a possible future domestic assault is considered an example of victim concern.

Scoring Criteria

All of the following must be present:

- a statement made by the female partner who is the victim of the index assault
- *and* a statement made in the victim's first reports to the police, or to victim services if this information was not available to police, even if she subsequently expressed no concern
- *and* a statement that indicates concern, fear, worry, or certainty pertaining to a possible future domestic assault.

If any one of these criteria is absent, then score 0 for the item, even if every other criterion is present. These criteria are all required.

At least one of the following must be present:

- a statement pertaining to possible future assaults against the female partner who is the victim of the index assault
- *and/or* a statement pertaining to possible future assaults against the children

Either of these criteria must be present to score 1 for the item. They do not both have to be present. If neither of these criteria is met, then score 0 for the item.

Do not include

- the victim's fear for safety during the index assault,
- statements made by the victim on a separate occasion before the index assault,
- or inferences about concern based on protective action taken by the victim.

Frequently Asked Questions

Question. The victim went to a women's shelter, and she went back to her home to gather her property only when accompanied by a shelter support worker for protection. Obviously she is afraid of the perpetrator. Can I use this information to score Victim Concern?

Answer. No. A verbal statement by the victim is required. In the research, this variable was coded on the basis of overt behavior, usually a statement made to police, and was not inferred from other behavior.

Question. The victim states that the perpetrator would certainly assault her again if he had the opportunity; however, she is moving to another city, so he will no longer be in contact with her. How should this response be scored?

Answer. Victim Concern should be scored 1 because the victim's statement indicates certainty that he will assault her again. This item is not scored on the basis of a conditional probability (e.g., "Would he assault you again if you stayed in the city . . . or moved out of state . . . or left the country?"), nor can we assume that moving to another city or taking other measures to limit the perpetrator's opportunity to recidivate will guarantee that he will not assault her again.

8. More Than One Child

Add up the number of children the perpetrator has, plus any additional children the victim has. There must be more than one child in total to score 1 for this item.

Scoring Criteria

Include the following:

- biological or adopted children of the man being assessed,
- biological or adopted children of the female partner who is the victim of the index assault,
- minor or adult children, and
- children living with the victim or living elsewhere.

Do not include

- children who were unborn at the time of the index assault,
- children who were deceased before the index assault,
- or children of a former partner who are not biologically related to or adopted by the man being assessed or the victim.

Frequently Asked Questions

Question. The perpetrator's ex-wife had children from a previous relationship. These children lived with the perpetrator during the marriage, and he was like a father to them. The children now visit the perpetrator and the index victim every other weekend. Can I use this information to score Victim Concern?

Answer. No. Only children born to or adopted by the perpetrator and/or the index victim count. This item concerns offspring that are part of the current relationship and not the perpetrator's parenting role.

Question. The perpetrator has one son and the index victim has one daughter, but they have no joint children. How should I score More Than One Child?

Answer. Score the item 1 because both these children count toward the total.

9. Victim's Biological Child From a Previous Partner

Scoring Criteria

To score 1 for this item, the victim of the index assault must have a biological child whose father is not the perpetrator. Only one child is needed to score 1 for this item.

Include the following:

- biological children of the female partner who is the victim of the index assault,
- minor or adult children, and
- children living with the victim or living elsewhere.

Do not include

- children who were adopted by the victim,
- children who are not the victim's biological children, or
- children who were deceased before the index assault.

Frequently Asked Questions

Question. The victim adopted a child at birth before her relationship with the perpetrator began. She feels just as much love and devotion to this child as if she were the biological mother. Can I use this information to score Victim's Biological Child From a Previous Partner?

Answer. No. In the ODARA development research, children who were known to be adopted were coded separately from biological children. It was biological children that predicted recidivism.

Question. The victim had a child with a previous partner, but the perpetrator has no contact with this child and does not play the role of a father with this child in any way. Does this child still count?

Answer. Yes. The criteria pertain to the living existence of the child, not the perpetrator's relationship with that child.

Question. The index assault was committed by the perpetrator against his ex-wife. She has a new partner and has a child from this new relationship. Can I count this child to score Victim's Biological Child From a Previous Partner?

Answer. No. In the ODARA development research, we coded children separately according to whether they were from the relationship between the perpetrator and victim, from a previous relationship, or from a subsequent relationship. It was the partner's children from a previous relationship that predicted recidivism.

10. Violence Against Others

Scoring Criteria

All of the following must be present:

- an act of violence (as defined above) carried out by the man being assessed
- *and* an incident that occurred on a separate occasion before the index assault
- *and* a victim who is any person other than a current or previous female domestic partner of the man being assessed or her children.

If any one of these criteria is absent, then score 0 for the item. These criteria are all required.

Police involvement is not required, and information used to score this item can come from sources other than criminal justice documentation. The required criteria for this item are a subset of the criteria for Prior Nondomestic Incident, so if Prior Nondomestic Incident is scored 1, then Violence Against Others is automatically scored 1.

Frequently Asked Questions

Question. The perpetrator had a reputation for being a tough guy in his teens, and people talk about him being in fights, although there is no information about a specific event. Can I use this information to score Violence Against Others?

Answer. No. A specific incident is required. Reputations are too vague to score this item.

Question. The perpetrator has a police record for a violent assault, and a presentence report indicates that the victim was a dating partner. They had never lived together. Can I use this information to score Violence Against Others?

Answer. Yes. A domestic partner is a woman that the perpetrator lives or did live with for any length of time. A dating partner with whom the perpetrator did not cohabit does not meet the criteria for domestic partner, so she counts as a nondomestic victim or "other."

11. Substance Abuse

Scoring Criteria

To score 1 for this item, there must be more than one element of substance abuse present; alcohol use at the index assault is not sufficient by itself. The elements are listed from most common to least common according to the ODARA development research.

At *least two* of the following must be present:

- he consumed alcohol immediately before or during the index assault,
- he used drugs immediately before or during the index assault,
- he abused drugs and/or alcohol in the days or weeks before the index assault (e.g., alcohol intoxication, frequent alcohol use, use of street drugs, misuse of medication),
- he noticeably increased his abuse of drugs and/or alcohol in the days or weeks before the index assault (without a return to normal consumption prior to the index assault),
- he had been more angry or violent when using drugs and/or alcohol before the index assault,
- he consumed alcohol before or during a criminal offense predating the index assault,
- his alcohol use before the index assault but since age 18 resulted in some problems or interference in his life, and
- his drug use before the index assault but since age 18 resulted in some problems or interference in his life.

Any two of these criteria must be present to score 1 for the item. Not all of the criteria have to be present. If only one of these criteria is met, then score 0 for the item.

For the purposes of scoring this item, evidence for an alcohol or drug use problem or interference in the perpetrator's life can come from alcohol or drug use related to law violations resulting in a charge or revocation of conditional release; withdrawal symptoms or inability to decrease use; or financial, job, relationship, legal, or health problems or other problems attributable to alcohol or drug use. Drugs that count for this item are illicit or street drugs or misused prescription medications.

Do not include medications taken as prescribed.

Frequently Asked Question

Question. The perpetrator did not use alcohol or drugs for several months before the index incident and is not known for becoming more angry or violent when using alcohol. In the past, however, he was charged with driving under the influence of alcohol. How should I score Substance Abuse?

Answer. This item should be scored 1. If the perpetrator has been charged with an alcohol-related criminal offense before the index incident, then he consumed alcohol before or during a prior criminal offense *and* his alcohol use resulted in problems (i.e., charge for a law violation), thus satisfying two of the elements.

12. Assault on Victim When Pregnant

Information for scoring this item can come from sources other than criminal justice documentation, and the incident does not need to be known to the police.

Scoring Criteria

All of the following must be present:

- an act of violence (as defined above) carried out by the man being assessed
- *and* an incident against the female partner who is the victim of the index assault
- *and* the victim's pregnancy at the time of the assault.

If any one of these criteria is absent, then score 0 for the item, even if every other criterion is present. These criteria are all required. The index assault can count for this item.

Do not include

- incidents involving only pets or property
- or incidents that occurred when the victim was not pregnant.

Frequently Asked Questions

Question. The perpetrator was convicted of an assault against a previous domestic partner who is not the index victim. The ex-partner was 5 months pregnant. Can I use this information to score Assault on Victim When Pregnant?

Answer. No. In the ODARA development research, this question was coded with respect to the index victim only.

Question. How pregnant does the victim have to be to score this item 1?

Answer. In the ODARA development research, pregnancy was treated as a dichotomous variable (i.e., pregnant vs. not pregnant). Pregnancy of any duration at the time of the assault counts.

13. Barriers to Victim Support

This item covers the victim's circumstances at the time of the index assault and should be scored on the basis of information documented as close to the time of the index assault as possible. The elements are listed from most common to least common according to the ODARA development research.

Scoring Criteria

At *least one* of the following must be present:

- the victim of the index assault has one or more children age 18 or under who live with her and for whom she provides care
- *and/or* she has no telephone (i.e., no cell phone *and* no landline telephone in the home)
- *and/or* she has no transportation (i.e., no access to a vehicle *and* no public transportation in the vicinity of her home *and* no money for a taxi)
- *and/or* she is geographically isolated (i.e., living in a rural area with nobody living close by)
- *and/or* she consumed alcohol or drugs just before or during the index incident or has a history of alcohol or drug abuse (e.g., alcohol intoxication, frequent alcohol use, use of street drugs, abuse of medication).

Any one of these criteria must be present to score 1 for the item. Not all the criteria have to be present. If none of these criteria are met, then score 0 for the item.

Frequently Asked Question

Question. None of the suggested barriers to support apply to the victim, but she is of an ethnic minority in which a woman traditionally is subservient to her husband; in addition, there are no services for assaulted women in her minority language. Can I use this information to score Barriers to Victim Support?

Answer. No. In the ODARA development research, we recorded immigration issues and language barriers as circumstances that might increase the victim's vulnerability; however, we obtained insufficient numbers on these variables to establish an association with recidivism.

ADJUSTING ONTARIO DOMESTIC ASSAULT RISK ASSESSMENT SCORES FOR ASSESSMENTS WITH MISSING INFORMATION

If the available documentation indicates that an item might be present but the information is unclear or incomplete, the item may be treated as unknown or missing. It is better to seek more information before treating an item as missing, and this caveat is especially true for the perpetrator's criminal history (including prior domestic and nondomestic incidents and correctional and conditional dispositions). In some circumstances, however, some items are truly unknown. For example, a victim might recall that the perpetrator assaulted her on many occasions in the past, but she may not be able either to recall or to rule out a specific occasion on which she was pregnant during an assault, despite having given birth at least once during this time. In this case, Assault on the Victim When Pregnant could be treated as missing.

Prorating is a standard assessment procedure for dealing with missing information. Prorating replaces missing information with data estimated from all items that are not missing. Prorating is preferable to scoring 0 for missing items, which could underestimate risk. It is also preferable to scoring 1 for missing items, which could overestimate risk.

The ODARA score can be prorated for missing information using the adjusted scores shown in Table A.1. This table can be used for up to five missing items. Our research shows that missing more than five items reduced the accuracy of the ODARA to a point at which it was not statistically different from zero. To use Table A.1, first add up the scores for the items that are present and find this score in the Raw Score column. Then identify the column for the number of items that are missing. The number in the square where the row and column meet is the adjusted score.

For example, the perpetrator scores 2 on the ODARA, but there is a charge of assault on his criminal record without supplementary information indicating whether the assault met the criteria for a Prior Domestic Incident or for a Prior Nondomestic Incident and thus Violence Against Others. With a raw score of 2, start from "2" in the Raw Score column and follow along the row until it meets the Number of Missing Items column "3." The adjusted score is 3.

TABLE A.1
Adjusted Scores for Assessments With Missing Information

Raw score	No. of missing items				
	1	2	3	4	5
0	0	0	0	0	0
1	1	1	1	1	2
2	2	2	3	3	3
3	3	4	4	4	5
4	4	5	5	6	7+
5	5	6	7+	7+	7+
6	7+	7+	7+	7+	7+

APPENDIX B: SAMPLE RISK ASSESSMENT REPORT SUMMARY AND NORMS FOR THE ONTARIO DOMESTIC ASSAULT RISK ASSESSMENT (ODARA)

The ODARA is an actuarial risk assessment that ranks men with respect to their risk of domestic violence recidivism. The higher the ODARA score, the more likely the man is to assault a female cohabiting partner again, the more frequent and severe future assaults will be, and the sooner he will assault again. The ODARA was developed in a study of 589 men known to police in the Province of Ontario, Canada, for physically assaulting their female partners, and it was validated in three further studies. In an average follow-up of approximately 5 years after an index incident of domestic violence, 30% of men recidivated. The ODARA consists of 13 unique predictors of domestic violence recidivism, including domestic and nondomestic criminal history, threat and confinement during the index incident, children in the relationship, substance abuse, and barriers to victim support. In the ODARA development research, only acts of physical violence met the definition of domestic violence recidivism. Of the men who recidivated, most assaulted the same partner as before.

The ODARA score for Mr. X was based on information ascertained at or before the index assault, which occurred on December 26, 2008, using available information from the correctional file compiled at the Probation and Parole Office in Madelton, Ontario, and the clinical file compiled during pretrial assessment in the South Ontario Psychiatric Hospital Intake Assessment Unit. According to the information contained in these records, Mr. X scores 6 on the ODARA. As indicated by the normative data table (Table B.1), fewer than 10% of the men in the studies described above obtained higher scores than Mr. X. When followed up for approximately 5 years, more than 50% of men in Mr. X's risk category committed a new domestic assault.

Portions of this appendix have been adapted from "Ontario Domestic Assault Risk Assessment General Scoring Criteria" (2005) with permission.

TABLE B.1
Normative Data for the Distribution of Ontario Domestic Assault Risk Assessment (ODARA) Scores in a Population of Men With a Police Occurrence Report of Assault Against a Female Domestic Partner

ODARA score	Recidivism (%)	Percentage in this range of scores	Percentage scoring lower	Percentage scoring higher
0	7	9	0	91
1	17	17	9	74
2	22	21	26	53
3	34	20	47	33
4	39	13	67	20
5–6	53	14	80	6
7–13	74	6	94	0

Note. *Recidivism* is defined as a new assault against a female domestic partner identified by an occurrence report in police records or a charge in the criminal record during an average follow-up of 4.9 years after the index assault. Data from Hilton et al. (2004); Hilton and Harris (2009b); and Hilton, Harris, Rice, Houghton, and Eke (2008).

APPENDIX C: SCORING CRITERIA FOR THE DOMESTIC VIOLENCE RISK APPRAISAL GUIDE (DVRAG)

With the exception of the score on the Psychopathy Checklist—Revised (PCL–R; R. D. Hare, 2003), all items on the DVRAG follow the same inclusion and exclusion criteria as the Ontario Domestic Assault Risk Assessment (ODARA), detailed in Appendix A and summarized here; however, most DVRAG items have nonunitary weights, and several are scored as continuous rather than dichotomous items. The score sheet in Exhibit C.1 (see p. 178) enables simultaneous scoring of the ODARA and DVRAG.

ITEM SCORING

1. Number of Prior Domestic Incidents

Count the number of physical assaults by the perpetrator against a current or previous female cohabiting partner or her children on a separate occasion before the index assault and recorded in a police occurrence report or criminal record. Include any current or previous female domestic partner or her children, but exclude incidents involving only abused pets or damaged property.

No. of assaults	Score
0	−1
1	0
≥2	+5

2. Number of Prior Nondomestic Incidents

Count the number of physical assaults by the perpetrator on any person other than a current or previous female cohabiting partner or her children on a separate occasion before the index assault and recorded in a police occurrence report or criminal record. Exclude incidents involving only abused pets or damaged property.

No. of assaults	Score
0	−1
≥ 1	+5

3. Prior Custodial Sentence of 30 Days or More

Score *no* if the perpetrator did not spend any time incarcerated as a result of a sentence handed down by the court for a criminal offense before the index assault. Score *yes* for any continuous or intermittent admission to training school, jail, or federal correctional facility or a provincial or state correctional facility if the sentence was for at least 30 days. Exclude time spent in custody awaiting trial unless time served is explicitly stated as part of the sentence.

Response	Score
No	−1
Yes	+2

4. Failure on Prior Conditional Release

Score *no* if the perpetrator was not on conditional release at or before the index assault or, if he was, if he completed the conditions of release without failure. Score *yes* for any failure to obey a conditional release order that commenced prior to the index assault, whether or not the failure led to arrest, criminal charge, or revocation of conditional release.

Response	Score
No	−1
Yes	+2

5. Threat to Harm or Kill at the Index Assault

Score *yes* if the perpetrator made a threat of physical harm toward any person other than himself or incurred a criminal charge of threatening, uttering threats, threatening with a weapon, or equivalent charge arising from events at the index assault.

Response	Score
No	0
Yes	+1

6. Confinement of the Partner at the Index Assault

Score *yes* if the perpetrator detained the female victim in a locked or barricaded physical space or physically intervened with her attempt to leave the location.

Response	Score
No	0
Yes	+1

7. Victim Concern

Score *yes* if, at the time of her first report to police or documented interview with a victim service agency regarding the index assault, the female victim of the index assault verbally stated that she was concerned, afraid, worried, or certain that the perpetrator would assault her or her children in the future.

Response	Score
No	0
Yes	+2

8. Number of Children

Add up the number of living, minor or adult, biological or adopted children of the perpetrator, plus the additional children of the victim.

No. of children	Score
0–1	−1
≥2	+1

9. Victim's Biological Children From a Previous Partner

Count all the living, minor or adult, biological children of the female victim of the index assault whose father is not the perpetrator. Exclude adopted children.

No. of children	Score
0	−1
1	0
≥ 2	+2

10. Violence Against Others

Score *yes* for any physical assault by the perpetrator on any person other than a current or previous female cohabiting partner or her children on a separate occasion before the index assault, whether or not recorded in a police occurrence report or criminal record.

Response	Score
No	0
Yes	+8

11. Substance Abuse Score

Allot one point for each of the following: alcohol use at the index assault, drug use at the index assault, alcohol or drug abuse in days or weeks before the index assault, increased drug or alcohol use in days or weeks before the index assault, more angry or violent when using drugs or alcohol, alcohol involved in a prior criminal offense, adult alcohol problem, and adult drug problem. Exclude use of medications taken as prescribed. For the purposes of scoring this item, *problems* include law violations resulting in a charge or revocation of conditional release; financial, job, relationship, legal, or health problems; withdrawal symptoms or inability to decrease use; or any other problem resulting from substance use (alcohol, street drugs, or abuse of prescription medication).

No. of factors present	Score
≤ 1	−2
≥ 2	+2

12. Assault on Victim When Pregnant

Score *yes* for any physical assault by the perpetrator on the female victim of the index assault when she was pregnant on any occasion before or including the index assault, whether or not recorded in a police occurrence report or criminal record.

Response	Score
No	0
Yes	+5

13. Number of Barriers to Victim Support

Allot one point for each of the following: victim has a child age less than 18 years to care for, victim has neither telephone nor access to transportation, victim is isolated geographically or from the community, victim alcohol use in the index assault, or victim adult alcohol or drug problem. Note that the lack of both telephone and transportation counts as one barrier.

No. of factors	Score
0	−1
1	0
≥ 2	+4

14. Psychopathy Checklist—Revised Score

Full scoring criteria are available in R. D. Hare (2003).

PCL–R score	Score
≤ 9	−1
10–16	+1
≥ 17	+6

ADJUSTING DOMESTIC VIOLENCE RISK APPRAISAL GUIDE SCORES FOR ASSESSMENTS WITH MISSING INFORMATION

On the ODARA, if there were no prorating system, leaving an item out would have the same effect on the total score as scoring the item 0. Any item that is left blank reduces the total score and possibly over- or underestimates the perpetrator's risk. That is why we developed a prorating system, which can be used for up to five items if the available information indicates that the item might be present but the details are unclear or incomplete for scoring purposes. Prorating is a standard assessment procedure for dealing with missing information that gives credit for a missing item based on the score obtained for the items that were not missing. The prorating table in Appendix A makes this procedure easy for ODARA users.

Prorating is more laborious for the DVRAG than the ODARA because of the Nuffield system. Prorating, however, retains more predictive power than scoring items 0 and so is a desirable procedure if it can be done accurately. There is no simple table for prorating DVRAG scores, but assessors can use the detailed steps provided in the next section.

An alternative to prorating is afforded by the DVRAG's use of both addition and subtraction to derive the final score, which results in a wide range of possible scores. For each item, a value of 0 indicates that perpetrators having this characteristic reoffended at a rate that was very close (within 5%) to the base rate. Because of the item weighting, scoring a missing item 0 gives credit for a missing item based on the normative average. Thus, on the DVRAG, assessors can leave an item out or give it a score of 0.

Our calculations of the DVRAG's predictive accuracy in the combined sample of 649 cases revealed that it is quite robust in the face of up to five missing items, still predicting recidivism significantly better than the most accurate nonactuarial risk assessment. Results were best when the four criminal history items and the PCL–R were retained; consequently, we advise seeking more information if you have no criminal history information, just as with ODARA prorating. Any omission makes the estimated risk closer to the base rate than it might otherwise be, which could tend to underestimate risk (where the true score is positive) or to overestimate it (where the true score is negative). We suggest the following cautionary statements when communicating the assessment results with missing items:

- When prorating is used: "It should be noted that there were [*insert number up to 5*] items missing for Mr. Y, and his DVRAG score was prorated for these items."
- When missing items are scored 0: "It should be noted that there were [*insert number up to 5*] items missing for Mr. Y, so his score is closer to the middle risk category than might be expected if complete information had been available."

STEPS FOR PRORATING THE DOMESTIC VIOLENCE RISK APPRAISAL GUIDE

If the available documentation indicates that an item might be present but the information is unclear or incomplete, the item may be treated as unknown or missing. It is better to seek more information before treating an item as missing, and this caveat is especially true for the perpetrator's criminal history (including prior domestic and nondomestic incidents and custodial and noncustodial dispositions). In some circumstances, however, some items are truly unknown.

If the Raw Sum of the Items That Are Scored Is Positive

1. Note the maximum possible positive score on each of the missing items, and sum them.

___ + ___ + ___ + ___ + ___ = Total _____   (a)

2. Note the maximum possible positive scores on each of the scored items, and sum them.

___ + ___ + ___ + ___ + ___ + ___ + ___ + ___ + ___ + ___ + ___ + ___ + ___ = Total _____ (b)

3. Note the actual obtained values on each of the items that are scored, and sum them.

___ + ___ + ___ + ___ + ___ + ___ + ___ + ___ + ___ + ___ + ___ + ___ + ___ = Total _____ (c)

4. Divide the obtained sum (c) by the maximum possible (b): c ÷ b = _____ (d)

5. Multiply the obtained proportion (d) by the maximum possible on missing items (a): d × a = _____ (e)

6. Add the prorated score for missing items (e) to the obtained sum (c): e + c = _____ (f)

7. Round this result (f) to the nearest positive whole number for the final DVRAG score: _____

If the Raw Sum of the Items That Are Scored Is Negative

1. Note the most negative possible score on each of the missing items, and sum them.

___ + ___ + ___ + ___ + ___ = Total – _____ (a)

2. Note the most negative possible score on each of the scored items, and sum them.

___ + ___ + ___ + ___ + ___ + ___ + ___ + ___ + ___ + ___ + ___ + ___ + ___ = Total – _____ (b)

3. Note the actual obtained values on each of the items that are scored, and sum them.

___ + ___ + ___ + ___ + ___ + ___ + ___ + ___ + ___ + ___ + ___ + ___ + ___ = Total – _____ (c)

4. Divide the obtained sum (c) by the most negative possible (b): $c \div b =$ _____ (d)

5. Multiply the obtained proportion (d) by the most negative possible on missing items (a): $d \times a = -$ _____ (e)

6. Subtract the absolute value of the prorated score for missing items (e) from the obtained sum (c): $c - |e| = -$ _____ (f)

Note that f should be a more extreme negative number than c.

7. Round this result (f) to the nearest negative whole number for the final DVRAG score: _____

EXHIBIT C.1
Simultaneous Score Sheet for ODARA and DVRAG

ODARA items		Item name	DVRAG items			
0 or 1	Or circle ?		Circle one			
	?	1. Prior domestic incident	−1	0	+5	
	?	2. Prior nondomestic incident	−1		+5	
	?	3. Prior custodial sentence of 30 days or more	−1		+2	
	?	4. Failure on prior conditional release	−1		+2	
	?	5. Threat to harm or kill at the index assault		0	+1	
	?	6. Confinement of partner at index assault		0	+1	
	?	7. Victim concern		0	+2	
	?	8. More than one child	−1		+1	
	?	9. Victim's biological children from a previous partner	−1	0	+2	
	?	10. Violence against others		0	+8	
	?	11. Substance abuse	−2		+2	
	?	12. Assault on victim when pregnant		0	+5	
	?	13. Barriers to victim support	−1	0	+4	
NA	NA	14. Psychopathy Checklist—Revised score	−1	0	+1	+6
.	# ?	← Raw total score Sums of columns →	−	+	+	+
		← Adjusted score Final score →				

Note. ODARA = Ontario Domestic Assault Risk Assessment (Hilton et al., 2004); DVRAG = Domestic Violence Risk Appraisal Guide (Hilton, Harris, Rice, Houghton, & Eke, 2008). NA = not applicable.

APPENDIX D: SAMPLE RISK ASSESSMENT REPORT SUMMARY AND NORMS FOR THE DOMESTIC VIOLENCE RISK APPRAISAL GUIDE (DVRAG)

The DVRAG is an actuarial risk assessment tool that ranks men with respect to risk of domestic violence recidivism and its frequency and severity. The higher the DVRAG score, the more likely the man is to assault a female cohabiting partner again, the more frequent and severe future assaults will be, and the sooner he will assault again. The DVRAG was developed in a study of 649 men who were known to police in the Province of Ontario, Canada, for physically assaulting their female partners and who had a corrections file permitting in-depth assessment. In an average follow-up of nearly 5 years after an index incident of domestic violence, 45% of men recidivated, most against the same partner as at the index. The DVRAG consists of 14 unique predictors of domestic violence recidivism, including score on the Hare Psychopathy Checklist—Revised (PCL–R; R. D. Hare, 2003), domestic and nondomestic criminal history, threat and confinement during the index incident, children in the relationship, substance abuse, and barriers to victim support. In the DVRAG development research, only acts of physical violence met the definition of domestic violence recidivism.

The DVRAG score for Mr. Y was based on information ascertained at or before the index assault, which occurred on June 28, 2005, using information available in the file compiled at the Arbor Correctional Center. According to the information in these records, Mr. Y scores +26 on the DVRAG. As indicated by the normative data table, 97% of men in the study described above obtained lower scores than Mr. Y (see Table D.1). When followed up for nearly 5 years, all (100%) men in Mr. Y's risk category committed a new domestic assault that was recorded by police (see Table D.2).

TABLE D.1
Normative Data for the Distribution of Domestic Violence Risk Appraisal Guide (DVRAG) Scores

DVRAG score	% scoring lower	DVRAG score	% scoring lower
≤ 10	0	8	74
−9	≤ 2	9	77
−8	2	10	78
−7	4	11	81
−6	9	12	84
−5	15	13	86
−4	22	14	87
−3	27	15	89
−2	32	16	91
−1	38	17	92
0	43	18	93
1	48	19	94
2	54	20	95
3	58	21	96
4	63	24	97
5	65	26	98
6	68	≥31	≥ 99
7	71		

Note. Data from Hilton, Harris, Rice, Houghton, and Eke (2008).

TABLE D.2
Normative Data and Probability of Recidivism for the Domestic Violence Risk Appraisal Guide (DVRAG) Risk Categories in a Population of Men With a Police Occurrence Report of Assault Against a Female Domestic Partner and an In-Depth Correctional File

Risk category	DVRAG score	Recidivism	Percentage		
			In this category	Scoring lower	Scoring higher
1	−10 to −9	14	2	0	98
2	−8 to −5	24	20	2	78
3	−4 to −1	34	20	22	58
4	0 to +3	44	20	43	37
5	+4 to +10	51	19	63	19
6	+11 to +23	71	16	81	3
7	+24 to +41	100	3	97	0

Note. Recidivism is defined as a new assault against a female domestic partner identified by an occurrence report in police records or a charge in the criminal record during an average follow-up of 4.8 years. Data from Hilton, Harris, Rice, Houghton, and Eke (2008).

APPENDIX E:
PRACTICE CASE MATERIALS

The case materials in this appendix are provided for scoring practice. Cases E1 through E3 provide sufficient information for scoring the Ontario Domestic Assault Risk Assessment (ODARA), and Case E4 provides sufficient information to score the Domestic Violence Risk Appraisal Guide (DVRAG). All materials are based on cases drawn from our research, but many details have been modified to preserve anonymity and to provide a variety of scoring challenges. All names and locations have been fictionalized. We created the clinical interview transcripts with liberal modifications to fit the interview format. The transcripts themselves are not intended to illustrate exemplary interviewing techniques; in fact, some items are deliberately left unclear to challenge the practice scorer to examine the scoring criteria carefully and to consider the handling of missing information. Each case is followed by a table providing the correct scores for each case and brief explanations of the scores.

The psychosocial report for Case E4 was created according to the Guidelines for the Compilation of a Psychosocial History Suitable for Risk Appraisal (Quinsey, Harris, Rice, & Cormier, 2006) and was adapted from actual forensic assessment material. Thus, although it has been modified to provide anonymity and scoring practice, it is a realistic example of a perpetrator's psychosocial history. The information on which we based our scoring of the Psychopathy Checklist—Revised (PCL–R) is indicated in the psychosocial report by PCL–R items in parentheses at the end of the relevant paragraphs.

CASE E1: POLICE DOCUMENTATION,
ANDREW ROBITAILLE

Occurrence 01-0101768 (Domestic Assault)

Victim: Robitaille, Nancy, 98 Bridge Street, Riverdown, ON. Date of birth 1972-03-15. Employer: The Country Shoppe.
Witness, complainant: Gagnon, Rain (age 14), 98 Bridge Street, Riverdown, ON. Date of birth 1990-05-21. Employer: Student.
Accused: Robitaille, Andrew, 98 Bridge Street, Riverdown, ON. Date of birth 1966-04-09. Employer: Eldin Construction. Relationship to victim: Spouse.

Charges: Assault (spousal), 2004-06-21. Held for bail hearing, Riverdown Courthouse 1000 hr 2004-07-14.

History

The accused and victim have been married for 6 years and live with the victim's three children from her first marriage. The youngest son was present during the assault. The victim states that the accused has never threatened or hit her before. The accused had been consuming a significant amount of alcohol (six to seven bottles of beer) prior to the incident. His record indicates one previous conviction for impaired driving.

Incident

At approximately 2000 hr, the accused and victim were in their kitchen discussing the payment of a large phone bill. The accused was very upset at the expense, saying that someone would have to pay for it and it wouldn't be him. He felt the eldest son, who had made long distance calls, should be responsible for the cost. The victim did not agree. The argument became heated and loud. When the victim tried to leave the kitchen, the accused hit her across the face and then left the room himself. The youngest son called 911 at this time.

The victim called a girlfriend to see if she and the children could stay for the night, but the accused returned to the kitchen and ripped the phone off the wall, saying, "That has caused enough problems already." The victim decided not to call again, although she had a cell phone. The police arrived at 2030 hr. The accused was taken into custody without incident.

Criminal Record

Date	Location	Charge	Sentence
2002-07-27	Riverdown, ON	Operating a vehicle while impaired	6 months probation (license suspension, refrain from consuming alcohol, keep the peace)

(See Table E.1 for Andrew Robitaille's ODARA score sheet.)

TABLE E.1

Ontario Domestic Assault Risk Assessment (Hilton et al., 2004)
Score Sheet for Andrew Grant, With Explanations

Score	Item	Explanation
0	1. Prior domestic incident	No prior assaults in police record
0	2. Prior nondomestic incident	No prior assaults in police record
0	3. Prior custodial sentence of 30 days or more	No correctional sentences in record
0	4. Failure on prior conditional release	Prior conditional release in police record; no evidence suggesting failure
0	5. Threat to harm or kill at the index assault	No evidence of threat in police occurrence report
0	6. Confinement of the partner at the index assault	No evidence of confinement in police occurrence report (ripping phone does not meet criteria)
0	7. Victim concern	No evidence of statement indicating concern about future assault in police report
1	8. More than one child	Three children
1	9. Victim's biological child from a previous partner	Victim has children from her first marriage
0	10. Violence against others	No evidence of prior violent incident against a person other than a partner or children
1	11. Substance abuse	Alcohol use at index, prior offense (impaired)
0	12. Assault on victim when pregnant	No evidence of pregnancy in police report, statement that no prior assaults occurred
1	13. Barriers to victim support	Children in home to care for

Raw total (sum of items scored 1): 4
Adjusted score (prorated for missing information): 4

Note. For scoring criteria, see Appendix A, this volume.

CASE E2: POLICE VICTIM INTERVIEW, GREGORY SMITH

Interview Transcript

Officer: Ms. Williams, your boyfriend has been arrested for assault and has been transported to the station. We're going to keep him in custody until his bail hearing. I need to take a statement from you regarding what happened here this evening. Are you feeling up to giving me a statement at this time?

Ms. Williams: I've already told you pretty much all of it: He hit me in the face and pushed me.

Officer:	By "he," you mean Gregory Smith, correct? Can you start from when he came home?
Ms. Williams:	Greg, yes. Well, he came home kind of drunk. I was really upset because he was supposed to help me get the house ready for having his mother over this weekend, and I told him that, but he ignored me and turned on the TV. That's when I looked at him, and I could see he'd been drinking. So I said, "Where have you been? Did you go out for a beer after work or something? Why didn't you call?" I was just surprised because he's not usually like that. That's when he got up and slapped me and started pushing me into the wall.
Officer:	Then what happened?
Ms. Williams:	I was crying and telling him to stop.
Officer:	Did he stop?
Ms. Williams:	Yes, sort of. I went into the kitchen, but I could hear him in the living room crashing around, swearing at the dog. I was just in shock. That's why I called 911. I just didn't know what to do. I didn't want Sarah to wander in and get hurt.
Officer:	Did he say anything to you?
Ms. Williams:	No, he just sat there—until I started talking to him, then he just flipped.
Officer:	Did he threaten you?
Ms. Williams:	No, just hitting and pushing.
Officer:	And when you went to the kitchen?
Ms. Williams:	Like I said, he just stayed there, crashing around, swearing at the dog.
Officer:	Has he ever done this kind of thing before?
Ms. Williams:	No, no. He's just not like this. He's not a violent man.
Officer:	How long have you been together?
Ms. Williams:	Seven months. I knew him vaguely a long time ago, before he moved out to British Columbia. But he's traveled around a lot, with different jobs. Then he came back to Ontario to live with his mom late in 2008, and we got together; then he moved in with us a few months ago.
Officer:	Who is "us"?
Ms. Williams:	Just my kids and me.

Officer:	Does he have any children?
Ms. Williams:	No.
Officer:	Were your kids in the house tonight?
Ms. Williams:	Just my 5-year-old daughter. My son is at his dad's place for the weekend.
Officer:	Now, I know you said he's not usually like that, but have you ever seen him act this way before?
Ms. Williams:	Honestly, no. When we first got together he was so kind and gentle. Very helpful—he was always bringing me gifts, and he treated the kids really well. I guess the last couple of months he has been more irritated about little things. I think he's under a lot of stress, you know. He doesn't have a driver's license because he got too many speeding tickets, so he feels stuck in this little town, and his work is hard and stressful.
Officer:	So how does he get to work if he can't drive?
Ms. Williams:	I guess he gets a lift from one of the other guys who work there.
Officer:	You guess? Are you not sure?
Ms. Williams:	I'm usually gone when he's still in bed. But I see him coming home with other guys.
Officer:	And what is he usually like when gets home?
Ms. Williams:	He's usually fine.
Officer:	Have you ever seen him irritated, or has he ever behaved in a threatening way?
Ms. Williams:	No. Well, about 2 months ago we had a disagreement about how to discipline my son. It was pretty heated because he just wouldn't accept that I'm going to be the one to punish my kids if they do something wrong. My son had spilled something on the couch, and it got on some CDs that I guess I should have put away. My boyfriend was really mad. At one point he raised his fist in the air, but he didn't do anything. He just said, "Forget it!" and left the house. That's the only time besides today that I felt worried.
Officer:	Are you afraid that he will act like he did tonight again?
Ms. Williams:	Not really. I just called because I didn't know what to do to stop the situation. He's never hit me before, and I don't think he'd do it again. I don't want to make trouble for him.

Officer:	Do you know if he has ever assaulted anyone else?
Ms. Williams:	I'm sure he hasn't. He's not that kind of guy. When he was younger, he had a reputation as a troublemaker. But we talked about that, and I think people were wrong about him.
Officer:	You mentioned that he came home "kind of drunk" tonight. Tell me a bit about his drinking habits in the past and what he's like now.
Ms. Williams:	Like I said, he had a reputation when he was younger. He was supposed to be into partying and drugs, but I never saw it, and he says he wasn't like that. He just had to hang out with his big brother because his parents were never there for him. His brother would get nearly unconscious, but my boyfriend didn't drink a drop because he had to get his brother home and take care of him. I know that when we first met he didn't drink at all. I think he was on a special diet. Then he started having one or two drinks, and we might go out for a beer or something, but I have never seen him drunk. That's why I was so surprised tonight.
Officer:	Do you think he may have been using drugs earlier tonight, too?
Ms. Williams:	No, he doesn't use drugs.
Officer:	How would you describe how he acts when he does drink alcohol?
Ms. Williams:	I would say that he's normal. I've never seen him angry or agitated like some people get. He's just relaxed.
Officer:	So drugs and alcohol aren't usually a problem. What about weapons: Do you know if he's used firearms or other weapons in the past?
Ms. Williams:	No.
Officer:	Does he own any weapons or keep any in the house?
Ms. Williams:	No. Not here, anyway. His brother hunts, so he has some guns, but not Greg.
Officer:	Is there anything else you would like to add to your statement?
Ms. Williams:	No. That's it. I just want things to be the way they were.
Officer:	Let me tell you what is going to happen. . . . [*Officer completes interview and returns to police station to check criminal history.*]

Criminal Record

Date	Location	Charge	Sentence
1998-07-19	Wycombe, BC	Assault (spousal)	6 months probation (refrain from consuming alcohol, keep the peace)
2007-04-18	Cheshire, ON	Assault (spousal)	6 months probation (refrain from consuming alcohol, keep the peace)
2008-11-18	Tynemouth, ON	Operating a vehicle while impaired	8 months probation (license suspension, refrain from consuming alcohol, keep the peace)

(See Table E.2 for Gregory Smith's ODARA score sheet.)

TABLE E.2
Ontario Domestic Assault Risk Assessment (Hilton et al., 2004)
Score Sheet for Gregory Smith, With Explanations

Score	Item	Explanation
1	1. Prior domestic incident	Two domestic assault charges in criminal record (note victim was not aware of history)
0	2. Prior nondomestic assault	No other violent offenses in criminal record
0	3. Prior custodial sentence of 30 days or more	No custodial sentences in record
?	4. Failure on prior conditional release	Prior conditional release in police record; victim has incomplete knowledge; vague information about alcohol use; he might have been drinking in violation of the 2008 probation conditions
0	5. Threat to harm or kill at the index assault	No evidence of threat at index incident in police investigation interview
0	6. Confinement of the partner at the index assault	No evidence of confinement in police interview
0	7. Victim concern	Victim reported, "I don't think he'd do it again."
1	8. More than one child	Two children
1	9. Victim's biological child from a previous partner	Victim has children from previous partner
0	10. Violence against others	No evidence of prior violent incident to any person other than a partner or the children
1	11. Substance abuse	Alcohol use at index, prior offense (impaired)
0	12. Assault on victim when pregnant	No evidence of pregnancy in police report
1	13. Barriers to victim support	Children in home to care for

Raw total (sum of items scored 1): 5
Adjusted score (prorated for missing information): 5–6

Note. For scoring criteria, see Appendix A, this volume.

CASE E3: ODARA CLINICAL INTERVIEW TRANSCRIPT, MARK DOE

Interviewer: Jennifer, we've talked a lot about your situation and what happened tonight. We can talk in a few minutes, if you like, about some of the programs we have here at the shelter. But first, if you want, we can do this risk assessment. It's called the ODARA, the Ontario Domestic Assault Risk Assessment. The assessment will tell us his risk of domestic assault in the future. It takes about 10 minutes. Are you interested in doing this?

Jennifer: OK, yes.

Interviewer: All right, then. The first questions are about what happened tonight. This time, did Mark, your husband, threaten to harm or kill you or anyone else?

Jennifer: Yes. After he threw the first bottle at my head, he was yelling, "I'm going to get you. I'm gonna smash your face!" As if I did anything—he's the one I found with another woman.

Interviewer: This time, did he do anything to prevent you leaving the location?

Jennifer: Not really. I mean, he's in his truck, and I'm standing outside it, because I'm driving home from work when I see his truck, and I think, where's he going in his truck at this time of night? So I follow him, and when he pulled over, I got out of my car and went over to him in the truck. I wanted to talk to him, but he wouldn't get out. Then I see this woman. That's when I got mad, got my tire iron and broke the window. I was screaming at him that I'd had enough of his messing around and I was going to leave him. That's when he got out of the truck and started threatening me. He grabbed my wrist and started hitting me in the head with the beer bottle.

Interviewer: How did you manage to get away?

Jennifer: I twisted around, trying to throw him off balance. When he let go, I ran for the car.

Interviewer: Did he grab your keys or hold onto you when you were trying to get away?

Jennifer: No, once I started toward my car, he kind of just stood there yelling. He threw the broken bottle at me, but it missed.

Interviewer:	You mentioned beer. Did he drink alcohol just before or during the assault?
Jennifer:	Yes, he and that woman were both drunk. They were parked in the truck, on the side of the road. They had just come from a party, and they've got the empties in the truck. I guess the beer bottle was the closest thing he could find to hit me with.
Interviewer:	Did he use drugs just before or during this assault?
Jennifer:	I've never seen Mark use drugs. I don't know this woman, but I didn't see any tonight.
Interviewer:	Did he abuse alcohol in the past few days or weeks?
Jennifer:	Well, besides tonight, I haven't seen him drunk in the past few weeks. He's made it home at some point every night, so I would have known if he'd been drinking a lot.
Interviewer:	Is he more angry or violent when he uses drugs or alcohol?
Jennifer:	He's way more violent when he drinks a lot. That's the only time he gets into fights.
Interviewer:	Before this time, have police ever come because he was hitting you?
Jennifer:	No. I almost called them once when he knocked my son against the wall, but . . . I didn't.
Interviewer:	Have they ever come because he was threatening you?
Jennifer:	No.
Interviewer:	Or threatening your son?
Jennifer:	No, they never came before.
Interviewer:	Do you know if the police have dealt with him because he was hitting or threatening another partner?
Jennifer:	No, I don't know any of them, and he doesn't really talk about stuff like that to me.
Interviewer:	Before this time, have the police ever had to deal with him for any other kind of violence?
Jennifer:	No one has ever called the police on him, even when they should have. I guess we weren't sure if they would be able to make a difference.
Interviewer:	So is he violent to people other than you and your son?

Jennifer:	Well, he's always shouting at people, especially when he has been drinking. If they talk back to him, he gets really annoyed and will punch out at them. He fights his brother a lot after they've been drinking. Two years ago, I saw him hit his mom! But no one has ever called the police on him. Except once, his boss accused him of stealing some fishing licenses, but the police cleared him. He's never done any jail time for anything, never even been to court.
Interviewer:	I'd like to ask a bit more about your children now. How many do you have?
Jennifer:	Our son—that's my only kid—he's 16 years old. He just moved out with his girlfriend 3 months ago. I think he really wanted to get away from here, get a job and be independent.
Interviewer:	By "our son," do you mean he is your husband's biological child?
Jennifer:	Yeah.
Interviewer:	What about your husband; has he had any other children?
Jennifer:	No. At least, he's never mentioned any.
Interviewer:	Has he ever hit you when you were pregnant?
Jennifer:	No. He was really nice when I was pregnant. He didn't drink as much back then.
Interviewer:	Are you concerned that he will assault you again in the future?
Jennifer:	No, but it doesn't matter anyway because I'm leaving him. This girlfriend is the last straw; I'm tired of putting up with this.
Interviewer:	I would like to ask you a few more questions about your situation where you're living right now. Is that OK? Do you have a phone in your home?
Jennifer:	We have a phone.
Interviewer:	Do you have access to transportation?
Jennifer:	Well, yeah, we have the car and the truck, so I can always use one of them.
Interviewer:	Do you have neighbors living close by?
Jennifer:	Our house is actually joined to our neighbor's on the left.

Interviewer: So they would be able to hear you shout.

Jennifer: Oh, yes! Sometimes she complains when my husband yells at the hockey on TV.

Interviewer: Tonight you've mentioned that your husband had been using alcohol. Did you have anything to drink this evening?

Jennifer: No. I had just come from work and was driving home when I saw him driving and decided to follow. I'm not much of a drinker anyway; I don't enjoy it.

Jennifer declines involvement with the police, so she and the interviewer now discuss the ODARA results based on Jennifer's responses, given in Table E.3, and prepare a safety plan.

TABLE E.3
Ontario Domestic Assault Risk Assessment (Hilton et al., 2004)
Score Sheet for Mark Doe, With Explanations

Score	Item	Explanation
0	1. Prior domestic incident	Not to victim's knowledge—police record check advised
0	2. Prior nondomestic incident	Not to victim's knowledge—police record check advised
0	3. Prior custodial sentence of 30 days or more	Not asked because victim indicated no police history—police record check advised
0	4. Failure on prior conditional release	Not asked because victim indicated no police history—police record check advised
1	5. Threat to harm or kill at the index assault	Victim reported that accused stated, "I'm gonna smash your face."
0	6. Confinement of the partner at the index assault	Victim reported, "He kind of just stood there yelling."
0	7. Victim concern	Victim reported, "No, I don't think so."
0	8. More than one child	One son
0	9. Victim's biological child from a previous partner	Victim's son is the perpetrator's biological child
1	10. Violence against others	Victim reported, "I saw him hit his mom."
1	11. Substance abuse	Alcohol at index (client report), more angry or violent when drinking
0	12. Assault on victim when pregnant	Victim reported, "He was really very nice and kind when I was pregnant."
0	13. Barriers to victim support	Son moved out, has phone and car, neighbors nearby, no alcohol use

Raw total (sum of items scored 1): 3
Adjusted score (prorated for missing information): 3

Note. For scoring criteria, see Appendix A, this volume.

CASE E4: DOMESTIC VIOLENCE RISK APPRAISAL GUIDE
CASE MATERIAL, GARY MILLER

Police Occurrence Reports

Occurrence 01-0101458 (Domestic Assault)

Victim: Miller, Bertie, 379 Westgrove Street, Port Vebris, ON. Date of birth: 1953-02-21. Employer: Port Vebris Drug Store.
Witness, complainant: Jackson, Galilee (age 30), 24 Marie Street, Port Vebris, ON. Date of birth: 1973-05-12. Employer: Port Vebris Tourism Bureau.
Accused: Miller, Gary, 379 Westgrove Street, Port Vebris, ON. Date of birth: 1948-06-17. Employer: Port Vebris Marina. Relationship to victim: Spouse.
Charges: Assault (spousal), 2004-03-11. Held for bail hearing, Vebris County courthouse, 1000 hr 2004-04-14.

History. The accused and victim have been married since May 23, 1983. They do not have any joint children. They have lived at 379 Westgrove Street, Port Vebris, for 7 years. Police have attended this residence in the past for a domestic dispute (01-036475). Police have also attended once to bring assault charges against the accused in an unrelated matter (01-0204594). The accused has two alcohol- and driving-related charges on record (01-0621351, 01-0549873).

Incident. On March 11, 2004, at approximately 1815 hr, the accused and victim and the victim's son, "Lee" Jackson, were present at their residence. The victim had been consuming alcoholic beverages at the Vebris Bell restaurant prior to returning to the residence. The accused had been consuming alcoholic beverages at the residence prior to the victim's return.

The accused and the victim became involved in a heated argument regarding the victim's late return from work and the dinner. The victim then hit the accused across the back with a metal TV dinner tray. The accused grabbed the tray from the victim and struck her with it several times. The accused proceeded to punch the victim about the face and head with a closed hand. The victim then left the living room and went to the bathroom. The accused remained in the living room. At that time, Lee contacted the police.

Police attended the residence at 1840 hr. The accused answered the door and was observed to be in a state of intoxication. The victim was interviewed as the accused was charged and taken to the police station. The victim sustained extensive bruising to her face and head. Medical attention was obtained, and victim services were notified. The victim says there has been a recent escalation in frequency of threats from the accused. As well, she says he recently bought a revolver and has been threatening to kill himself.

Occurrence 01-0204594 (Assault, Fail to Comply)

Victim, complainant: Chapman, Karen, 248 Hill Road, Port Vebris, ON. Date of birth: 1955-05-01. Employer: Starboard Cuts Salon.
Witness: Miller, Bertie, 379 Westgrove Street, Port Vebris, ON. Date of birth: 1953-02-21. Employer: Port Vebris Drug Store.
Accused: Miller, Gary, 379 Westgrove Street, Port Vebris, ON. Date of birth: 1948-06-17. Employer: Port Vebris Marina. Relationship to victim: none.
Charges: Assault, fail to comply with probation order, 2000-10-19. Vebris County Courtroom 75 at 1430 hr, put over to 2000-10-20, 2000-12-08.

History. The accused and victim are acquainted with each other through the accused's wife, Bertie Miller. Victim reports she and the accused have verbally fought on a number of occasions, but it has never been violent before. The accused is presently on probation for a spousal assault (01-036475). The accused has two prior alcohol- and driving-related convictions.

Incident. Police received a call from the victim at 1437 hr Saturday, October 19, 2000. The victim reported being assaulted by an acquaintance at his residence. Constables Morris and Bouchard-Smith attended the victim's home and located the victim. The victim was observed to have bruising around her wrists and on her right shoulder and a cut above the left eye.

The victim reported that while attending a bonfire party the previous evening, the accused called her a "whore." The victim stated that both parties had been consuming alcoholic beverages at that time. On October 19, at approximately 1330 hr, the victim went to the accused's residence to confront the accused and request an apology. The accused attempted to force her out of his residence by holding her wrists together and pushing her out the door by her shoulder. The victim broke free and went to her vehicle. The accused followed the victim to the driveway and punched her in the face. Victim services were notified.

Police then attended the accused's residence. The accused's spouse answered the front door. The police interviewed the spouse, who confirmed the victim's story. The accused was observed sleeping on the living room sofa, and the wife was unwilling to disturb him. Police awoke the accused, arrested him for assault, and escorted him to the station. At that time, the accused was also charged with breach of probation. On October 20, 2000, at 1000 hr, he was denied bail and remains in custody until his court date.

Occurrence 01-036475 (Domestic Assault)

Victim, complainant: Miller, Bertie, 379 Westgrove Street, Port Vebris, ON. Date of birth: 1953-02-21. Employer: Port Vebris Drug Store.
Accused: Miller, Gary, 379 Westgrove Street, Port Vebris, ON. Date of birth: 1948-06-17. Employer: Port Vebris Marina. Relationship to victim: Spouse.

Charges: Assault (spousal), 2000-08-25. Remand for next court date, 2000-08-30, Vebris County Courthouse.

History. The accused and victim have been married since May 23, 1983. They do not have any joint children. They have lived at the current residence for 3 years. The accused has two impaired driving convictions on record (01-0621351, 01-0549873). There are no prior domestic incidents. Prior to this incident, the accused had been consuming alcoholic beverages at a local pub.

Incident. This incident occurred on August 25, 2000, at approximately 1700 hr. The accused had returned to his residence after going to a pub when he had finished work. The victim had prepared a dinner. The accused began an argument by insulting her housekeeping and cooking abilities. He threatened her while holding a raised beer bottle in his hand. The accused then threw his plate of food, which shattered on the wall, just missing the victim's head. The victim called the police when the accused went into the other room.

Police arrived at 1805 hr, entering the residence through the kitchen door. The accused was observed sitting in the living room, drinking beer and watching television. The accused was arrested and charged with assault without incident. In response to required domestic assault victim interview items, the victim states that she does not fear the accused and that he has never attempted to choke her or attack her while pregnant. She states she does not believe that he is more angry when drinking alcohol because he is "always angry." The victim was given medical attention for minor cuts, and victim services were notified.

Occurrence 01-0549873 (Driving While Impaired)

Accused: Miller, Gary, 255 Lodge Road, Bradley Sound, ON. Date of birth: 1948-06-17. Employer: Port Vebris Central Marine Service & Supply.

Charges: Impaired operation of a motor vehicle, 1999-08-03. Held for court on 2000-08-30, Vebris County Courthouse. Released on bail, 1999-08-10. Sentenced 90 days plus 6 months probation, 1999-09-10.

History. The accused has one previous impaired conviction on record. He served 30 days and completed probation.

Incident. On August 3, 1999, at 0024 hr, the accused was observed driving 20 km/hr on Birchwood Crescent, Port Vebris. When stopped by police, the accused was observed to be drowsy and intoxicated. He was cooperative as he was taken to the police station.

Occurrence 01-0621351 (Driving While Impaired, Fail to Provide Sample)

Accused: Miller, Gary, 255 Lodge Road, Bradley Sound, ON. Date of birth: 1948-06-17. Employer: Sound Boat Repairs.

Charges: Impaired operation of a motor vehicle, fail to provide breath sample upon demand, 1988-05-11. Released on bail, 1988-05-14, sentenced 30 days plus 12 months probation, suspended license, 1988-05-22.

History. The accused has no criminal record. The accused had been consuming alcoholic beverages at a downtown pub since 1130 hr.

Incident. On May 11, 1988, at 0240 hr, police observed the accused driving erratically on First Street, downtown Bradley Sound. When police stopped the accused, he was observed to be in an extremely intoxicated state. He refused to cooperate in providing a breath sample. The accused was taken to the station and interviewed.

Psychosocial Assessment Report

Name: Gary Reginald Miller
Case number: 2004-458
Date of admission: July 6, 2004
Date of report: July 24, 2004
Legal documentation: Found guilty of assault (spousal) and sentenced to 90 days plus 18 months probation on June 28, 2004
Parole eligibility date: July 28, 2004
Warrant expiry: March 1, 2006
Date of birth: June 17, 1948 (Vebris Lake, ON, Canada)
Marital status: Married to Bertha (Bertie) Louise Miller
Occupation: Marine laborer
Information sources: Offender, spouse, stepson, brother, Ontario Provincial Police report, Royal Canadian Mounted Police Fingerprint Service, Simcoe Provincial Correctional Institution, Vebris Lake Collegiate
Case historian: Stella Li, MSW

Circumstances Leading to Admission

Mr. Gary Miller, a 56-year-old, married, White man was admitted to the South Ontario Psychiatric Hospital Intake Assessment (SOPHIA) unit on July 6, 2004. He had been charged and subsequently found guilty of assault against his wife of 21 years. He was sentenced by the Port Vebris Provincial Court on June 28, 2004, to 90 days plus 18 months probation. He was detained in the Simcoe Provincial Correctional Institution since that date and was brought to this facility for assessment following repeated disruptive behavior while in the institution. (*PCL–R item 20*)

Current Offense Information

The police report indicates that on March 11, 2004, the victim, 51-year-old Mrs. Bertie Miller, arrived home from work later than usual while

Mr. Miller was at home drinking alcohol and waiting for Mrs. Miller to return home to prepare dinner. Mrs. Miller states that she drank two beers with a female friend before she came home. According to reports from the offender, from Mrs. Miller, and from her son (Mr. Miller's stepson), on her return, a heated argument began, which continued while Mrs. Miller was preparing dinner. Mrs. Miller states that Mr. Miller insulted her cooking skills and complained that she was a "miserable" wife and that he deserved better than a microwave TV dinner. As Mr. Miller turned to go back to watching TV, Mrs. Miller hit him across the back with the metal TV tray that she had in her hands. Mr. Miller then turned around, grabbed the tray, and hit Mrs. Miller with it several times. He also punched her several times. The victim sustained bruising to the head and face requiring four stitches close to the eye. Mrs. Miller called the police, who arrested Mr. Miller at the home. *(PCL–R items 10, 14)*

Mr. Miller remained on bail without incident until he was convicted of assault for the above offense. According to correspondence from the Simcoe Provincial Correctional Institution, Mr. Miller was in a subdued mood on his arrival at the institution, but within 48 hours he began to display agitated and verbally aggressive behavior. He complained of inability to sleep and nausea. He was observed to be restless and often startled without obvious external stimulation. Following a violent altercation with another inmate, Mr. Miller was placed in isolation until transfer to this facility could be arranged. Transfer was delayed for several days because of the Canada Day long weekend. *(PCL–R items 10, 14)*

Family History

The father, Reginald Dyer Miller, was born in 1921 and worked as a farm laborer most of his life. Reginald Miller had a son, the offender's half-brother, from a brief marriage to an English woman while he served overseas in the Canadian Armed Forces. He married the offender's mother in 1948 because of her pregnancy with the offender. They remained married until Reginald Miller's death, although the marriage was a stormy one. The offender and his brother report that Reginald Miller often drank heavily and beat their mother and both boys regularly. He apparently died of natural causes at the age of 46 in 1967. Reports are sketchy, but his death may have been related to liver complaints that he suffered from during the last few years of his life. The offender, who was 18 at the time, did not attend the funeral. According to the offender's brother, this has always been a sore point with his mother, but the offender states that he was "too emotionally upset" to attend.

The mother, Maria Magdalena Miller, age 72, dropped out of school to marry and raise her family. She describes herself as a devout Roman Catholic and believed in keeping the family together despite the repeated beatings they received from the offender's father. After the offender was born, she suffered at least three miscarriages and one stillborn son before having a second healthy child. She did not remarry and now resides with the offender's brother in MacRory, ON, but has had several hospital admissions for failing physical health in the past year.

Younger brother Robert William Miller, age 44, is employed as a nurse in the MacRory District Hospital. His earliest memories of his father include physical beatings, but he also recalls happy times and states that he missed having a father when he was growing up. He drank to excess as a teenager and made two failed attempts at suicide at ages 15 and 17. He reports to be in good physical and mental health for the past 25 years and describes himself as a social drinker. He lives with his long-term partner, John, who also helps care for Magdalena Miller.

Bertha (Bertie) Louise Miller, age 51, married the offender in 1983 at the age of 30 years. She was previously a single mother. She enjoys her work as an office clerk. She describes herself as a social drinker, usually going to a licensed restaurant or to her girlfriends' homes for a few beers on weekend evenings. She met Mr. Miller in the parking lot of a fast food restaurant and was attracted to his car, a 1962 Firebird. She expressed some lasting regret that he lost the car in 1985 for nonpayment of the loan, and since that time his poor credit rating has meant that they have been able only to purchase vehicles in poor condition or to borrow vehicles from friends. Mrs. Miller complains of declining physical health due to the stressful nature of her marriage, but she states that she wants "someone to grow old with." When asked if she was concerned whether Mr. Miller would assault her again in the future, she stated, "I know he will. Just give him time, and he'll be angry about some stupid thing and it'll happen again." She appears resigned to it, regretting only that she no longer has the strength to stand up for herself that she used to have.

Mrs. Miller has one son, Galilee ("Lee") Jackson, age 31. Mr. Miller has no children.

Childhood

Mr. Miller describes himself as a loner since early childhood. He was an only child until the age of 12. The offender states that he never developed a close relationship with his brother and would be irritated by the child's presence. According to his brother, Robert Miller, the mother was kind but not overtly affectionate. Both Mr. Miller and his brother report being repeatedly beaten by their father; Mr. Miller states that he eventually learned to stay out of the way when his father was drinking. Both the offender and his brother deny involvement with child protection services.

Mr. Miller states that all his problems in adolescence date from the birth of his brother. He ran away when his brother was born. He and a friend broke into a cottage, where they stayed for 3 nights until the owners arrived on the weekend. The owners called the police, who took him home, and no charges were laid. During the rest of that summer, he broke into at least five more cottages on his own and stole food, alcohol, and music records. Eventually he was charged with breaking and entering and theft under. The family moved from Vebris Lake into Port Vebris with the result that the offender had easier access to alcohol and drugs and to antisocial peers. During his teenage years, he amassed a number of petty offenses, including trespass, mischief, break and enter, taking auto without consent, theft under, and possession of narcotics, and he served two stints in juvenile detention centers. *(PCL–R items 18, 20)*

Schooling

Mr. Miller began school at the age of 5 and left school during grade 11 at the age of 17 due to lack of interest. His elementary education was uneventful and he was a fair student, but after moving to Port Vebris in Grade 7 and becoming involved in drugs, his performance and attendance dropped off. He states that one Grade 8 teacher picked on him because of his small size and that this encouraged his peers to bully him, which resulted in several fights and two suspensions. He describes his high school education as "irrelevant." In adulthood, however, he completed various practical courses as requirements for his laborer positions and worked toward his high school equivalency diploma on and off, eventually obtaining a marine engineering diploma at the age of 37. *(PCL–R item 12)*

Occupational

Mr. Miller has worked as a marine laborer on a seasonal basis during the past 23 years, except for 2 years during the recession in the early 1990s and in 2002 when he experienced some health problems. He did various unskilled jobs during the off-season until about 7 years ago, when he decided to "slow down," but he still occasionally works for friends and family for cash or beer. In this manner, he has been able to contribute to the household finances more or less consistently. He states that he has always got on well with his bosses and coworkers, who are his drinking buddies. He was fired from one marina halfway through the season, which he blames on one coworker who was "a stupid rich kid from the city" who didn't know anything but was trying to impress the boss and complained about the quality of Mr. Miller's work. The offender is not interested in going back to work after his incarceration, stating, "They'll never accept me now." He also complains that this incarceration is "the bitch's fault" and that she'll have to support him now. *(PCL–R item 16)*

Medical

Mr. Miller reports no awareness of pregnancy difficulties and states that he was "about average" weight when he was born, with no major childhood injuries. He reports spending a few weeks in a sanatorium for tuberculosis at the age of 6 in 1953, but he recovered without complications. By all reports, he was small for his age after this illness. He reports "some" blackout episodes from alcohol and drug use as a teenager. He was diagnosed with a degenerative spinal disorder after an episode of severe pain, for which he was hospitalized for 3 days in 2002 and remained off work for several months. The pain is now managed with anti-inflammatory and analgesic medications.

Psychiatric

This is the offender's first admission to a psychiatric facility. He denies any prior psychiatric problems, although he admits to being "screwed up" as a teenager. Upon admission to the SOPHIA unit, Mr. Miller displayed agitation and restless behavior and repeatedly and loudly demanded to be released and to have his cigarettes returned. Results of psychiatric testing by Dr. See, which can be found in her report dated July 10, 2004, indicated a diagnosis of alcohol dependence; personality disorder with antisocial features; and possible substance-induced psychosis, in remission. Mrs. Miller reports that the offender has made threats to kill himself in the past. He purchased a revolver that he showed to her on at least three occasions, stating that he planned to "end it all." In our interview, however, and in psychiatric testing, Mr. Miller denied any suicidal thoughts or despondent mood. (PCL–R items 3, 5)

Substance Use

Mr. Miller states that he first consumed alcohol when he broke into the cottage with his friend at 12 years of age and drank from a liquor bottle. He continued to drink small amounts of liquor when breaking into cottages and with his new acquaintances in Grade 7. He continued to drink beer and liquor as a teenager and claims that he could "handle half a Mickey no problem" at the age of 16, which would gain him some status among his peers. Currently his preferred drink is beer, of which he consumes two to six bottles on a daily basis, together with whiskey on weekends. He also began smoking marijuana at the age of 14 or 15 and declined to comment on his current use of this or other illicit substances except to describe himself as a "social smoker." He also states that he began smoking cigarettes at age 12, at first by stealing from his father's unattended packs, and currently he and his wife smoke a carton per week between the two of them. He experienced great difficulty with the smoke-free policy at this facility, despite receiving nicotine patches and purchasing his own nicotine gum. Although police records indicate that Mr. Miller was intoxicated at the time of the index assault,

Mrs. Miller described this to me as being unusual, stating that "he hadn't been that drunk in a long time."

Criminal History

Consistent with Mr. Miller's statements, records indicate that Mr. Miller began engaging in breaking and entering and petty theft, and received his first criminal charges, at the age of 12. He was convicted and sentenced to community service. His first custodial sentences were served at juvenile detention centers, the first (14 days) for taking auto without consent, driving while impaired, and failure to remain at the scene of an accident, at the age of 15, and the second (2 months) for 12 counts of break and enter at the age of 17. *(PCL–R item 20)*

Mr. Miller was charged with possession of stolen property and possession of a narcotic in 1972 and again with possession in 1974. All charges were withdrawn. More recently, he has two convictions for impaired driving, one in 1988 and one in 1999, and he served 1 month for each in the Bradley Jail. In September 2000, the offender was convicted of assault after threatening his wife with a beer bottle and received 6 months probation. While on probation, he was charged with assault after pushing and punching his wife's friend, and he was subsequently convicted of the lesser charge of failure to comply and received 18 months probation. *(PCL–R items 19, 20)*

Adult Relationships and Sexual History

Mr. Miller states that he reached puberty later than many of his peers and that his small physical stature was a source of teasing and bullying by his peers until he was about 15. He states that he had his first girlfriend when he was 16, but she did not want to have sexual intercourse. His earliest sexual intercourse was at age 17, at a house party, with a girl he knew from school. In his late teens and early 20s, he had two or three heterosexual relationships that he called serious, but he also had sex with other women at house parties during that time. He describes the other women as usually consuming alcohol and very interested in sex with him. He states that on one occasion, he was beaten up by the boyfriend of a young woman he had had sex with; apparently she claimed that he had raped her, but the offender believes that was just an excuse she made to her boyfriend. At age 28, he moved in with a woman 5 years his junior who was an office worker at the marina. This relationship lasted for 6 years, ending when he moved in with his current wife. Mrs. Miller describes having a violent argument with this girlfriend, who came to her home to confront her about sleeping with the offender while he was still living with the girlfriend. Mrs. Miller is of the opinion that, caught in a deception, Mr. Miller moved in with her to avoid having to face the girlfriend himself. *(PCL–R item 11)*

Mr. Miller describes his marriage as "good" and states that fighting a lot is what keeps them together. He states that they have had a good arrangement, as he brings in the money and she takes care of the cooking and cleaning. He states that her full-time employment is so that she can have money for beer and bingo. He admits that he has not always been sexually faithful to her, but he states that he is "slowing down" and that if his wife really minded that much, then she would leave him. *(PCL–R items 7, 11, 16)*

Interviewer's Impressions

I spoke with Mr. Miller briefly the day he was admitted to the SOPHIA unit and for 3 hours 1 week later. The first interview was terminated because of his disinterest and verbal aggression. During the second interview, he was calm and keen to co-operate in order to facilitate his discharge. He presented as an unkempt, moderately overweight, and balding man who made jocular conversation and vague attempts at flirtatious behavior (e.g., calling me "darlin'" and commenting on my attire) at the onset of the interview. He answered all my questions and elaborated without prompting, occasionally having to be brought back to the topic in question and reminded of the serious nature of his incarceration. He stated that he preferred the unit to the jail. He expressed concern and irritation about the no-smoking policy on the unit but seemed pleased that nicotine substitutes were readily available. He stated that "the inmates" are more accepting of him here than at the jail, and he likes having the option to participate in work or recreation activities if he feels like it or just to watch TV. He asked me to recommend that he remain at the unit until he has completed one third of his sentence, at which point he feels he will be ready to "make a fresh start in the community." When asked what programs he plans to take advantage of while at the unit, he identified bingo and movie nights. *(PCL–R items 1, 5, 7)*

With respect to his childhood, he stated that he had a normal childhood and a close family. He described his father, however, as a "useless bastard" but was not able to describe his character further, giving only a list of the various items his father had used to beat him when he was drunk (belts, a rake, a rotten plank, a two-hole punch). He did not seem to bear ill will toward his father or to blame his childhood for his adolescent and adult criminal activity. He described his mother as "a saint" but was unable to elaborate on his feelings for her. He does not like to visit her often because, according to Mr. Miller, his brother lectures him about his smoking and objects to the derogatory terms Mr. Miller habitually uses to refer to his brother's partner.

As stated above, he reported having a good relationship with his wife, although she has also been physically violent to him in the past. He believes the fact that her violent behavior has been relatively minor and infrequent shows that she is acknowledging that he is right. With respect to his own violent behavior, he acknowledges that he "went a bit overboard." (*PCL–R items 6, 8, 10*)

(See Table E.4 for Gary Miller's DVRAG score sheet.)

TABLE E.4
Domestic Violence Risk Appraisal Guide (Hilton, Harris, Rice, Houghton, & Eke, 2008). Score Sheet for Gary Miller, With Explanations

Item	Possible scores	Score	Reason
1. Number of Prior domestic incidents	0 = –1 1 = 0 ≥ 2 = +5	0	Police occurrence 01-036475, Domestic assault
2. Number of Prior non-domestic incidents	0 = –1 ≥ 1 = +5	+5	Police occurrence 01-0204594 indicates that he assaulted acquaintance Karen Chapman
3. Prior custodial sentence of 30 days or more	No = –1 Yes = +2	+2	Police occurrences 01-0621351 and 01-0549873 cite prior sentences of 30 and 90 days for impaired driving
4. Failure on prior con-ditional release	No = –1 Yes = +2	+2	Police occurrence 01-0204594 took place while he was on probation for a prior domestic assault (and he was charged with breach)
5. Threat to harm or kill at the index assault	No = 0 Yes = +1	0	No evidence of threat in police occurrence report
6. Confinement of the partner at the index assault	No = 0 Yes = +1	0	Police report states, "Victim was able to leave."
7. Victim concern	No = 0 Yes = +2	+2	In the interview for psychosocial report, the victim stated, "I know he will."
8. Number of children	≤ 1 = –1 ≥ 2 = +1	–1	Police occurrence 01-036475 states, "The couple do not have joint children," and psychosocial report states, "Mrs. Miller has one son. . . . Mr. Miller has no children."
9. Victim's biological children from a pre-vious partner	0 = –1 1 = 0 ≥2 = +2	0	Psychosocial report states, "Mrs. Miller has one son."
10. Violence against others	No = 0 Yes = +8	+8	Same as for Prior Nondomestic Incident

TABLE E.4
Domestic Violence Risk Appraisal Guide (Hilton, Harris, Rice, Houghton, & Eke, 2008). Score Sheet for Gary Miller, With Explanations   *(Continued)*

Item	Possible scores	Score	Reason
11. Substance abuse score	$\leq 1 = -2$ $\geq 2 = +2$	+2	Police occurrence 01-0101458 states, "The accused had been drinking alcoholic beverages." Psychosocial report indicates he noticeably increased his alcohol abuse (the victim reported, "He hadn't been that drunk in a long time"). Police occurrences 01-0621351 and 01-0549873 show prior impaired driving, indicating he consumed alcohol before or during a prior criminal offense and has engaged in alcohol use resulting in problems. Psychosocial report shows offenses, including possession of narcotics, indicating drug problem.
12. Assault on victim when pregnant	No = 0 Yes = +5	0	Police report 01-036475 states the victim reported that "he has never attempted to . . . attack her while pregnant."
13. Number of barriers to victim support	$0 = -1$ $1 = 0$ $\geq 2 = +4$	0	Police report 01-0101458 states, "The victim had been consuming alcoholic beverages."
14. Psychopathy Checklist—Revised score (full scoring criteria available in R. D. Hare, 2003)	$\leq 9 = -1$ $10–16 = +1$ $\geq 17 = +6$	+6	PCL–R score is higher than 17 based on information available in the psychosocial report and other documents.

Total score: 26
Percentile: > 97

Note. For scoring criteria, see Appendix C, this volume.

APPENDIX F: GRAPHICAL AIDS FOR THE STATISTICAL INTERPRETATION OF THE ONTARIO DOMESTIC ASSAULT RISK ASSESSMENT (ODARA)

0 According to the client's responses and the available information in the perpetrator's records, the perpetrator scores 0 on the ODARA. This score represents the lowest of seven risk categories. One out of 10 known wife assaulters scores 0.

1 According to the client's responses and the available information in the perpetrator's records, the perpetrator scores 1 on the ODARA. This score represents the second lowest of seven risk categories. One quarter of known wife assaulters scores 1 or lower.

2 According to the client's responses and the available information in the perpetrator's records, the perpetrator scores 2 on the ODARA. Half of known wife assaulters score 2 or lower.

3 According to the client's responses and the available information in the perpetrator's records, the perpetrator scores 3 on the ODARA. Seven out of 10 known wife assaulters score 3 or lower.

4 According to the client's responses and the available information in the perpetrator's records, the perpetrator scores 4 on the ODARA. Eight out of 10 known wife assaulters score 4 or lower.

5-6 According to the client's responses and the available information in the perpetrator's records, the perpetrator scores 5 (or 6) on the ODARA. This score represents the second highest of seven risk categories. Nine out of 10 known wife assaulters score 6 or lower.

7-13 According to the client's responses and the available information in the perpetrator's records, the perpetrator scores 7 (or higher) on the ODARA. This score represents the highest of seven risk categories. Fewer than 1 of 10 known wife assaulters score in this category.

Figure F.1. How does the perpetrator rank among wife assaulters?

ODARA score = 0: 7% of such wife assaulters commit another assault against their partner (or, in some cases, a future partner) that comes to the attention of the police within an average of about 5 years.

 ODARA score = 1: 17% of such wife assaulters commit another assault against their partner (or, in some cases, a future partner) that comes to the attention of the police within an average of about 5 years

 ODARA score = 2: 22% of such wife assaulters commit another assault against their partner (or, in some cases, a future partner) that comes to the attention of the police within an average of about 5 years

 ODARA score = 3: 34% of such wife assaulters commit another assault against their partner (or, in some cases, a future partner) that comes to the attention of the police within an average of about 5 years

 ODARA score = 4: 39% of such wife assaulters commit another assault against their partner (or, in some cases, a future partner) that comes to the attention of the police within an average of about 5 years

 ODARA score = 5–6: 53% of such wife assaulters commit another assault against their partner (or, in some cases, a future partner) that comes to the attention of the police within an average of about 5 years

 ODARA score = 7–13: 74% of such wife assaulters commit another assault against their partner (or, in some cases, a future partner) that comes to the attention of the police within an average of about 5 years

Figure F.2. How likely is the perpetrator to assault a female domestic partner again?

REFERENCES

Ægisdóttir, S., White, M. J., Spengler, P. M., Maugherman, A. S., Anderson, L. A., Cook, R. S., et al. (2006). The meta-analysis of clinical judgment project: Fifty-six years of accumulated research on clinical versus statistical prediction. *Counseling Psychologist, 34,* 341–382.

Andrews, D., & Bonta, J. (2001). *LSI–R user's manual.* Toronto, Ontario, Canada: Multi-Health Systems.

Andrews, D., & Bonta, J. (2006). *The psychology of criminal conduct* (4th ed.). Cincinnati, OH: Anderson Publishing.

Andrews, D. A., Bonta, J., & Wormith, J. S. (2006). The recent past and near future of risk and/or need assessment. *Crime & Delinquency, 52,* 7–27.

Andrews, D. A., & Dowden, C. (2006). Risk principle of case classification in correctional treatment. *International Journal of Offender Therapy and Comparative Criminology, 50,* 88–100.

Andrews, D. A., Zinger, I., Hoge, R. D., Bonta, J., Gendreau, P., & Cullen, F. T. (1990). Does correctional treatment work? A clinically relevant and psychologically informed meta-analysis. *Criminology, 28,* 369–404.

Apsler, R., Cummins, M. R., & Carl, S. (2003). Perceptions of the police by female victims of domestic partner violence. *Violence Against Women, 9,* 1318–1335.

Archer, J. (2000). Sex differences in aggression between heterosexual partners: A meta-analytic review. *Psychological Bulletin, 126,* 651–680.

Babcock, J. C., Green, C. E., & Robie, C. (2004). Does batterers' treatment work? A meta-analytic review of domestic violence treatment. *Clinical Psychology Review, 23,* 1023–1053.

Baldwin, L. (Chair). (1999). *Working toward a seamless community and justice response to domestic violence: A five year plan for Ontario.* Unpublished report to the Attorney General of Ontario by the Joint Committee on Domestic Violence, Toronto, Ontario, Canada.

Barbaree, H. E. (2005). Psychopathy, treatment behavior, and recidivism: An extended follow-up of Seto and Barbaree. *Journal of Interpersonal Violence, 20,* 1115–1131.

Belfrage, H. (2008). Police-based structured spousal violence risk assessment: The process of developing a police version of the SARA. In A. C. Baldry & F. W. Winkel (Eds.), *Intimate partner violence prevention and intervention: The risk assessment and management approach* (pp. 33–44). New York: Nova Science.

Berk, R. (2007). Statistical inference and meta-analysis. *Journal of Experimental Criminology, 3,* 247–270.

Berk, R. A., Campbell, A., Klap, R., & Western, B. (1992). A Bayesian analysis of the Colorado Springs spouse abuse experiment. *Journal of Criminal Law and Criminology, 83,* 170–200.

Blair, P. R., Marcus, D. K., & Boccaccini, M. T. (2008). Is there an allegiance effect for assessment instruments? Actuarial risk assessment as an exemplar. *Clinical Psychology: Science and Practice, 15,* 346–360.

Blais, E., & Dupont, B. (2005). Assessing the capability of intensive police programmes to prevent severe road accidents. *British Journal of Criminology, 45,* 914–937.

Boase, P., Jonah, B. A., & Dawson, N. (2004). Occupant restraint use in Canada. *Journal of Safety Research, 35,* 223–229.

Boles, A. B., & Patterson, J. C. (1997). *Improving community response to crime victims.* Thousand Oaks, CA: Sage.

Bonta, J., & Andrews, D. A. (2007). *Risk–need–responsivity model for offender assessment and rehabilitation.* Ottawa, Ontario, Canada: Public Safety Canada. Retrieved February 12, 2009, from http://www.publicsafety.gc.ca/res/cor/rep/_fl/Risk_Need_2007-06_e.pdf

Bonta, J., Law, M., & Hanson, K. (1998). The prediction of criminal and violent recidivism among mentally disordered offenders: A meta-analysis. *Psychological Bulletin, 123,* 123–142.

Brantingham, P., & Brantingham, P. (1984). *Patterns in crime.* New York: Macmillan.

Brown, D. (2001). Turning domestic violence into a religion: Inquest on epic social debate. *The Ottawa Citizen—Online.* Retrieved February 12, 2009, from http://www.fact.on.ca/news/news0112/oc011207.htm

Brownridge, D. A. (2006). Partner violence against women with disabilities: Prevalence, risk, and explanations. *Violence Against Women, 12,* 805–822.

Bryant, G. D., & Norman, G. R. (1980). Expressions of probability words and numbers. *New England Journal of Medicine, 302,* 411.

Bureau of Justice Statistics. (2005). *Crime and victims statistics.* Retrieved February 12, 2009, from http://www.ojp.usdoj.gov/bjs/cvict.htm

Buzawa, E. S., & Buzawa, C. G. (2003). *Domestic violence: The criminal justice response* (3rd ed.). Thousand Oaks, CA: Sage.

Bybee, D., & Sullivan, C. M. (2005). Predicting re-victimization of battered women 3 years after exiting a shelter program. *American Journal of Community Psychology, 36,* 85–96.

Byrne, C. A., Kilpatrick, D. G., Howley, S. S., & Beatty, D. (1999). Female victims of partner versus nonpartner violence. *Criminal Justice and Behavior, 26,* 275–292.

Campbell, J. C. (1986). Nursing assessment for risk of homicide with battered women. *Advances in Nursing Science, 8,* 36–51.

Campbell, J. C. (2004). Helping women understand their risk in situations of intimate partner violence. *Journal of Interpersonal Violence, 19,* 1464–1477.

Campbell, J. C. (2007). Prediction of homicide of and by battered women. In J. C. Campbell (Ed.), *Assessing dangerousness* (pp. 85–104). New York: Springer.

Campbell, J. C., Glass, N., Sharps, P. W., Laughon, K., & Bloom, T. (2007). Intimate partner homicide. *Trauma, Violence, & Abuse, 8,* 246–269.

Campbell, J. C., Webster, D., Koziol-McLain, J., Block, C. R., Campbell, D., Curry, M. A., et al. (2003). Assessing risk factors for intimate partner homicide. *National Institute of Justice Journal, 250,* 14–19.

Campbell, M. A., French, S., & Gendreau, P. (in press). The prediction of violence in adult offenders: A meta-analytic comparison of instruments and methods of assessment. *Criminal Justice and Behavior.*

Capaldi, D. M., & Crosby, L. (1997). Observed and reported psychological and physical aggression in young, at-risk couples. *Social Development, 6,* 184–206.

Capaldi, D. M., & Kim, H. K. (2007). Typological approaches to violence in couples: A critique and alternative conceptual approach. *Clinical Psychology Review, 27,* 253–265.

Carter, A. M., & Hilton, N. Z. (2007, June). *Using non-numerical descriptors of violence risk: Low, moderate, or high risk?* Poster presented at the Seventh Annual Conference of the International Association of Forensic Mental Health Services, Montreal, Quebec, Canada.

Cattaneo, L. B. (2007). Contributors to assessments of risk in intimate partner violence: How victims and professionals differ. *Journal of Community Psychology, 35,* 57–75.

Cattaneo, L. B., & Goodman, L. A. (2003). Victim-reported risk factors for continued abusive behavior: Assessing the dangerousness of arrested batterers. *Journal of Community Psychology, 31,* 349–369.

Cattaneo, L. B., & Goodman, L. A. (2005). Risk factors for reabuse in intimate partner violence. *Trauma, Violence, & Abuse, 6,* 141–175.

Cercone, J. J., Beach S. R., & Arias, H. (2005). Gender symmetry in dating intimate partner violence: Does similar behavior imply similar constructs? *Violence and Victims, 20,* 207–218.

Chen, G., & Warburton, R. N. (2006). Do speed cameras produce net benefits? Evidence from British Columbia, Canada. *Journal of Policy Analysis and Management, 25,* 661–678.

Cohen, J. (1992). A power primer. *Psychological Bulletin, 112,* 155–159.

Cohen, M. M., Forte, T., DuMont, J., Hyman, I., & Romans, S. (2005). Intimate partner violence among Canadian women with activity limitations. *Journal of Epidemiology and Community Health, 59,* 834–839.

Coker, A. L., Smith, P. H., & Fadden, M. K. (2005). Intimate partner violence and disabilities among women attending family practice clinics. *Journal of Women's Health, 14,* 829–838.

Coohey, C. (2007). The relationship between mothers' social networks and severe domestic violence: A test of the social isolation hypothesis. *Violence and Victims, 22,* 503–512.

Cooke, D. J., Wozniak, E., & Johnstone, L. (2008). Casting light on prison violence in Scotland: Evaluating the impact of situational risk factors. *Criminal Justice and Behavior, 35,* 1065–1078.

Cornelius, W. A., & Rosenblum, M. R. (2005). Immigration and politics. *Annual Review of Political Science, 8*, 99–119.

Correctional Service of Canada. (2006). *The Aboriginal offenders—Overview*. Retrieved February 12, 2009, from http://csc-scc.gc.ca/text/prgrm/abinit/know/7_e.shtml

Corrections and Conditional Release Act of 1992, Section 233, SC 1992, c20. Retrieved February 12, 2009, from http://www.canadianprisonlaw.com/ccra/frontpage.htm

Cross, P. (2002). *The Hadley inquest: Commentary*. Toronto, Ontario, Canada: Ontario Women's Justice Network. Retrieved October 25, 2007, from http://www.owjn.org/issues/w-abuse/hadley.htm

Dalton, B. (2007). What's going on out there? A survey of batterer intervention programs. *Journal of Aggression, Maltreatment & Trauma, 15*, 59–74.

Dawes, R. M. (2005). The ethical implications of Paul Meehl's work on comparing clinical versus actuarial prediction methods. *Journal of Clinical Psychology, 61*, 1245–1255.

Dawes, R. M., Faust, D., & Meehl, P. E. (1989, March 31). Clinical versus actuarial judgment. *Science, 243*, 1668–1674.

Dobash, R. E., & Dobash, R. (1979). *Violence against wives*. New York: Free Press.

Doob, A. N. (2006). *Understanding pretrial remand*. Paper presented at the Biannual Conference of the Ontario Ministry of Correctional Services and Community Safety, PESAR, and Nippising University, North Bay, Ontario, Canada.

Dopson, S., Locock, L., Gabbay, J., Ferlie, E., & Fitzgerald, L. (2003). Evidence-based medicine and the implementation gap. *Health: An Interdisciplinary Journal for the Social Study of Health, Illness and Medicine, 7*, 311–330.

Douglas, K. S., & Ogloff, J. R. P. (2003). Multiple facets of risk for violence: The impact of judgmental specificity on structured decisions about violence risk. *International Journal of Forensic Mental Health, 2*, 19–34.

Douglas, K. S., Ogloff, J. R., & Hart, S. D. (2003). Evaluation of a model of violence risk assessment among forensic psychiatric patients. *Psychiatric Services, 54*, 1372–1379.

Douglas, K. S., Ogloff, J. R. P., Nicholls, T. L., & Grant, I. (1999). Assessing risk for violence among psychiatric patients: The HCR–20 Violence Risk Assessment Scheme and the Psychopathy Checklist: Screening Version. *Journal of Consulting and Clinical Psychiatry, 67*, 917–930.

Douglas, K. S., & Skeem, J. L. (2005). Violence risk assessment: Getting specific about being dynamic. *Psychology, Public Policy, and Law, 11*, 347–383.

Douglas, K. S., Yeomans, M., & Boer, D. P. (2005). Comparative validity analysis of multiple measures of violence risk in a sample of criminal offenders. *Criminal Justice and Behavior, 32*, 479–510.

Dunford, F. W., Huizinga, D., & Elliott, D. S. (1990). The role of arrest in domestic assault: The Omaha police experiment. *Criminology, 28*, 183–206.

Dunford-Jackson, B. L. (2004). The role of family courts in domestic violence: The U.S. experience. In P. D. Jaffe, L. L. Baker, & A. J. Cunningham (Eds.), *Protecting children from domestic violence: Strategies for community intervention* (pp. 188–199). New York: Guilford Press.

Dutton, D. G. (1988). *The domestic assault of women*. Boston: Allyn & Bacon.

Dutton, D. G., & Corvo, K. (2006). Transforming a flawed policy: A call to revive psychology and science in domestic violence research and practice. *Aggression and Violent Behavior, 11*, 457–483.

Dutton, D. G., & Corvo, K. (2007). The Duluth model: A data-impervious paradigm and a failed strategy. *Aggression and Violent Behavior, 12*, 658–667.

Dutton, D. G., & Nicholls, T. L. (2005). The gender paradigm in domestic violence research and theory: Part I—The conflict theory and data. *Aggression and Violent Behavior, 10*, 680–714.

Dvoskin, J. A., & Heilbrun, K. (2001). Risk assessment and release decision-making: Toward resolving the great debate. *Journal of the American Academy of Psychiatry and Law, 29*, 6–10.

Eckhardt, C. I., Murphy, C., Black, D., & Suhr, L. (2006). Intervention programs for perpetrators of intimate partner violence: Conclusions from a clinical research perspective. *Public Health Reports, 121*, 369–381.

Edens, J. F., Marcus, D. K., Lilienfeld, S. C., & Poythress, N. G. (2006). Psychopathic, not psychopath: Taxometric evidence for the dimensional structure of psychopathy. *Journal of Abnormal Psychology, 115*, 131–144.

Edleson, J. L., Gassman-Pines, J., & Hill, M. B. (2006). Defining child exposure to domestic violence as neglect: Minnesota's difficult experience. *Social Work, 51*, 167–174.

Ehrensaft, M. K., Cohen, P., Brown, J., Smailes, E., Chen, H., & Johnson, J. C. (2003). Intergenerational transmission of partner violence: A 20-year prospective study. *Journal of Consulting and Clinical Psychology, 71*, 741–753.

Eke, A., Hilton, N. Z., Harris, G. T., Rice, M. E., & Houghton, R. (2008). *Intimate partner homicide: Prospects for prediction*. Manuscript submitted for publication.

Elbogen, E. B., Huss, M. T., Tomkins, A. J., & Scalora, M. J. (2005). Clinical decision making about psychopathy and violence risk assessment in public sector mental health settings. *Psychological Services, 2*, 133–141.

Esses, V. M., & Webster, C. D. (1988). Physical attractiveness, dangerousness, and the Canadian Criminal Code. *Journal of Applied Social Psychology, 18*, 1017–1031.

FACT Ontario. (2000). *Timeline of events around the murder–suicide of Gillian and Ralph Hadley*. Retrieved February 12, 2009, from http://fact.on.ca/hadley/timeline.htm

Fals-Stewart, W., Leonard, K. E., & Birchler, G. R. (2005). The occurrence of male-to-female intimate partner violence on days of men's drinking: The moderating effects of antisocial personality disorder. *Journal of Consulting and Clinical Psychology, 73*, 239–248.

Farrington, D. P. (1985). Predicting self-reported and official delinquency. In D. P. Farrington & R. Tarling (Eds.), *Prediction in criminology* (pp. 150–173). New York: State University of New York Press.

Farrington, D. P. (2002). *What has been learned from self-reports about criminal careers and the causes of offending?* Retrieved February 12, 2009, from http://www. homeoffice.gov.uk/rds/pdfs/farrington.pdf

Feder, L., & Wilson, D. B. (2005). A meta-analytic review of court-mandated batterer intervention programs: Can courts affect abusers' behavior? *Journal of Experimental Criminology, 1*, 239–262.

Ford, D. A., & Regoli, M. J. (1993). The criminal prosecution of wife assaulters: Process, problems, and effects. In N. Z. Hilton (Ed.), *Legal responses to wife assault* (pp. 127–164). Newbury Park, CA: Sage.

Freeman, N. J., & Sandler, J. C. (2008). Female and male sex offenders: A comparison of recidivism patterns and risk factors. *Journal of Interpersonal Violence, 23*, 1394–1413.

Gendreau, P., & Smith, P. (2007). Influencing the "people who count": Some perspectives on the reporting of meta-analytic results for prediction and treatment outcomes with offenders. *Criminal Justice and Behavior, 34*, 1536–1559.

Gigerenzer, G. (2008). Why heuristics work. *Perspectives on Psychological Science, 3*, 20–29.

Gladwell, M. (2005). *Blink: The power of thinking without thinking.* London: Little, Brown.

Gondolf, E. W., & Deemer, C. (2004). Phoning logistics in a longitudinal follow-up of batterers and their partners. *Journal of Interpersonal Violence, 19*, 747–765.

Gondolf, E. W., & Heckert, D. A. (2003). Determinants of women's perceptions of risk in battering relationships. *Violence and Victims, 18*, 371–386.

Gondolf, E. W., & Wernik, H. (2008). Clinician ratings of batterer treatment behaviors in predicting reassault. *Journal of Interpersonal Violence.* doi:10.1177/0886260508325493

Goodman, G. S., Ghetti, S., Quas, J. A., Edelstein, R. S., Alexander, K. W., Redlich, A. D., et al. (2003). A prospective study of memory for child sexual abuse: New findings relevant to the repressed-memory controversy. *Psychological Science, 14*, 113–118.

Goodman, L. A., Dutton, M. A., & Bennett, L. (2000). Predicting repeat abuse among arrested batterers. *Journal of Interpersonal Violence, 15*, 63–74.

Graham-Kevan, N., & Archer, J. (2003). Physical aggression and control in heterosexual relationships: The effect of sampling. *Violence and Victims, 18*, 181–196.

Grann, M., & Pallvik, A. (2002). An empirical investigation of written risk communication in forensic psychiatric evaluations. *Psychology, Crime & Law, 8*, 113–130.

Grann, M., & Wedin, I. (2002). Risk factors for recidivism among spousal assault and spousal homicide offenders. *Psychology, Crime & Law, 8*, 5–23.

Green, A. G., & Green, D. (2004). The goals of Canada's immigration policy: A historical perspective. *Canadian Journal of Urban Research, 13*, 102–139.

Green, L. W., Orleans, C. T., Ottoson, J. M., Cameron, R., Pierce, J. P., & Bettinghaus, E. P. (2006). Inferring strategies for disseminating physical activity policies, programs, and practices from the successes of tobacco control. *American Journal of Preventive Medicine, 31*, 81.

Greenhalgh, T., Robert, G., Macfarlane, F., Bate, P., & Kyriakidou, O. (2004). Diffusion of innovations in service organizations: Systematic review and recommendations. *Milbank Quarterly, 82*, 581–629.

Grove, W. M. (2005). Clinical versus statistical prediction: The contribution of Paul E. Meehl. *Journal of Clinical Psychology, 61*, 1233–1243.

Grove, W. M., & Meehl, P. E. (1996). Comparative efficiency of informal (subjective, impressionistic) and formal (mechanical, algorithmic) prediction procedures: The clinical–statistical controversy. *Psychology, Public Policy, and Law, 2*, 293–323.

Grove, W. M., Zald, D. H., Lebow, B. S., Snitz, B. E., & Nelson, C. (2000). Clinical versus mechanical prediction: A meta-analysis. *Psychological Assessment, 12*, 19–30.

Gurmankin, A. D., Baron, J., & Armstrong, K. (2004). The effect of numerical statements of risk on trust and comfort with hypothetical physician risk communication. *Medical Decision Making*, 265–271.

Hammond, D., Fong, G. T., Zanna, M. P., Thrasher, J. F., & Borland, R. (2006). Tobacco denormalization and industry beliefs among smokers from four countries. *American Journal of Preventive Medicine, 31*, 225–231.

Hanson, R. K., & Bussière, M. T. (1998). Predicting relapse: A meta-analysis of sexual offender recidivism studies. *Journal of Consulting and Clinical Psychology, 66*, 348–362.

Hanson, R. K., Helmus, L., & Bourgon, G. (2007). *The validity of risk assessments for intimate partner violence: A meta-analysis* (Report No. 2007-07). Ottawa, Ontario, Canada: Public Safety Canada.

Hanson, R. K., & Morton-Bourgon, K. E. (2005). The characteristics of persistent sexual offenders: A meta-analysis of recidivism studies. *Journal of Consulting and Clinical Psychology, 73*, 1154–1163.

Hanson, R. K., & Morton-Bourgon, K. E. (2009). The accuracy of recidivism risk assessments for sexual offenders: A meta-analysis. *Psychological Assessment, 21*, 1–21.

Hanson, R. K., & Wallace-Capretta, S. (2004). Predictors of criminal recidivism among male batterers. *Psychology, Crime & Law, 10*, 413–427.

Hardesty, J. L., & Campbell, J. C. (2004). Safety planning for abused women and their children. In P. D. Jaffe, L. L. Baker, & A. J. Cunningham (Eds.), *Protecting children from domestic violence: Strategies for community intervention* (pp. 89–100). New York: Guilford Press.

Hare, R. D. (1991). *Psychopathy Checklist—Revised: Manual*. Toronto, Ontario, Canada: Multi-Health Systems.

Hare, R. D. (2003). *Hare Psychopathy Checklist—Revised (PCL–R)* (2nd ed.). Toronto, Ontario, Canada: Multi-Health Systems.

Hare, S. C. (2006). What do battered women want? Victims' opinions on prosecution. *Violence and Victims, 21*, 611–628.

Harris, G. T., & Hilton, N. Z. (2001). Interpreting moderate effects in interpersonal violence. *Journal of Interpersonal Violence, 16*, 1094–1098.

Harris, G. T., Hilton, N. Z., Rice, M. E., & Eke, A. W. (2007). Children killed by genetic versus step-parents. *Evolution and Human Behavior, 28*, 85–95.

Harris, G. T., & Rice, M. E. (2003). Actuarial assessment of risk among sex offenders. *Annals of the New York Academy of Science, 989*, 198–210.

Harris, G. T., & Rice, M. E. (2006). Treatment of psychopathy: A review of empirical findings. In C. Patrick (Ed.), *The handbook of psychopathy* (pp. 555–572). New York: Guilford Press.

Harris, G. T., & Rice, M. E. (2007). Characterizing the value of actuarial violence risk assessment. *Criminal Justice and Behavior, 34*, 1638–1658.

Harris, G. T., Rice, M. E., & Cormier, C. A. (2002). Prospective replication of the Violence Risk Appraisal Guide in predicting violent recidivism among forensic patients. *Law and Human Behavior, 26*, 377–394.

Harris, G. T., Rice, M. E., Hilton, N. Z., Lalumière, M. L., & Quinsey, V. L. (2007). Coercive and precocious sexuality as a fundamental aspect of psychopathy. *Journal of Personality Disorders, 21*, 1–27.

Harris, G. T., Rice, M. E., & Quinsey, V. L. (1993). Violent recidivism of mentally disordered offenders. *Criminal Justice and Behavior, 20*, 315–335.

Harris, G. T., Rice, M. E., & Quinsey, V. L. (1994). Psychopathy as a taxon: Evidence that psychopaths are a discrete class. *Journal of Consulting and Clinical Psychology, 62*, 387–397.

Harris, G. T., Rice, M. E., Quinsey, V. L., Lalumière, M. L., Boer, D., & Lang, C. (2003). A multi-site comparison of actuarial risk instruments for sex offenders. *Psychological Assessment, 15*, 413–425.

Harris, G. T., Skilling, T. A., & Rice, M. E. (2001). The construct of psychopathy. *Crime and Justice, 28*, 197–264.

Hart, S. D., Cox, D. N., & Hare, R. D. (1995). *The Hare PCL:SV: Psychopathy Checklist: Screening Version.* Toronto, Ontario, Canada: Multi-Health Systems.

Hart, S. D., Michie, C., & Cooke, D. J. (2007). Precision of actuarial risk assessment instruments. *British Journal of Psychiatry, 190*, 60–65.

Harvey, A. B. (1944). *Treemar's annotated criminal code Canada* (5th ed.). Toronto, Ontario, Canada: Burroughs.

Haslam, N. (2003). The dimensional view of personality disorders: A review of the taxometric evidence. *Clinical Psychology Review, 23*, 75–93.

Hawthorne, L. (2005). "Picking winners": The recent transformation of Australia's skilled migration policy. *International Migration Review, 39*, 663–696.

Heckert, D. A., & Gondolf, E. W. (2004). Battered women's perceptions of risk versus risk factors and instruments in predicting repeat reassault. *Journal of Interpersonal Violence, 19*, 778–800.

Heilbrun, K. (1997). Prediction versus management models relevant to risk assessment: The importance of legal decision-making context. *Law and Human Behavior, 21*, 347–360.

Heilbrun, K., Dvoskin, J., Hart, S., & McNiel, D. (1999). Violence risk communication: Implications for research, policy, and practice. *Health, Risk and Society, 1*, 91–106.

Heilbrun, K., O'Neill, M. L., Stevens, T. N., Strohman, L. K., Bowman, Q., & Yi-Wen, L. (2004). Assessing normative approaches to communicating violence risk: A national survey of psychologists. *Behavioral Sciences and the Law, 22*, 187–196.

Heilbrun, K., O'Neill, M. L., Strohman, L. K., Bowman, Q., & Philipson, J. (2000). Expert approaches to communicating violence risk. *Law and Human Behavior, 24*, 137–148.

Heilbrun, K., Philipson, J., Berman, L., & Warren, J. (1999). Risk communication: Clinicians' reported approaches and perceived values. *Journal of the American Academy of Psychiatry and Law, 27*, 397–406.

Hendricks, B., Werner, T., Shipway, L., & Turinetti, G. J. (2006). Recidivism among spousal abusers: Predictions and program evaluation. *Journal of Interpersonal Violence, 21*, 703–716.

Henning, K., & Feder, L. (2004). A comparison of men and women arrested for domestic violence: Who presents the greater threat? *Journal of Family Violence, 19*, 69–80.

Hiebert, D. (2006). Winning, losing, and still playing the game: The political economy of immigration in Canada. *Royal Dutch Geographical Society, 97*, 38–48.

Hilton, N. Z. (1991). Mediating wife assault: Battered women and the "new family." *Canadian Journal of Family Law, 9*, 29–54.

Hilton, N. Z. (1992). Battered women's concerns about their children witnessing wife assault. *Journal of Interpersonal Violence, 7*, 77–86.

Hilton, N. Z. (2000). The role of attitudes and awareness in anti-violence education. *Journal of Aggression, Maltreatment & Trauma, 3*, 221–238.

Hilton, N. Z., Carter, A. M., Harris, G. T., & Sharpe, A. J. (2008). Does using non-numerical terms to describe risk aid violence risk communication? Clinician preference, agreement, and decision-making. *Journal of Interpersonal Violence, 23*, 171–188.

Hilton, N. Z., & Harris, G. T. (2005). Predicting recidivism among serious wife assaulters: A critical review and implications for policy and practice. *Trauma, Violence, & Abuse, 6*, 3–23.

Hilton, N. Z., & Harris, G. T. (2007). Assessing risk of intimate partner violence. In J. C. Campbell (Ed.), *Assessing dangerousness* (pp. 105–125). New York: Springer.

Hilton, N. Z., & Harris, G. T. (2009a). Criminal justice responses to partner violence: History, evaluation, and lessons from interventions for criminal conduct. In D. Whitaker & J. Lutzker (Eds.), *Preventing partner violence: Research and evidence-based intervention strategies* (pp. 219–243). Washington, DC: American Psychological Association.

Hilton, N. Z., & Harris, G. T. (2009b). How nonrecidivism affects predictive accuracy: Evidence from a cross-validation of the Ontario Domestic Assault Risk Assessment (ODARA). *Journal of Interpersonal Violence, 24*, 326–337.

Hilton, N. Z., Harris, G. T., & Holder, N. L. (2008). Actuarial violence risk assessment in hospital-based partner assault clinics. *Canadian Journal of Nursing Research, 40,* 56–70.

Hilton, N. Z., Harris, G. T., Rawson, K., & Beach, C. A. (2005). Communicating violence risk information to forensic decision makers. *Criminal Justice and Behavior, 32,* 97–116.

Hilton, N. Z., Harris, G. T., & Rice, M. E. (1998). On the validity of self-reported rates of interpersonal violence. *Journal of Interpersonal Violence, 13,* 58–72.

Hilton, N. Z., Harris, G. T., & Rice, M. E. (2000). Functions of aggression by male teenagers. *Journal of Personality and Social Psychology, 79,* 988–994.

Hilton, N. Z., Harris, G. T., & Rice, M. E. (2001). Predicting violent recidivism by serious wife assaulters. *Journal of Interpersonal Violence, 16,* 408–423.

Hilton, N. Z., Harris, G. T., & Rice, M. E. (2003). Adolescents' perceptions of the seriousness of sexual aggression: Influence of gender, traditional attitudes, and self-reported experience. *Sexual Abuse: A Journal of Research and Treatment, 15,* 201–214.

Hilton, N. Z., Harris, G. T., & Rice, M. E. (2006). Sixty-six years of research on the clinical versus actuarial prediction of violence. *Counseling Psychologist, 34,* 400–409.

Hilton, N. Z., Harris, G. T., & Rice, M. E. (2007). The effect of arrest on wife assault recidivism, controlling for pre-arrest risk. *Criminal Justice and Behavior, 34,* 1334–1344.

Hilton, N. Z., Harris, G. T., Rice, M. E., Eke, A. W., & Lowe-Wetmore, T. (2007). Training front-line users in the Ontario Domestic Assault Risk Assessment (ODARA), a tool for police domestic investigations. *Canadian Journal of Police and Security Services, 5,* 92–96.

Hilton, N. Z., Harris, G. T., Rice, M. E., Houghton, R., & Eke, A. W. (2008). An in-depth actuarial risk assessment for wife assault recidivism: The Domestic Violence Risk Appraisal Guide. *Law and Human Behavior, 32,* 150–163.

Hilton, N. Z., Harris, G. T., Rice, M. E., Lang, C., Cormier, C. A., & Lines, K. J. (2004). A brief actuarial assessment for the prediction of wife assault recidivism: The Ontario Domestic Assault Risk Assessment. *Psychological Assessment, 16,* 267–275. [Erratum *17,* 131].

Hilton, N. Z., Harris, G. T., Rice, M. E., Smith Krans, T., & Lavigne, S. E. (1998). Antiviolence education in high schools. *Journal of Interpersonal Violence, 13,* 726–742.

Hilton, N. Z., & Simmons, J. L. (2001). The influence of actuarial risk assessment and clinical judgments in tribunal decisions about mentally disordered offenders. *Law and Human Behavior, 4,* 391–406.

Hines, D. A., & Saudino, K. J. (2002). Intergenerational transmission of intimate partner violence. *Trauma, Violence, & Abuse, 3,* 210–225.

Hirschel, J. D., & Hutchison, I. W. (1996). Realities and implications of the Charlotte Spousal Abuse Experiment. In E. S. Buzawa & C. G. Buzawa (Eds.), *Do arrests and restraining orders work?* (pp. 51–82). Thousand Oaks, CA: Sage.

Hoffman, P. (1994). Twenty years of operational use of a prediction instrument: The United States Parole Commission's salient factor score. *Journal of Criminal Justice, 22*, 477–494.

Holtzworth-Munroe, A. (2000). A typology of men who are violent toward their female partners: Making sense of the heterogeneity in husband violence. *Current Directions in Psychological Science, 9*, 140–143.

Holtzworth-Munroe, A., Meehan, J. C., Stuart, G. L., Herron, K., & Rehman, U. (2003). Do subtypes of maritally violent men continue to differ over time? *Journal of Consulting and Clinical Psychology, 71*, 728–740.

Hornsveld, R. H. J., Bezuijen, S., Leenaars, E. E. M., & Kraaimaat, F. W. (2008). Domestically and generally violent forensic psychiatric outpatients: Personality traits and behavior. *Journal of Interpersonal Violence, 23*, 1380–1393.

Houry, D., Reddy, S., & Parramore, C. (2006). Characteristics of victims coarrested for intimate partner violence. *Journal of Interpersonal Violence, 21*, 1483–1492.

Houston, D. J., & Richardson, L. E. (2005). Getting Americans to buckle up: The efficacy of state seat belt laws. *Accident Analysis and Prevention, 37*, 1114–1120.

Huizinga, D., & Elliott, D. S. (1986). Reassessing the reliability and validity of self-report delinquency measures. *Journal of Quantitative Criminology, 2*, 293–324.

Huss, M. T., & Langhinrichsen-Rohling, J. (2000). Identification of the psychopathic batterer: The clinical, legal, and policy implications. *Aggression and Violent Behavior, 5*, 403–422.

Huss, M. T., & Langhinrichsen-Rohling, J. (2006). Assessing the generalization of psychopathy in a clinical sample of domestic violence perpetrators. *Law and Human Behavior, 30*, 571–586.

Immican. (2003). *Immigration points*. Retrieved February 12, 2009, from http://www.immican.ca/point_system.htm

Jacobson, N. S., Gottman, J. M., Waltz, J., Rushe, R., Babcock, J., & Holtzworth-Munroe, A. (1994). Affect, verbal content, and psychophysiology in the arguments of couples with a violent husband. *Journal of Consulting and Clinical Psychology, 62*, 982–988.

Jaffe, P., & Burris, C. A. (1984). *An integrated response to wife assault: A community model* (Rep. No. 1984-27). Ottawa, Ontario, Canada: Ministry of the Solicitor General of Canada.

Jaffe, P. G., Hastings, E., Reitzel, D., & Austin, G. W. (1993). The impact of police laying charges. In N. Z. Hilton (Ed.), *Legal responses to wife assault* (pp. 62–95). Newbury Park, CA: Sage.

Jaffe, P. G., Sudermann, M., Reitzel, D., & Killip, S. M. (1992). An evaluation of a secondary school primary prevention program on violence in intimate relationships. *Violence and Victims, 7*, 129–146.

Johnson, S. (2006). *The ghost map: The story of London's deadliest epidemic—And how it changed the way we think about disease, cities, science, and the modern world*. New York: Putnam.

Kahneman, D., & Tversky, A. (2000). *Choices, values, and frames*. New York: Cambridge University Press.

Karelitz, T. M., & Budescu, D. V. (2004). You say "probable" and I say "likely": Improving interpersonal communication with verbal probability phrases. *Journal of Experimental Psychology: Applied, 10*, 25–41.

Kernic, M. A., & Bonomi, A. E. (2007). Female victims of domestic violence: Which victims do police refer to crisis intervention? *Violence and Victims, 22*, 463–473.

Kim, J., & Gray, K. A. (2008). Leave or stay? Battered women's decision after intimate partner violence. *Journal of Interpersonal Violence, 23*, 1465–1482.

Klein, E., Campbell, J., Soler, E., & Ghez, M. (1997). *Ending domestic violence: Changing public perceptions/halting the epidemic*. Thousand Oaks, CA: Sage.

Konečni, V. J., & Ebbesen, E. B. (1984). The mythology of legal decision making. *International Journal of Law and Psychiatry, 7*, 5–18.

Koziol-McLain, J., Webster, D., McFarlane, J., Block, C. R., Ulrich, Y., Glass, N., et al. (2007). Risk factors for femicide–suicide in abusive relationships: Results from a multisite case control study. In J. C. Campbell (Ed.), *Assessing dangerousness* (pp. 127–149). New York: Springer.

Krajewski, S. S., Rybarik, M. F., Dosch, M. E., & Gilmore, G. D. (1996). Results of a curriculum intervention with seventh graders regarding violence in relationships. *Journal of Family Violence, 11*, 93–112.

Krauss, D. A. (2004). Adjusting risk of recidivism: Do judicial departures worsen or improve recidivism prediction under the Federal Sentencing Guidelines? *Behavioral Sciences and the Law, 22*, 731–750.

Krauss, D. A., & Lee, D. H. (2003). Deliberating on dangerousness and death: Jurors' ability to differentiate between expert actuarial and clinical predictions of dangerousness. *International Journal of Law and Psychiatry, 26*, 113–137.

Kroner, D. G. (2005). Issues in violent risk assessment. *Journal of Interpersonal Violence, 20*, 231–235.

Kropp, P. R. (2008a). Development of the Spousal Assault Risk Assessment Guide (SARA) and the Brief Spousal Assault Form for the Evaluation of Risk (B–SAFER). In A. C. Baldry & F. W. Winkel (Eds.), *Intimate partner violence prevention and intervention: The risk assessment and management approach* (pp. 19–31). New York: Nova Science.

Kropp, P. R. (2008b). Intimate partner violence risk assessment and management. *Violence and Victims, 23*, 202–220.

Kropp, P. R., & Hart, S. D. (2000). The Spousal Assault Risk Assessment (SARA) guide: Reliability and validity in adult male offenders. *Law and Human Behavior, 24*, 101–118.

Kropp, P. R., Hart, S. D., Webster, C. D., & Eaves, D. (1999). *Spousal Assault Risk Assessment guide*. Toronto, Ontario, Canada: Multi-Health Systems.

Lalumière, M. L., Harris, G. T., Quinsey, V. L., & Rice, M. E. (2005). *The causes of rape*. Washington, DC: American Psychological Association.

Landau, T. C. (2000). Women's experiences with mandatory charging for wife assault in Ontario, Canada: A case against the prosecution. *Domestic Violence: Global Responses, 7*, 141–157.

Langford, D. R. (2000). Developing a safety protocol in qualitative research involving battered women. *Qualitative Health Research, 10*, 133–142.

Langhinrichsen-Rohling, J. (2005). Top 10 greatest "hits." *Journal of Interpersonal Violence, 20*, 108–118.

Langhinrichsen-Rohling, J., Huss, M. T., & Ramsey, S. (2000). The clinical utility of batterer typologies. *Journal of Family Violence, 15*, 37–53.

Lavoie, F., Vézina, L., Piché, C., & Boivin, M. (1995). Evaluation of a prevention program for violence in teen dating relationships. *Journal of Interpersonal Violence, 10*, 516–524.

Leistico, A. R., Salekin, R. T., DeCoster, J., & Rogers, R. (2007). A large-scale meta-analysis relating the Hare measures of psychopathy to antisocial conduct. *Law and Human Behavior, 32*, 28–45.

Leonard, K. E., & Senchak, M. (1996). Prospective prediction of husband marital aggression within newlywed couples. *Journal of Abnormal Psychology, 105*, 369–380.

Li, G. (2008). Homicide in Canada, 2007 [Statistics Canada Catalogue No. 85-002-X]. *Juristat, 28*.

Litwack, T. R., Zapf, P. A., Groscup, J. L., & Hart, S. D. (2006). Violence risk assessment: Research, legal, and clinical considerations. In I. B. Weiner & A. K. Hess (Eds.), *The handbook of forensic psychology* (3rd ed., pp. 487–533). Hoboken, NJ: Wiley.

Loftus, E. F. (1997). Memory for a past that never was. *Current Directions in Psychological Science, 6*, 60–65.

Logan, TK, Walker, R., Jordan, C. E., & Leukefeld, C. G. (2006). *Women and victimization: Contributing factors, interventions, and implications*. Washington, DC: American Psychological Association.

MacCoun, R. J. (1990). The emergence of extralegal bias during jury deliberation. *Criminal Justice and Behavior, 17*, 303–314.

Macgowan, M. J. (1997). An evaluation of a dating violence prevention program for middle school students. *Violence and Victims, 12*, 223–235.

Mamuza, J. M. (2001). Do actuarial assessments fall victim to base rate neglect? *Dissertation Abstracts International, 61* (10), 5617B.

Manguno-Mire, G. M., Thompson, J. W., Bertman-Pate, L. J., Burnett, D. R., & Thompson, H. W. (2007). Are release recommendations for NGRI acquittees informed by relevant data? *Behavioral Sciences and the Law, 25*, 43–55.

Martin, A. J., Berenson, K. R., Griffing, S., Sage, R. E., Madry, L., Bingham, L. E., et al. (2000). The process of leaving an abusive relationship: The role of risk assessments and decision-certainty. *Journal of Family Violence, 15*, 109–122.

Martin, J. C. (1955). *The criminal code of Canada*. Toronto, Ontario, Canada: Cartwright.

Martin, M. E. (1997). Double your trouble: Dual arrest in family violence. *Journal of Family Violence, 12*, 139–157.

Maxwell, C. D., Garner, J. H., & Fagan, J. A. (2001, June). The effects of arrest on intimate partner violence: New evidence from the Spouse Assault Replication Program. *National Institute of Justice Research Briefs*, 1–15.

McBurnett, K., Kerckhoff, C., Capasso, L., Pfiffner, L. J., Rathouz, P. J., McCord, M., et al. (2001). Antisocial personality, substance abuse, and exposure to parental violence in males referred for domestic violence. *Violence and Victims, 16*, 491–506.

McKee, S. A., Harris, G. T., & Rice, M. E. (2007). Improving forensic tribunal decisions: The role of the clinician. *Behavioral Sciences and the Law, 25*, 485–506.

Mears, D. P. (2003). Research and interventions to reduce domestic violence. *Trauma, Violence, & Abuse, 4*, 127–147.

Meehl, P. E. (1973). *Psychodiagnosis: Selected papers*. Minneapolis: University of Minnesota Press.

Melton, H. C., & Belknap, J. (2003). He hits, she hits: Assessing gender differences and similarities in officially reported intimate partner violence. *Criminal Justice and Behavior, 30*, 328–348.

Ménard, K. S., Anderson, A. L., & Godboldt, S. M. (2009). Gender differences in intimate partner recidivism: A 5-year follow-up. *Criminal Justice and Behavior, 36*, 61–76.

Miles v. Commonwealth of Virginia. (2006). Retrieved February 13, 2009, from http://www.courts.state.va.us/opinions/opnscvtx/1052568.txt

Miller, J. (2003). An arresting experiment. *Journal of Interpersonal Violence, 18*, 695–716.

Mills, J. F., & Kroner, D. G. (2006). The effects of base-rate information on the perception of risk for reoffense. *American Journal of Forensic Psychology, 24*, 45–56.

Mills, J. F., Kroner, D. G., & Hemmati, T. (2007). The validity of violence risk estimates: An issue of item performance. *Psychological Services, 4*, 1–12.

Mohandie, K., Meloy, J. R., McGowan, M. G., & Williams, J. (2006). The RECON typology of stalking: Reliability and validity based upon a large sample of North American stalkers. *Journal of Forensic Sciences, 51*(1), 147–155.

Monahan, J. (1981). *Predicting violent behavior: An assessment of clinical techniques*. Beverly Hills, CA: Sage.

Monahan, J. (2006). A jurisprudence of risk assessment: Forecasting harm among prisoners, predators, and patients. *Virginia Law Review, 92*, 391–435.

Monahan, J., Steadman, H. J., Appelbaum, P. S., Grisso, T., Mulvey, E. P., Loren, H., et al. (2006). The classification of violence risk. *Behavioral Sciences and the Law, 24*, 721–730.

Monahan, J., Steadman, H. J., Clark Robbins, P., Appelbaum, P., Banks, S., Grisso, T., et al. (2005). An actuarial model of violence risk assessment for persons with mental disorders. *Psychiatric Services, 56*, 810–815.

Monahan, J., Steadman, H. J., Silver, E., Appelbaum, P. S., Robbins, P., & Mulvey, E. P. (2001). *Rethinking risk assessment: The MacArthur study of mental disorder and violence*. New York: Oxford University Press.

Morse, B. J. (1995). Beyond the Conflict Tactics Scale: Assessing gender differences in partner violence. *Violence and Victims, 10*, 251–272.

Mossman, D. (1994). Assessing predictions of violence: Being accurate about accuracy. *Journal of Consulting and Clinical Psychology, 62*, 783–792.

Murphy, A. H. (1991). Probabilities, odds, and forecasts of rare events. *Weather and Forecasting, 6*, 302–307.

Murphy, C. M., Morrel, T. M., Elliott, J. D., & Neavins, T. M. (2003). A prognostic indicator scale for the treatment of partner abuse perpetrators. *Journal of Interpersonal Violence, 18*, 1087–1105.

Neumann, C. S., Kosson, D. S., Forth, A. E., & Hare, R. D. (2006). Factor structure of the Hare Psychopathy Checklist: Youth Version (PCL:YV) in incarcerated adolescents. *Psychological Assessment, 18*, 142–154.

Nicolaidis, C., Curry, M. A., Ulrich, Y., Sharps, P., McFarlane, J., Campbell, D., et al. (2003). Could we have known? A qualitative analysis of data from women who survived an attempted homicide by an intimate partner. *Journal of General Internal Medicine, 18*, 788–794.

O'Keefe, M. (1997). Predictors of dating violence among high school students. *Journal of Interpersonal Violence, 12*, 546–568.

O'Leary, K. D., Slep, A. M., & O'Leary, S. G. (2007). Multivariate models of men's and women's partner aggression. *Journal of Consulting and Clinical Psychology, 75*, 752–764.

Ontario Ministry of the Solicitor General. (2000). *A guide to the Domestic Violence Supplementary Report form.* Toronto, Ontario, Canada: Author.

Ontario Office of the Chief Coroner. (1998). *Inquest into the deaths of Arlene May and Randy Iles, February 16–July 2, 1998, Coroners Courts, Toronto, Ontario: Synopsis by Dr. Bonita, presiding coroner.* Retrieved February 13, 2009, from http://www.owjn.org/archive/arlene3.htm

Pate, A. M., & Hamilton, E. E. (1992). Formal and informal deterrents to domestic violence: The Dade County spouse assault experiment. *American Sociological Review, 57*, 691–697.

Payton, M. E., Greenstone, M. H., & Schenker, N. (2003). Overlapping confidence intervals or standard error intervals: What do they mean in terms of statistical significance? *Journal of Insect Science, 34*, 1–6.

Pechmann, C., Dixon, P., & Layne, N. (1998). An assessment of U.S. and Canadian smoking reduction objectives for the year 2000. *American Journal of Public Health, 88*, 1362–1367.

Pence, E. (2002). The Duluth domestic abuse intervention project. In E. Aldarondo & F. Mederos (Eds.), *Programs for men who batter* (pp. 2–46). Kingston, NJ: Civic Research Institute.

Pence, E. L., & Shepard, M. F. (1999). Developing a coordinated community response. In M. F. Shepard & E. L. Pence (Eds.), *Coordinating community responses to domestic violence* (pp. 3–24). Thousand Oaks, CA: Sage.

Pleck, E. (1989). Criminal approaches to family violence, 1640–1980. In L. Ohlin & M. Tonry (Eds.), *Family violence* (pp. 19–57). Chicago: University of Chicago Press.

Popham, S., & Hilton, N. Z. (2006, October). *The ODARA: Development, application to corrections, and scoring criteria.* Paper presented at the Biannual Conference of the Ontario Ministry of Correctional Services and Community Safety and Nippising University, North Bay, Ontario, Canada.

Pritchard, D. A. (1977). Linear versus configural statistical prediction. *Journal of Consulting and Clinical Psychology, 45,* 559–563.

Public Safety Canada. (2000). *Response to the report of the Sub-Committee on Corrections and Conditional Release Act of the Standing Committee on Justice and Human Rights: A work in progress: The Corrections and Conditional Release Act.* Retrieved February 12, 2009, from http://ww2.ps-sp.gc.ca/publications/ccra/CcraOct2000_e.pdf

Quinsey, V. L., & Ambtman, R. (1978). Psychiatric assessment of the dangerousness of mentally ill offenders. *Crime and Justice, 6,* 249–257.

Quinsey, V. L., & Ambtman, R. (1979). Variables affecting psychiatrists' and teachers' assessments of the dangerousness of mentally ill offenders. *Journal of Consulting and Clinical Psychology, 47,* 353–362.

Quinsey, V. L., Harris, G. T., Rice, M. E., & Cormier, C. A. (2006). *Violent offenders: Appraising and managing risk* (2nd ed.). Washington, DC: American Psychological Association.

Quinsey, V. L., Jones, G. B., Book, A. S., & Barr, K. N. (2006). The dynamic prediction of antisocial behavior among forensic psychiatric patients. *Journal of Interpersonal Violence, 21,* 1539–1565.

Quinsey, V. L., Khanna, A., & Malcolm, P. B. (1998). A retrospective evaluation of the regional treatment centre sex offender treatment program. *Journal of Interpersonal Violence, 13,* 621–644.

Reitz, J. G. (2002). Host societies and the reception of immigrants: Research themes, emerging theories and methodological issues. *International Migration Review, 4,* 1005–1019.

Rice, M. E., & Harris, G. T. (1995). Violent recidivism: Assessing predictive validity. *Journal of Consulting and Clinical Psychology, 63,* 737–748.

Rice, M. E., & Harris, G. T. (1988). An empirical approach to the classification and treatment of maximum security psychiatric patients. *Behavioral Sciences and the Law, 6,* 497–514.

Rice, M. E., & Harris, G. T. (2005). Comparing effect sizes in follow-up studies: ROC area, Cohen's *d*, and *r*. *Law and Human Behavior, 29,* 615–620.

Rice, M. E., Harris, G. T., & Hilton, N. Z. (in press). The Violence Risk Appraisal Guide and Sex Offender Risk Appraisal Guide for violence risk assessment and the Ontario Domestic Assault Risk Assessment and Domestic Violence Risk Appraisal Guide for wife assault risk assessment. In R. Otto & K. Douglas (Eds.), *Handbook of violence risk assessment.* Oxford, England: Routledge/Taylor & Francis.

Rice, M. E., Harris, G. T., Varney, G. W., & Quinsey, V. L. (1989). *Violence in institutions: Understanding, prevention, and control.* Toronto, Ontario, Canada: Hans Huber.

Rivett, M., & Kelly, S. (2006). "From awareness to practice": Children, domestic violence and child welfare. *Child Abuse Review, 15,* 224–242.

Roberts, T. A., Auinger, P., & Klein, J. D. (2006). Predictors of partner abuse in a nationally representative sample of adolescents involved in heterosexual dating relationships. *Violence and Victims, 21*, 81–89.

Roehl, J., & Guertin, K. (2000). Intimate partner violence: The current use of risk assessments in sentencing offenders. *Justice System Journal, 21*, 171–198.

Salekin, R., Rogers, R., & Sewell, K. (1996). A review and meta-analysis of the Psychopathy Checklist and Psychopathy Checklist—Revised: Predictive validity of dangerousness. *Clinical Psychology: Science and Practice, 3*, 203–215.

Sartin, R. M., Hansen, D. J., & Huss, M. T. (2006). Domestic violence treatment response and recidivism: A review and implications for the study of family violence. *Aggression and Violent Behavior, 11*, 425–440.

Schauss, S. L., Chase, P. N., & Hawkins, R. P. (1997). Environment–behavior relations, behavior therapy and the process of persuasion and attitude change. *Journal of Behavior Therapy and Experimental Psychiatry, 28*, 31–40.

Schwarz, N. (1999). How the questions shape the answers. *American Psychologist, 54*, 93–105.

Sedgwick, P., & Hall, A. (2003). Teaching medical students and doctors how to communicate risk. *British Medical Journal, 327*, 694–695.

Seto, M. C. (2005). Is more better? Combining actuarial risk scales to predict recidivism among adult sex offenders. *Psychological Assessment, 17*, 156–167.

Shackelford, T. K. (2001). Cohabitation, marriage, and murder: Woman-killing by male romantic partners. *Aggressive Behavior, 27*, 284–291.

Shaw, N. J., & Dear, P. R. (1990). How do parents of babies interpret qualitative expressions of probability? *Archives of Disease in Childhood, 65*, 520–523.

Shepard, M. (1992). Predicting batterer recidivism five years after community intervention. *Journal of Family Violence, 7*, 167–178.

Sherman, L. W., & Berk, R. A. (1984). The specific deterrent effects of arrest for domestic assault. *American Sociological Review, 49*, 261–272.

Sherman, L. W., Schmidt, J. D., Rogan, D. P., Smith, D. A., Gartin, P. R., Cohen, E. G., et al. (1992). The variable effects of arrest on criminal careers: The Milwaukee domestic violence experiment. *Journal of Criminal Law and Criminology, 83*, 137–169.

Skilling, T. A., Harris, G. T., Rice, M. E., & Quinsey, V. L. (2002). Identifying persistently antisocial offenders using the Hare Psychopathy Checklist and DSM antisocial personality disorder criteria. *Psychological Assessment, 14*, 27–38.

Skogan, W. G. (1986). Methodological issues in the study of victimization. In E. A. Fattah (Ed.), *From crime policy to victim policy* (pp. 80–99). London: Macmillan.

Skogan, W. G. (1990). The polls—A review. *Public Opinion Quarterly, 54*, 256–272.

Slovic, P., & Monahan, J. (1995). Probability, danger, and coercion. *Law and Human Behavior, 19*, 49–65.

Smuts, B. (1992). Male aggression against women. *Human Nature, 3*, 1–44.

Spidel, A., Vincent, G., Huss, M. T., Winters, J., Thomas, L., & Dutton, D. (2007). The psychopathic batterer: Subtyping perpetrators of domestic violence. In H. Hervé & J. C. Yuille (Eds.), *The psychopath* (pp. 327–342). Mahwah, NJ: Erlbaum.

Stallings, W. M., & Gillmore, G. M. (1971). A note on "accuracy" and "precision." *Journal of Educational Measurement, 8,* 127–129.

Stark, E., & Flitcraft, A. (1996). *Women at risk: Domestic violence and women's health.* Thousand Oaks, CA: Sage.

Statistics Canada. (2006). *Measuring violence against women: Statistical trends 2006.* Ottawa, Ontario, Canada: Ministry of Industry.

Straus, M. A. (1979). Measuring intrafamily conflict and violence: The Conflict Tactics (CT) Scales. *Journal of Marriage and the Family, 41,* 75–88.

Straus, M. A., Hamby, S. L., Boney-McCoy, S., & Sugarman, D. B. (1996). The revised Conflict Tactics Scales (CTS2). *Journal of Family Issues, 17,* 283–316.

Streiner, D. L., & Cairney, J. (2007). What's under the ROC? An introduction to receiver operating characteristics curves. *Canadian Journal of Psychiatry, 52,* 121–128.

Stuart, E. P., & Campbell, J. C. (1989). Assessment of patterns of dangerousness with battered women. *Issues in Mental Health Nursing, 10,* 245–260.

Stuart, G. L., Moore, T. M., Gordon, K. C., Ramsey, S. E., & Kahler, C. W. (2006). Psychopathology in women arrested for domestic violence. *Journal of Interpersonal Violence, 21,* 376–389.

Stuart, R. B. (2005). Treatment for partner abuse: Time for a paradigm shift. *Professional Psychology: Research and Practice, 36,* 254–263.

Swanson, J. H. W. (1994). Mental disorder, substance abuse, and community violence: An epidemiological approach. In J. Monahan & H. J. Steadman (Eds.), *Violence and mental disorder: Developments in risk assessment* (pp. 101–136). Chicago: University of Chicago Press.

Swets, A., Dawes, R. M., & Monahan, J. (2000). Psychological science can improve diagnostic decisions. *Psychological Science in the Public Interest, 1,* 1–26.

Swogger, M. T., Walsh, Z., & Kosson, D. S. (2007). Domestic violence and psychopathic traits: Distinguishing the antisocial batterer from other antisocial offenders. *Aggressive Behavior, 33,* 253–260.

Tanasichuk, C. L., & Wormith, J. S. (2008). Does treatment make psychopaths worse? A meta-analytic review. In G. Bourgon, R. K. Hanson, J. D. Pozzulo, K. E. Morton-Bourgon, & C. L. Tanasichuk (Eds.), *Proceedings of the North American Correctional & Criminal Justice Psychology Conference* (pp. 50–54). Ottawa, Ontario, Canada: Public Safety Canada.

Taylor, P. J., Goldberg, E., Leese, M., Butwell, M., & Reed, A. (1999). Limits to the value of mental health review tribunals for offender patients. *British Journal of Psychiatry, 174,* 164–169.

Todd, P. M., & Gigerenzer, G. (2000). Précis of *Simple heuristics that make us smart. Behavioral and Brain Sciences, 23,* 723–780.

Todd, P. M., & Gigerenzer, G. (2007). Environments that make us smart. *Current Directions in Psychological Science, 16*, 167–171.

Trevethan, S., Moore. J. P., & Rastin, C. J. (2002). A profile of Aboriginal offenders in federal facilities and serving time in the community. *FORUM on Corrections Research, 14*, 17–19. Retrieved March 6, 2009, from http://www.csc-scc.gc.ca/text/pblct/forum/e143/e143f-eng.shtml

Trujillo, M. P., & Ross, S. (2008). Police response to domestic violence: Making decisions about risk and risk management. *Journal of Interpersonal Violence, 23*, 454–473.

U.S. Sentencing Commission. (2004) *Measuring recidivism: The criminal history computation of the Federal Sentencing Guidelines.* Retrieved October 30, 2007, from http://www.ussc.gov/publicat/recidivism_general.pdf

Vasey, M. W., Kotov, R., Frick, P. J., & Loney, B. R. (2005). The latent structure of psychopathy in youth: A taxometric investigation. *Journal of Abnormal Child Psychology, 33*, 411–429.

Virginia Secretary of Health and Human Resources. (2008). *Sexually violent predator referral, commitment, and bed utilization forecast for FY2009–2014.* Retrieved February 13, 2009, from http://leg2.state.va.us/dls/h&sdocs.nsf/By+Year/RD3032008/$file/RD303.pdf

Volokh, A. (1997). n guilty men. *University of Pennsylvania Law Review, 146*, 173–216.

Walsh, Z., & Kosson, D. S. (2007). Psychopathy and violent crime: A prospective study of the influence of socioeconomic status and ethnicity. *Law and Human Behavior, 31*, 209–229.

Webster, C. D., Harris, G. T., Rice, M. E., Cormier, C. A., & Quinsey, V. L. (1994). *The violence prediction scheme.* Toronto, Ontario, Canada: University of Toronto.

Weisz, A. N., Tolman, R. M., & Saunders, D. G. (2000). Assessing the risk of severe domestic violence. *Journal of Interpersonal Violence, 15*, 75–90.

Williams, A. F., Wells, J. K., & Reinfurt, D. W. (2004). Increasing seat belt use in North Carolina. In R. Hornik (Ed.), *Public health communication: Evidence for behavior change* (pp. 85–96). Mahwah, NJ: Erlbaum.

Williams, K. R., & Grant, S. R. (2006). Empirically examining the risk of intimate partner violence: The revised Domestic Violence Screening Instrument (DVSI–R). *Public Health Reports, 121*, 400–408.

Williams, K. R., & Houghton, A. B. (2004). Assessing the risk of domestic violence reoffending: A validation study. *Law and Human Behavior, 28*, 437–455.

Wilson, C. (1995). N. D. P. stumbles. *Nation, 24*, 77–78.

Wilson, E. B. (1927). Probable inference, the law of succession, and statistical inference. *Journal of the American Statistical Association, 22*, 209–212.

Wilson, M., & Daly, M. (1993). Spousal homicide risk and estrangement. *Violence and Victims, 8*, 3–16.

Wilson, M., & Daly, M. (1996). Male sexual proprietariness and violence against wives. *Current Directions in Psychological Science, 5*, 2–7.

Winkel, F. W. (2008). Identifying domestic violence victims at risk of hyper-accessible traumatic memories and/or re-victimization through validated screening: The predictive performance of the Scanner and the B–SAFER. In A. C. Baldry & F. W. Winkel (Eds.), *Intimate partner violence prevention and intervention: The risk assessment and management approach* (pp. 61–81). New York: Nova Science.

Winkel, F. W., & de Kleuver, E. (1997). Communication aimed at changing cognitions about sexual intimidation. *Journal of Interpersonal Violence, 12*, 513–529.

Wormith, J. S., & Goldstone, C. S. (1984). The clinical and statistical prediction of recidivism. *Criminal Justice and Behavior, 11*, 3–34.

Zink, T., & Putnam, F. (2005). Intimate partner violence research in the health care setting. *Journal of Interpersonal Violence, 20*, 365–372.

INDEX

Wife assault
    explanations of, 146–147
    mandatory arrest for, 114–116
    no-drop prosecution policies for, 116–118
    prediction of, VRAG, 9, 10
    as term, 6

Women
    and criminal justice system, 21
    recidivism predictions by, 34, 140–141
    violence by. *See* Female domestic offenders
Women's shelters, 123, 161

ABOUT THE AUTHORS

N. Zoe Hilton, PhD, is a senior research scientist at the Mental Health Centre Penetanguishene, Ontario, Canada, and an adjunct assistant professor of psychiatry at the University of Toronto, Ontario, Canada. She holds degrees from the University of Southampton, Southampton, England; the University of Cambridge Institute of Criminology, Cambridge, England; and a PhD in psychology from the University of Toronto. Her research work and publications are primarily on the topic of violence in relationships, including women's perspectives, theoretical aspects, and risk assessment.

Grant T. Harris, PhD, is the director of research at the Mental Health Centre Penetanguishene (MHCP), Ontario, Canada. He is also an adjunct associate professor of psychology at Queen's University, Kingston, Ontario, Canada, and an adjunct associate professor of psychiatry at the University of Toronto, Ontario, Canada. Over the past 3 decades, he has received many research grants and has conducted extensive scientific research on violent and criminal behavior, psychopathy, sexual aggression, and deviance, all of which has resulted in more than 120 publications in the scientific and professional literature. He coauthored the American Psychological Association best-selling book *Violent Offenders: Appraising and Managing Risk*, now in its second edition, as well as others on rape and institutional violence. He obtained a BSc from the University of Toronto and a PhD in experimental psychology from McMaster University. He joined the staff of the MHCP in 1980 and for several years was responsible for the development and supervision of behavioral programs on a maximum security unit for dangerous and assaultive men. He has been the recipient of such awards as the Career Contribution Award from the Criminal Justice Section of the Canadian Psychological Association and the Amethyst Award for Outstanding Achievement by an Ontario Public Servant.

Marnie E. Rice, PhD, is a fellow of the Royal Society of Canada, Canada's senior national body of distinguished scientists and scholars. She has worked at the Mental Health Centre Penetanguishene, Ontario, Canada, for 33 years, as a clinical psychologist; researcher; and, for 14 years, director of research. She is currently research director emerita and part-time professor of psychiatry and behavioral neurosciences at McMaster University, Hamilton, Ontario, Canada; adjunct professor of psychiatry at the University of Toronto, Ontario, Canada; and adjunct associate professor of psychology at Queen's University, Kingston, Ontario, Canada. She has produced more than 130 scientific publications, including several on the topic of sex offenders. Her work has been cited more than 2,000 times in the scientific and scholarly literature. She is a coauthor of the American Psychological Association best-selling book *Violent Offenders: Appraising and Managing Risk*, now in its second edition, as well as three other books on rape, institutional violence, and risk assessment. She has been the recipient of many awards, including the American Psychological Association's Award for Distinguished Contribution to Research in Public Policy and the Career Contribution Award from the Criminal Justice Section of the Canadian Psychological Association.